GW00373912

TERENC

TERENCE

NICHOLAS IND

CONRAN

THE AUTHORIZED BIOGRAPHY

SIDGWICK & JACKSON

First published 1995 by Sidgwick & Jackson

This edition published 1996 by Sidgwick & Jackson
an imprint of Macmillan Publishers Ltd
25 Eccleston Place, London SW1W 9NF
and Basingstoke

Associated companies throughout the world

ISBN 0 283 06294 0

9 8 7 6 5 4 3 2 1

A CIP catalogue record for this book is available from
the British Library.

Typeset by Parker Typesetting Service, Leicester
Printed and bound in Great Britain by BPC Hazell Books Ltd
A member of The British Printing Company Ltd

I now realize that to allow your biography to be written while you are still alive is both foolish and egotistical. Nevertheless, I do hope that my involvement in design, marketing, retailing and restaurants over many years may be of interest to budding entrepreneurs of all ages. Remember: nothing ventured, nothing gained!

Terence Conran

CONTENTS

ACKNOWLEDGEMENTS

I would like to thank the many people and institutions who have helped in the research and writing of this book, not least of whom is Terence Conran. Not only did he give up much of his time to interviews, he also allowed me to write what I hope is a balanced account of his life. Access to friends, colleagues and perhaps foes was facilitated by Terence, and by the generous help of his P.A., Amanda Robinson.

Others I would like to thank, include all those who gave their time for interviews: Shirley Conran, Jasper Conran, Sebastian Conran, Tom Conran, Sophie Conran, Caroline Conran, Priscilla Carluccio, Robert Addington, Stephen Bayley, Brinsley Black, Francis Bruguière, Yves Cambier, Sir Hugh Casson, Stafford Cliff, Michel Cultru, Kate Currie, Brenda Davison, Geoff Davy, Robin and Lucienne Day, Pauline Dora, Raymond Elston, Rodney Fitch, Christopher Frayling, Charles Gordon, Loyd Grossman, Des Gunewardena, Maggie Heaney, Anthony Hill, Keith Hobbs, Sir Howard Hodgkin, Min Hogg, Simon Hopkinson, Toby Jellinek, Michael Likierman, Rodney Kinsman, Michael Julien, John Kasmin, Joel Kissin, Natasha Kroll, Maurice Libby, Gill Lingwood, Cynthia Manners, Geoff Marshall, John Mawer, Martin Moss, John Murray, Fiona MacCarthy, Eric O'Leary, Sir Eduardo Paolozzi, David Phillips, Philip Pollock, Don Potter, Mary Quant, David Queensberry, Martyn Rowlands, Desmond Ryman, Zimmie Sasson, Roger Seelig, Christina Smith, Betsy Smith, Jeremy Smith, Anita Storey, Deyan Sudjic, Sean Sutcliffe, Pagan Taylor, Andrina Waddington, Michael Wickham, Bernard Wiehahn, James Woudhuysen, Peter York.

The following people were also enormously helpful with information and support: Vittorio Radice and Ben Weaver of

Habitat, Alan Shrimpton of Bryanston School, Deidre Morrow of the CD Partnership, Sylvia Backermeyer at the Central School, Caroline Cuthbert of the Tate Gallery, Greta Ind and Vivi Ind; as were the following institutions – Highfield School, the Art and Design Library at the V & A, Langport Library and the Berkshire Records Office.

INTRODUCTION

'I am not interested in the past but only in the future. But I do believe in the inspiration of tradition.'

In reading the autobiography of the playwright John Osborne, I came across these words of George Devine, the first Artistic Director of the English Stage Company. Equally, they could be the words of Terence Conran. Like Devine, his life has been about challenging the accepted and questioning the unquestioned, of looking forward, of experimenting – failing occasionally, but mostly succeeding. It has made for a life of variety and excitement. It is not the life of an ordinary businessman – his interests are too rich and varied – nor is it the life of an aesthete – he is too commercial. It is the story of a man whose impact on our lives is profound, because he combines an unerring eye for the form of things with an energetic entrepreneurship.

I came to this project never having met Terence Conran. I read an interview with him in a newspaper, in which he put forward his forthright views about architecture, London (the need for a co-ordinated policy), politics (Socialist) and design. He seemed passionate and committed about the world around him, in a way that is rare for a businessman. I wrote to him about a biography and he agreed in principle. That accessibility to people was something that struck me as I got to know him better. Students and journalists, designers and businessmen contacted him continually. He would always make the time for them and if they had good ideas he would be supportive. As I reflect on the inaccessibility of most people – the unanswered letters and unreturned phone calls – the rarity of Terence's attitude is all the sharper. Terence has the undoubted ability to make people comfortable. There is no grandeur or pretension and the 'Sir' is a rarely used appendage.

Some forewarned me of his bullying; that I would never be able to write a balanced book, because he wouldn't let me. There was no bullying. Sometimes Terence would disagree with a view or a degree of emphasis, but he never insisted on anything. He let me write the book I wanted. The only limitation was Terence's lack of analysis of his past. As someone who is interested in the future, he does not dwell on his motivations. For example when asked why he did something as a twenty-year-old, he would not have a real answer. Perhaps this is not so rare. I am much younger than Terence and I'm not sure I could provide any real depth as to why I did things, except at particularly poignant moments. Nor has Terence kept much memorabilia – photographs are few, letters scarcer. The upside to Terence's limited recollections was the emphasis it placed on getting the views of others. His school friends, his family, his mentors and his colleagues all provided insight into his attitudes and behaviour. In the main they were almost frighteningly open about him. Some, such as Sir Hugh Casson, Michael Wickham, Sir Eduardo Paolozzi, Mary Qaunt and Terence's sister, Priscilla Carluccio were also extremely adept at painting a picture of the times in which Terence grew up.

The experience of researching and writing the book has been all consuming, occupying completely my available time. It has also been the most enjoyable project I have ever undertaken. Nothing could, nor did, divert me from the book. Although I have a design background, it taught me a lot about design. I learnt even more about restaurants, which I knew very little about before. I hope, as a reader, you get the same reward and enjoyment.

Nicholas Ind
London, September 1994

TERENCE CONRAN

CHAPTER ONE
EARLY LIFE

Terence Conran is a complex mixture of opposites. He is tactless, abrasive, bullying, impatient, charming and passionate. He loves women, yet he can also be misogynistic. He is a businessman who dislikes the routine of business. He has a superb eye for visual details, but is poor at the detail of administration. He dislikes the obvious, but hates the impractical. He likes originality, but can be derivative. He is a socialist with conservative impulses. He is supremely ambitious and egotistical, and yet little concerned with money. He is both generous and parsimonious. He is self-confident yet also shy and fragile. He is a puritan and a sensualist. He is all these incongruities, but consistently he is possessed of enormous energy and drive and an almost missionary-like desire to change the way we view the world.

His character is a fascinating concoction of nature and nurture. Certainly his mother and his early mentors played a key role in his adult personality, but his larger-than-life forebears also displayed the combination of passion and individualism that Terence embodies.

His father's side of the family came from County Mayo in the West of Ireland. The name, which was originally O'Conaráin, came from County Offaly, where it dates back to before Tudor times, but in County Wexford there is a place called Ballyconran, which suggests that influential families bearing the name once lived there. Terence's grandfather, Bertram, who was always known as Bertie, left Ireland to make his fortune in Australia, where he trained racehorses and farmed. While there, he met and married Marion Sloper, the daughter of Gerard Orby Sloper.

The Slopers had once owned a large property in St James's Place and the 1,400-acre estate of West Woodhay in Berkshire, including a large house designed by Inigo Jones. The first Sloper to own West

Woodhay was William, who acquired it around 1710. He was the Member of Parliament for Newbury, a Whig, a founder of the Georgia colony in America and a friend of the Prime Minister, Robert Walpole – a man whose 'connections and influence were far-flung and incalculable'.[1] His son, another William, achieved considerable fame as the lover of the most distinguished actress of the age, Susannah Cibber. She was the sister of Thomas Arne, who composed 'Rule Britannia', and the wife of the actor/manager Theophilus Cibber, who was the son of the Poet Laureate. When in 1739 William Sloper left his wife and children for Susannah, the affair became the stuff of tabloid journalism. Theophilus Cibber, who introduced his wife to Sloper, kidnapped her back at gunpoint – after having spies watch her make love to William. The full details came out in a much publicized court case, and a little book on the affair, *A Tryal of a Cause*, was so popular that it continued to be reprinted well into Victorian times.

In spite of the scandal, William was a man of strong beliefs and passions; even though they never married, his commitment to Susannah was total. Shunned by polite society, their household at West Woodhay became a magnet for her theatrical and musical friends: Handel would come to play the harpsichord, and her long-term acting partner David Garrick would entertain various Whig colleagues of William's with his impersonations of politicians.

It was only when William died, in 1789, that his wife came back to West Woodhay – some fifty years after their separation. William's son, Robert, was the next inhabitant of the house. Terence has a letter to William written in 1752 by the Lord Chief Justice of the Court of Common Pleas, Sir John Willes, who was furious with the 'villainous' Robert for eloping with his daughter Jane in a post-chaise. Willes says he 'will never see their faces again' and promises to make sure that Jane 'will never

---

1. Mary Nash, *The Provoked Wife: The Life and Times of Susannah Cibber* (Hutchinson, 1977), p.130.

receive one farthing'. Robert went on to become a general and a knight, and commander-in-chief of all His Majesty's forces in India. However, his reputation was tarnished when he was recalled from his post for misappropriating funds. His successor, Lord Cornwallis, thought his offence was a response to the large number of dependants, legitimate and illegitimate, that he had to look after.

During the nineteenth century the Sloper family went into something of a decline. The impressive library built by William Sloper Jr had become disordered by generations of 'unbookish descendants', while the church at West Woodhay had fallen into disuse, in spite of one of the Reverend Slopers' attempts to enforce attendance by rounding up his parishioners with a shotgun. Nevertheless the house was still beautiful. In 1829 a cousin of the Slopers had his honeymoon there. His bride thought West Woodhay was the 'perfection of an old manor'. Fifty years later, however, the Slopers left West Woodhay. Gerard Orby Sloper was short of money and sold the house to the Cole family – newly rich London importers and bankers – 'and went to live, it was said, in Paris'.[2]

Although the circumstances of Terence's grandparents' first meeting are not known, in 1905 they returned from Australia to Britain and settled in Berkshire. *En route*, Marion gave birth to a son, Rupert, in Johannesburg.

Bertie's Australian ventures had made sufficient money for the Conrans to live well. He became a stockbroker in the City of London, but it seems he enjoyed a leisurely lifestyle. Rupert was consigned to a nanny, while the grand and beautiful Marion and the debonair Bertie socialized. Priscilla, Terence's sister, thinks that Rupert's childhood was very unhappy: 'My father always said that his parents never knew of his existence, except when they were going out, when his father would give him a gold sovereign.'

2. Mary Nash, *The Provoked Wife: The Life and Times of Susannah Cibber* (Hutchinson, 1977), p.330.

Once he was old enough, Rupert was put not only out of mind but also out of sight. He was sent away first to Dover College and then, at the age of eleven, to a Jesuit-run boarding school called Beaumont, in Old Windsor, Berkshire. The choice was not due to his father's Irish Catholic heritage, but because his mother had decided to convert to Catholicism – a not uncommon occurrence among her generation and class. At Beaumont, Rupert excelled at sport, playing for the 1st XI at cricket and the 1st XV at rugby, and was also good at drawing. Overall, however, his school life was not enjoyable. He struggled with his lessons, and for his failings was beaten regularly by the monks.

In 1923, at the age of eighteen, he escaped from both home life and school to join the Army. But this was to be a short-lived experience: the discipline of the Army seemed to be an extension of the horrors of school, and after a couple of years he left and became a coffee merchant.

Rupert was not very ambitious or businesslike, but he had great charm. He was an able market clerk who got on well with colleagues and customers alike, but he was not driven by either the desire or the need to make money. Buoyed up by family funds, he enjoyed a hectic social life and indulged his passion for rugby, playing for Rosslyn Park in south-west London. It was through his membership of the club that he met his future wife, Christina Halstead – her cousin Jean knew some of the other players and had introduced her to them.

The Halsteads came from Chichester, in Sussex. Terence's maternal great-grandfather was reputedly Surveyor to the Fabric of Chichester Cathedral; his grandfather was a stockbroker and a great collector, travelling all over the world to put together collections of such curios as snuffboxes, many of which are now owned by the Victoria & Albert Museum. Christina grew up in a large house in Chichester and attended the local high school. Her parents seem to have been beset by ill health – as was she in later life – and her mother died when Christina was only a few years old; her father died when she was twelve.

For a time Christina lived with her grandmother, and then with her aunts. She showed an aptitude for drawing, but her relatives wanted to make sure she was not financially dependent on them and, rather than going to art school as she wanted, she was pushed off to London to attend a secretarial college. After studying she lived in a bedsit in Earls Court and worked in a solicitor's office. She was an intelligent woman with wide interests, but her opportunities were always likely to be limited by her circumstances. It must have been a frustrating and lonely existence for a young unmarried woman, with no close family, whose confidence had been undermined by her aunts' telling her how plain she was.

Her world changed when she met the handsome and affluent Rupert Conran, who 'swept her off her feet'. Although they were very different – Rupert urbane, gregarious and charming; Christina shy and introspective – 'they were mad about each other'. Rupert liked her sense of humour – which, like Terence's, was scatological – and her quiet determination. She had the sharper and more enquiring mind, but she was always grateful to Rupert for helping her break out of her humdrum existence. On 27 October 1928 they were married at St Cuthbert's Church in Kensington. Almost exactly one year later the great crash of stock-market prices around the world wiped out both the Halstead and the Conran family funds.

Even though both Rupert and Christina had worked for their living, there had always been family money in reserve. Now, although Rupert's mother provided him with a small income, most of the money was gone. All that were left were some beautiful pictures and family heirlooms, which would have to be sold when school fees and other bills had to be paid. For most of their lives the Conrans struggled to come to terms with their straitened circumstances – 'genteel semi-poverty'. Aspects of their former lifestyle, such as a nanny for the children, would be juxtaposed with the need to sell the family silver.

Initially the Conrans lived in Phillimore Gardens, in Kensington, and Rupert continued his job as a market clerk, but when Christina became pregnant, in 1931, they decided to buy a small house in Esher, Surrey, where property was affordable and it was possible for Rupert to commute to London.

The marriage of Rupert Conran and Christina Halstead, 1928

Terence Orby Conran was born on 4 October. Neither of his parents was religious – his father in particular having been put off religion by his experience at Beaumont School – so Terence was never christened, and he can't remember ever going to church when a child. Although the Conrans were soon to move back to London, Terence has two fleeting memories of Esher: he can recall lying in the garden under an apple tree in blossom and, later on, spilling green paint on the terracotta kitchen floor – the memory of the jarring colours has remained.

Driven by the economic necessity of having to support a family, and having had some experience of trading in commodities – he had worked on the Rubber Exchange – Terence's father decided to set up a company, Conran & Co., to import gum copal from the Congo. With the remains of the family funds, he bought some warehouse space on the north side of the Thames at Stepney. Here the gum copal was sorted and stored before being melted or 'cracked' to form a natural base for varnish. One of Terence's earliest memories as a young boy was visiting the warehouse and being excited by the energy and bustle of what was then a very busy river – a contrast to the much quieter views he now enjoys from his office and restaurants on the south side of the river at Tower Bridge.

To be nearer to Stepney, Terence's parents sold the house in Esher and bought a big apartment at the top of a block of flats in Canfield Gardens, just off the Finchley Road in north-west London. A tough but friendly and bright nanny called Jenny Envis, who had previously worked for the Duke of Westminster, was hired to look after Terence. She would remain with the family while the children were growing up, and became a lifelong companion to Terence's mother. Terence stayed in contact with her throughout her life, but, as in most of his relationships with women, he would occasionally display cruelty as well as warmth and fondness. Priscilla can remember Jenny Envis giving Terence some violets and him throwing them back at her. Terence would often find the emotion of close relationships uncomfortable and would need to push people away like this.

Terence remembers their new home as being spacious and nicely decorated by his mother, who mixed modern furniture with the more traditional paintings and artefacts they had inherited. He recalls beige-coloured furniture and a large carpet in the living-room which was ruined when his father dropped a bottle of black ink on it.

My taste in interior design is in part a reaction to the clutter that most of my generation grew up with. I was lucky because when I was a child my mother decided what the house should look like, and her taste was for Ambrose Heal's furniture. . . . She achieved great simplicity.[3]

Although his mother was not especially politically inclined, she was very well read and was leftward leaning in her attitudes. She believed in social justice and a more equal society – just the sort of ideals that defined the Arts and Crafts movement of which Ambrose Heal was a part. In fact her liking for Heal's furniture seems to have been in part aesthetic and in part ethical.

As Christina had missed out on the opportunity to use her own talents, she was very keen to develop her children's abilities and awareness of art and design, and she took Terence to exhibitions and to look at the displays at Heal's (where, in spite of the family's limited finances, his Christmas presents were bought). Along with the sculptor Eduardo Paolozzi and the Condé Nast photographer Michael Wickham, his mother was to be the great formative influence on Terence's taste and aesthetic sense.

In 1936 his parents had their second child, Priscilla. The next year Terence was sent to Arnold House School in Hampstead as a day boy. He can remember playing football there, the school's red blazers with green edging, and also the arrival of a group of Chinese children of indeterminate age. (As they spoke no English, the only way to tell how old they were was by inspecting their teeth!)

At Arnold House, Terence did a lot of drawing and painting. From an early age he had shown an aptitude for drawing which his parents, who both enjoyed sketching, nurtured. Priscilla recalls, 'I don't think he was an easy little boy, and it was through his pictures that I think they discovered he was going to be creative.' For Terence, drawing was a means of self-expression. He was a shy child – partly because he was so much in his

3. Terence Conran, *Terence Conran's New House Book* (Conran Octopus, 1985).

Terence and his sister, Priscilla

mother's world, and found it difficult to communicate with other children – and enjoyed his own inner world of fantasy and make-believe, which he expressed with his crayons and coloured pencils. As Terence got older the joy of drawing for its own sake diminished and his creativity found other outlets, but he has always retained a strong visual awareness.

Terence's stay at Arnold House was short-lived. After Chamberlain's visit to Munich to meet Hitler in September 1938, there was saturation coverage on the radio and in the press on the likelihood of conflict and its impact. Barrage balloons were installed, trenches were dug in London's parks, and the Conrans, like every family in Britain, received their gas masks.

It was the gas masks that did it, that and the trenches that appeared overnight in the public parks and private gardens in the last days of September 1938, crude pits dug as air-raid shelters, when for many in Britain war with Germany seemed inevitable before the month was out.[4]

'The least unexpected war in history' was still a year away, but after Hitler marched into Prague in March 1939, people knew that war was a question of when, not if. Terence's parents decided they would be better off out of London – a judgement that proved correct, as the roof of Canfield Gardens was blown off after they moved. While they looked for somewhere to live permanently, the Conrans went to stay with one of Christina's aunts – the strangely named Tom (short for Tomasina) – at Midhurst in Sussex, and Terence was moved to a prep school called Boxgrove. (The original school has since been demolished, and its records have been lost.) It was during Terence's short stay there that he first met Alexander Plunket-Greene, who later became a friend and the husband of Mary Quant.

His parents eventually managed to find a more permanent home at Old Shepherd's Farm at Liphook in Hampshire. It was a modern but quite large redbrick house owned by the Mills family, who also happened to run the nearby school of Highfield. The Conrans rented the house, and Terence was sent across the two fields to school. However, Liphook proved to be only marginally safer than London. The town was on the main London to Portsmouth railway line, and the ferrying of munitions to the naval dockyard at Portsmouth by train, via an ammunitions depot at Liphook, soon made the line a popular target for German bombers. Many evenings were spent underneath a table in front of a large fireplace. Priscilla remembers that she and Terence thought it was all rather exciting, but the danger was brought home when incendiary bombs set the adjacent farm alight. The next day Terence can remember the ground being covered with wild mushrooms – the heat having caused them to

4. Peter Hennessy, *Never Again* (Jonathan Cape, 1992) p. 6.

sprout. One day the reality of war was brought even closer, when a German plane flew low over his head firing its guns as he ran along the lanes between school and home.

Highfield was a conventional English preparatory school with a good academic reputation and a considerable emphasis on those twin pillars of private education, sport and religion. Terence recalls there being rather too much of the latter for his liking, which led to his lifelong denial of religion: 'Fairly early on I took the view that man had designed God rather than the other way round.' The headmaster was Canon Mills, who had moved the school up from Highfield in Southampton in 1907, acquiring some 170 acres of fields and woods and building a new schoolhouse and, of course, chapel. The broadcaster Ludovic Kennedy, who went there in the 1930s, describes the Canon in his memoirs:

> The headmaster was a portly clergyman with pince-nez and watery blue eyes whom we called the Bug and whose principal pleasures in life seemed to be commissioning stained glass pictures of saints for the school chapel and administering the cane.[5]

When Terence joined the school in the summer of 1941 the Canon was still known as the Bug – school nicknames rarely change – and he still seems to have administered the cane with excessive zeal. But, although the Bug was a strict disciplinarian, Thomas Goulder, a fellow pupil of Terence's, remembers that there was a softer side to him. On Sunday evenings the Canon would gather the school together in his study and, with the lights turned down, read them an adventure story – albeit bowdlerized for the benefit of the boys. This editing never quite worked, however, as someone was always positioned behind his shoulder to see the text and signal his expurgations.

There were only eighty-eight boys at Highfield, all of whom were borders except for Terence, who lived so close that he could

---

5. Ludovic Kennedy, *On My Way to the Club* (Collins, 1989), p. 40.

walk to school every day. This was probably an advantage in that Terence missed the daily cold baths and the Bug's contribution to rationing, which was to feed the boys day-old bread. However, it did mean he was not as involved in school life as the others, which made him seem something of an outsider. Terence was self-contained rather than gregarious. He preferred to be at home either making things or cataloguing his various collections rather than playing with his schoolfellows.

Terence may have not been particularly academic – unlike his mother, who was very bookish – but he did have passionate interests, which he pursued with total commitment. Before the days of television, hobbies assumed a great deal of importance in children's lives, and Terence loved his hobbies. Quoting from a set of books of orange-paper designs – one of his recently acquired collections – he says:

'A hobby is something about which you can grow enthusiastic. It consists of activities that arouse your deepest interest. And whatever it may be, do not acquire the idea that it is a waste of time. When you are interested you are always learning – broadening your intellect, your soul. Some make their hobby their business, and then they are able to play all through life.' That's really me. Most things I've done in my life have been what I wanted to do.

Terence was as driven as a child as he was later as an adult. Spurred on by the desire to prove himself to his mother and by his need for self-expression, he acquired a love of collecting which has remained with him. He was never much of a reader, but he acquired a breadth and depth of knowledge both through what people told him and through his own voyages of discovery as a hobbyist. First of all it was flowers and plants, then he moved on to butterflies and hawk moths. In later life it would be design and cooking.

The antecedents of his strong sense of smell, shape and colour that would feature so strongly in the success of Habitat can be found in his childhood hobbies. The appeal of lepidoptery for him was in the myriad colours and textures to be found in the hawk moths he loved. Rather than spend his evenings listening to the radio or doing his homework, Terence would be out in the woods setting his traps and decoys in the grounds of the school. He would then catalogue his collection and enjoy the overall effect of the moths together in a glass case. In those pre-DDT days, there was an amazing variety of moths and butterflies in the English countryside, and Terence worked hard to get every type he could. When he appeared on a television programme called *Memento* some fifty years later, he presented a display case of hawk moths as one of his most prized possessions.

Terence also liked making things. He worked in the school carpentry shop, and he built his own workshop at Old Shepherd's Farm. The pleasure of woodwork and later metalwork was in being able to see the tangible results of his efforts. It was through the physical reality of making, of working as a craftsman, that he came to design. He was not then and is not now a conceptual designer: Terence will design a product with the construction of it clearly defined in his own mind. He likes the beauty of simple and functional shapes – the sort of objects and furniture with which his mother furnished their house. Growing up in this sort of home, Terence acquired a fervent belief in the virtue of function in design.

> If you look at hand tools, they are things that are totally and completely functional and practical. I have not yet seen an ugly hand tool, so that really is a perfect example of form and function coming together to produce something that not only works but is also aesthetically beautiful.[6]

Notably it is the product – its look and its feel – that he loves, not the idea of the designer. Ask him to talk about a product and he will have to hold it, to touch it. He enthuses about beautiful objects, and his descriptions of both an everyday metal watering-can and a piece of Wedgwood porcelain will employ a language that is both reverent and sensual. Ornate or overly decorative

6. *The South Bank Show*, London Weekend Television, October 1987.

products, designed principally to convey status and wealth, not only lack truth but also obscure the construction and the form of the object, which, for Terence, represent its essence and delight. In contrast, a simple form has an integrity which can be seen and felt.

At Liphook Terence learned not only to make, but also to trade. With little money to buy things and with wartime rationing in force, the Conran children had to use their imagination and Terence's skill at handicrafts to entertain themselves. He produced precise, small-scale models of ships and trains, which they used to play with and which he also sold locally. Priscilla remembers the small model boats would be carved with minute details such as little bunk beds and even jamjars in the cupboards. Terence recalls selling his work: 'There was a man in Liphook at the Anchor pub called Charlie Lane, who had the most fantastic collection of old trains and a workshop that repaired them. I made him a model of some boat, and he swapped it for a three-and-a-half-inch Myford metal-turning lathe. I think I got the better deal.'

The lathe enabled Terence to be more adventurous, but it was also the cause of an accident when a piece of metal flew off and lodged in his left eye. Terence remembers little about the process of extracting the metal – although he thinks a magnet might have been involved – but the accident left him able only to see light and indistinct forms from that eye. It didn't affect his ability to read or work, but he found that when he tried to play cricket he couldn't see the ball when batting right-handed and had to retrain himself to bat with his left. To Terence's mind, however, the accident did have one beneficial effect, in that later on his disability meant he was excused National Service.

During the war years, the Conrans' family holidays were few and far between. There had been a summer trip just before the war to the beach at Felpham, near Bognor Regis, where Terence had an argument with the son of Nazi Germany's ambassador, Joachim von Ribbentrop. Terence resolved their differences by hitting his adversary on the head with a beach spade. Also there were visits to the Isle of Wight, where Terence was entranced by the shape of the boats he saw and the smell and industry of the boatyards. However his most memorable holiday as a child was during one summer in the middle of the war, when the Conrans went to stay with a rather exotic great-aunt on his mother's side of the family, called Dorothy Knowling. She lived near Cornwood, in south Devon, and Priscilla recalls that she had an amazing garden with rare plants from Tibet, where she used to go to visit the Dalai Lama. Terence remembers his aunt as exciting and bohemian. She had been educated in Vienna, spoke fluent French, and was a passionate collector. She stimulated his imagination with stories of her travels, and he enjoyed exploring her garden with her. Not only did he press new flowers in the book he had started, but he also added to his butterfly and moth collection – the Highfield Natural History Society was to report on the finding of a swallowtail butterfly in Devon that year, which was something of a rarity, as these large and brightly coloured butterflies are normally only found in Norfolk. As well as visits to the beach with their parents, Terence and Priscilla amused themselves on the river with miniature boats that Terence had constructed. When his parents went home, Terence stayed on with his great-aunt for the rest of the summer.

At Highfield, as at his previous school, Terence spent much time drawing. The school magazine did not have any illustrations, but in 1942 his house at school, Heathfield, produced its own magazine. Although the war was having a terrible effect on people at this time, and Terence could see how frightened many of those were who had fled the bombing of London, for a schoolboy there was a sense of adventure, and the magazine reflected this. There were many stories and drawings about the war – pictures of aerial dogfights, with bullets drawn in true schoolboy fashion as dotted lines streaking across the page. Terence's drawing, however, was non-militaristic: it was a nice simple drawing of a boy on a galloping horse, signed 'T. O. Conran, copied'. The school also ran a competition called Jacks, in which, on the last Sunday of each term, each class chose one boy as its representative to draw the most frightening thing you could meet in Highfield Woods. The pictures were then pinned up on the school notice-board and a winner was chosen. Terence was selected by his class and won. Thomas Goulder can remember that 'Terence painted a strange monster. He was a quite exceptional artist from the age of ten'.

Although Priscilla doesn't remember Terence as being particularly sporty, he was encouraged by his father to play rugby and cricket. Given the shortage of teachers because of the war, Terence's father also helped out in coaching the school's teams at cricket, rugby and football. In 1944, by which time the number of pupils at the school had risen to 111, Terence was playing as a forward in the rugby team. The next year he was awarded his school colours. He was also a success at cricket. In one game against St Edmund's School he took six wickets for eight runs and then batted the school to victory – the school magazine reported, 'Dobson and Conran somehow gathered 36 runs between them by methods which can hardly be described as orthodox.' Terence played football for the school, was in the shooting VIII, sang in the choir, and was a tough opponent in the boxing ring: '. . . the semi-final bout between Conran and Gout was decidedly so [spirited], as these two boys hammered at one another from the beginning to the end . . . a close fight was awarded to Gout.'

He also found time to be an active member of the debating society. The first debate he attended, in November 1943, was on an interesting topic in the light of his future career: 'In the opinion of this House the production of Utility goods should be continued after the war.' Utility was the system set up by the government in 1942 to produce simple yet sound furniture. The minutes of the society do not record Terence speaking, nor which way he voted, but the motion was defeated 16 to 11. However, they do record his contribution to later debates. He was against 'this House cannot foresee any future for sea power' and against 'war is more conducive to progress than peace', but he was for 'this country owes its greatness more to its writers and poets than its statesmen'.

At home, Terence's mother remained an inspiration. She encouraged his model-making and drawing, and when sometimes he would get frustrated with his inability to make something he had designed in his head, and would leave it half-finished or would throw it down the stairs, she would be there gently to persuade him to carry on. Priscilla recalls that her mother 'was quite passive to what we were doing, but the undercurrent was that she expected us to achieve excellence, partly because she hadn't had the opportunity herself. She wasn't tough – she was fey and very intelligent.'

Although Terence still talks about his mother with reverence, and was always driven by the desire for her approbation, he rarely mentions his father. Priscilla thinks Terence's relations with their father were difficult. Rupert's business was suffering because of the war, and his Thameside warehouse had been bombed. Although he had great charm and was a good salesman, he wasn't an easy or happy man. He seems to have been frustrated by the position he found himself in. Outside sport, he was unable to fulfil himself. Terence says, 'I think he found the transition from being a social, good-looking sportsman to being a hard-up parent very difficult.' Although Terence was fond of his father, Rupert tended to drink too much and veered between sentimentality and bullying. He was an intolerant man, who, having received little affection in his own childhood, gave little affection to his own children. Rather than learning from his own experience, he took his own frustrations and sense of failure out on Terence, whose wilfulness used to irritate him. Priscilla, who can remember once biting her father because he was hitting Terence, says, 'I think we ran rings round my father, and I think he found it very difficult. In retrospect I can understand him, but when you're young it's not easy to understand that your father has a problem with you.'

In spite of the five-year age-gap between Terence and Priscilla, the two Conran children grew up together in relative harmony. They were united in their devotion to their mother and a wariness of their father, and as they grew older they found they enjoyed a remarkable similarity of taste. As children, however, there was some inevitable sibling rivalry. Priscilla recalls that once Terence brought home a bowl which he said he had made, but

Terence at Highfield School, Summer 1942
(Fourth from left in middle row)

Priscilla was sure he hadn't: 'I can remember us all saying to him, "But you didn't make it." He swore he had. My mother said, "Let's not discuss it any more," but I thought why shouldn't we discuss it some more, so I kept on about it.'

Priscilla enjoyed teasing Terence, but if they were doing things together he always needed to be in control. If she was accompanying him anywhere, he insisted that she look impeccable. He could lead her astray and she remembers him encouraging her and the next-door children to strip the apple trees in the garden and have an apple fight.

Compared to earlier pictures of Terence, in which he looked rather angelic, photographs from the war years show a tough-looking boy with a somewhat surly expression. He looks determined and unapproachable. He had his friends at school, but he was not particularly close to anyone and he was not one of those boys whom everyone remembers. Thomas Goulder recalls that Richard Moore, who later became a senior member of the Liberal Party, was probably the real character in their class, not least because he was always in trouble with Canon Mills. Terence seems to have been a practical yet unacademic boy. Many of the traits of the adult Conran were already formed: the passion for collecting, for building a personal statement; the impatience to get things done; the creativity – and a difficulty in personal relations.

Priscilla remembers that at an early age Terence could show affection for her pets, but somewhere it seems his ability to express emotion was lost. This trait is probably fairly endemic in British private schools – the need to suppress emotion is born out of the tradition of the stiff upper lip and a fear of showing weakness to others – but it seems to have been emphasized in Terence. Partly this was due to his shy and introverted nature, but probably more important was his identification with his mother and a rejection of his father's overly emotional personality, which was emphasized when he drank. Later in life he would always shy away from people who wore their emotions on their sleeve.

In 1945, at the age of thirteen, Terence was due to leave Highfield. Most of the school's alumni would go on to the well-established public schools, such as Eton, Harrow and Winchester. Terence's mother recognized that such academic environments were unlikely to suit his abilities, and instead it was decided he should go to Bryanston, near Blandford in Dorset. Bryanston did not have the tradition of other public schools, having been founded only in 1928, but it did have a strong reputation in the arts and for allowing boys to express their individuality. It was particularly popular with parents who had artistic connections, such as the writer J. B. Priestley, who sent his son Tom there, and Norman Hartnell, the Queen's dressmaker, whose son Roy was a contemporary of Terence's. It also generated a fair number of artists and writers – the painter Lucian Freud went to Bryanston in the late thirties, and among Terence's generation were Alexander Plunket-Greene, Howard Hodgkin and the geometric abstract artist Anthony Hill. A 1942 prospectus set out the school's approach:

Stress is laid on training the boy as an individual as well as a member of society, because the fully developed individual is likely to become a good citizen. For this purpose wide scope and skilled training are provided in creative work (in school and out), not only intellectual, but artistic and manual. In school, by gradually decreasing the amount of *class* teaching over a period of years, boys are trained to work on their own.

The Bryanston approach was to see school as 'a training for life', rather than as a source of knowledge for knowledge's sake. Whereas most public schools focused on academic subjects and were quite overtly anti-business and anti-vocational, Bryanston embraced the practical. The curriculum included such subjects as forestry, agriculture, commerce, banking, architecture and engineering (Terence won the Bryanston Engineering Prize in 1947), and was approached through a combination of lessons, group work and private study – a style more akin to a university than a school. An article in the *Journal of Education* described the system:

A boy makes up his programme of subjects, with his tutor, so that the times add up to his number of work periods in the week. Such extra subjects as music can be included. The composition and size of a boy's programme can be suited to his individual needs.[7]

Bryanston was an inspired choice for Terence, and whereas school had been something to avoid at Highfield, now it would come to be something that was relished. However, just as the war ended and before Terence could take up his place at the new school, he fell ill. At first no one believed him: Priscilla says, 'He

7. D. R. Wigram, 'The Dalton Plan in an English Public School', in *The Journal of Education*, December 1942.

was always telling fibs about having tummy pains at school, because I suspect he didn't like school very much.' Then the school nurse realized he had acute peritonitis, and he was rushed off to hospital. After an operation, he was put into a nursing home in Hindhead for six months. Priscilla remembers that the sanatorium had 'nil desperandum' carved in stone above the door, and that Terence had pipes and tubes everywhere. For an active, practical boy with little interest in reading, the convalescence could have been unbearable, but one of the doctors encouraged Terence to make models, and he was soon producing miniature furniture for dolls' houses and little rabbit roundabouts. When he continued his convalescence at home, he sold his creations to the local shop.

In January 1946 Terence went off to Bryanston in his parents' Austin car with his trunk and tuck box strapped to the back. Although school life would isolate him to a certain extent from wider events, there was a great sense of optimism about the future. Despite the end of the war there was rationing, and large numbers of soldiers were still in uniform, but there was a desire for change. The feeling that the country was moving forward towards a more caring, egalitarian society was already evident, and would be emphasized by the time Terence left Bryanston and went on to art school. The social researchers Mass Observation found:

> The 'selfish' set of attitudes revealed in prewar studies gave way to a sense of purpose which went beyond self and immediate convenience . . . From 1943 people began to show a willingness to itemize what was wrong with British society and to suggest ways of putting it right.[8]

Bryanston was much bigger than Highfield. There were some four hundred acres of woodland and playing fields, and more than three hundred pupils. The writer Roger Longrigg, who was a fellow

8. Peter Hennessy, *Never Again* (Jonathan Cape, 1992), p. 78.

pupil, recalls that the school grounds and the surrounding countryside were spectacular. Bryanston was in the heart of Thomas Hardy's Wessex, and from the top of the school house (the former home of the Portman family) there were impressive views of the Stour Valley, which Hardy had eulogized in *Tess of the D'Urbervilles* as 'this fertile and sheltered tract of country in which the fields are never brown and the springs never dry'. Once inside the gates there was a two-mile-long drive from Blandford through thick woods and greenery which hid the geranium red and white school house from view until the last sweep of the road. The gently flowing Stour, which was used for rowing, fishing and swimming, cut through the grounds. The main part of the school was a late-Victorian building which had been designed by the leading country-house architect Norman Shaw:

The interior is yet more overwhelming, both in size and by the way Shaw uses great areas of Portland stone. The front door leads to a vestibule apsed at both ends, out of the centre of which steps rise through a mighty stone doorway into the great central saloon.[9]

To Terence overwhelming meant intimidating, and, having just come out of hospital, he was miserable about being separated from his home life, whatever its faults. The school food was also pretty terrible. His mother was a limited cook, because she had never been taught, but home food was always wholesome, in spite of rationing. At Bryanston, Terence can remember thin bread and margarine with jam that tasted of no known fruit. There were also whale meat, powdered egg and dripping. There was a tuck shop, but it had no tuck. Occasionally, however, the Bryanston diet would be alleviated when the boys caught a fish in the Stour.

9. M. C. Morgan, *Bryanston 1928–1978* (Bryanston School, 1978) – quoting from John Newman and Nikolaus Pevsner, *The Buildings of England: Dorset* (Penguin, 1972), pp. 118–20.

Even if the food was always something to be endured, after his initial homesickness Terence began to enjoy Bryanston. It was far more liberal than Highfield. Howard Hodgkin remembers, 'The school as a whole was intellectual, not in an academic way, but there were remarkable teachers. It was liberal and questioning. It prided itself in a positive way on the arts.'

Among Terence's remarkable teachers were two very strong influences: Charles Handley-Read, who taught art, and Don Potter, who taught pottery, sculpture and metalwork.

Handley-Read, who was the first Old Bryanstonian to become a teacher at the school, had a wide-ranging knowledge of art history. Although he had studied architecture at Cambridge, his real love was painting. He had become an expert on Paul Klee (a strong influence on Terence and other textile designers in the 1950s), was working on a book on the art of the Vorticist painter Wyndham Lewis (*The Art of Wyndham Lewis*, 1951), and was a great collector of Victorian painting. He gave his pupils individual tuition and helped develop their drawing skills. Handley-Read's influence can be seen in Terence's drawings from the period, some of which appeared in the school magazine, the *Bryanston Saga*. They include neat scraperboards (a method of illustration which involves scraping away a black ink layer to reveal white clay-surfaced card underneath) of the school boat-house he had helped to build and of flying geese as well as geometric abstracts.

Terence also produced two *Saga* covers which show the influence of the sculptor and typographer Eric Gill. This was not particularly surprising, as it was Eric Gill who had taught Don Potter to sculpt and carve. Potter passed on Gill's ideas on sculpture as well as the principles of pottery developed by Bernard Leach and Michael Cardew. Leach described in 1931 how he had made an ash glaze from brown Cornish bracken mixed with feldspars and quartz. Under the guidance of Don Potter, Terence also experimented with these ash glazes. Similarly, Leach's modest approach to design, assimilated in part from his experience of working in Japan, is clearly close to that espoused by Terence throughout his life. Leach, whose ideas were laid

**One of Terence's illustrations from the
Bryanston Saga, 1947**

down in what has become the potter's bible, *A Potter's Book* (1939), believed in simplicity of design and form:

. . . in the early nineteen twenties he [Leach] really was a voice crying out in the wilderness, and his work was, to an extent distressing to him and discreditable to the British public, despised and rejected. That public was not yet ready for such deliberately 'unshowy' work. Leach believed that 'potters must be artists, but they should make things that are useful as well as decorative, otherwise they are in danger of losing the common touch. Teapots, cups, dishes, casseroles, are just as interesting as pots for flowers . . .'[10]

From his early days at Bryanston, Terence was devoted to pottery. He says that, at that time, if anyone asked him what he wanted to be he would say 'a potter'. In many ways a career as a potter − albeit with a strong commercial orientation − would have been ideally suited to both his temperament and his skills.

10. Michael Cardew, 'Bernard Leach − recollections', in *The New Zealand Potter*, Special edition, 1960.

He liked using his hands, and had a strong affinity for the form of objects and a well-developed sense of colour and texture. Howard Hodgkin says, 'What Terence acquired at Bryanston was his feeling for materials,' and Don Potter remembers that Terence 'had a very good eye for proportion'.

Terence was very interested in the slipware of the seventeenth-century English potter Thomas Toft, which had been rediscovered by Leach, Cardew and the Japanese potter Shoji Hamada. Slipware is a method of decoration akin to icing a cake, which makes it a difficult technique with which to draw. Toft's skills as a draughts-man were such that he could nevertheless produce images of great charm and eloquence. The appeal to Terence, however, was in the actual making of slipware, and the pre-industrial, craft feel of the finished product.

Don Potter encouraged Terence's enthusiasms and experi-ments and admired the way he persevered in the face of difficulties – a sign that his mother's persistence in making sure he finished things was paying off. Potter also involved the boys in building a wood-fired kiln in the cellars of the school, and it wasn't long before Terence was building his own kiln in an outhouse at Old Shepherd's Farm. School holidays were spent either doing pottery and metalwork at Liphook or working at a local pottery, which specialized in earthenware. Priscilla remem-bers that home had become like a craft centre: 'There was a pottery wheel which he made at Bryanston and brought back. We had a lathe, which he got from a publican, and the kiln attached to one of the old wash-houses. Later he started doing textile screen printing.'

The quality of work produced by Terence and the other school potters was high. In the autumn of 1947 there was an exhibition of their work at Heal's. The *Times Educational Supplement* enthused over the pottery and sculpture, which included a very Gill-like kneeling lamb:

> Made of red clay, and with glazes of deep rich brown, cool terra-cotta and Chinese white and other unusual colours, there are some pots worthy of a master craftsman. The whole of the work is spontaneous and without

mannerisms, surely directed by the master, and yet expressing the individuality
of the various students. The slipware too has a definite personality without
being laboured. The forms are simple, strong and natural.

Terence's work also proved to be saleable. When the school
needed a leaving present for a master, they chose the gift from
the work of Don Potter's pottery students – a Conran pot, price
ten shillings.

However, pottery wasn't Terence's only passion: he continued his butterfly and moth collecting, under the auspices of
the Bryanston Natural History Society; he did woodwork with
Mr Muirhead in the well-equipped carpentry shop; and of
course he did metalwork with Don Potter, who taught him to
weld. (Potter still has a metal chair made by one of his students
from the forties which is not only ingenious in its construction
but also features the thin black metal legs Terence favoured in
his early designs.) There was a clear emphasis at Bryanston on
being able to do as well as think, which suited Terence's
personality. It also proved to be useful later in life. When he
was struggling to get himself established as a designer in the
early 1950s, he kept going by being able not only to design
furniture and fittings but also to make them. By understanding
the process of construction, he could make prototypes and one-
off items for clients.

At Bryanston the instilling of practical skills in the boys was
institutionalized in the form of something called Pioneers. The
official idea behind it was 'to provide boys with opportunities
for working together at useful construction jobs'; however, the
artist Anthony Hill thinks the school was as much motivated by
the need to stop its buildings falling down. Pioneering required
spending one and a half hours a week digging trenches, planting
trees, repairing the river-bank and in Terence's case building a
boat-house under the direction of the gang leader, who was a
big Welsh boy called Tom Ponsonby (who used the experience
to good effect later on, when he became Opposition Chief
Whip in the House of Lords). Terence enjoyed learning about
manual tasks, such as bricklaying – it all added to his practical

knowledge about how things were made. Ponsonby also helped to found the Da Vinci Society, of which Terence was a member. This was a sort of cultural appreciation group, and invited writers and artists such as John Piper, William Coldstream, Victor Pasmore and Hugh Casson along to speak. It introduced Terence to the London art world in which he would come to participate in the fifties.

Terence thrived on the Bryanston experience. Even if he wasn't very self-confident in his relationships with people, Bryanston developed a confidence in his practical abilities. To some he could seem arrogant and a bully, which was mostly a cover for his own insecurity; others liked his seeming sureness and strength of character. Howard Hodgkin thinks that 'Terence's knowing what's good for people, somehow comes from Bryanston. Though the school wasn't smug, it somehow established that feeling.' He adds, 'I think one of the secrets of Terence's success is that he's not really changed. Most people acquire guilt and self-doubt and things that are barriers to action. I think he never really has.' Alexander Plunket-Greene, who Hodgkin remembers as 'by far the most creative person at Bryanston', says, 'Terence was less of a child than the rest of us, and I was rather in awe of him. He was a surly lad with some very strong ideas – he still is if you don't know him.'[11] Although Plunket-Greene, Tom Ponsonby and Hodgkin – until he ran away from school – were all friends, Terence was often on his own or with Don Potter experimenting in the workshop. This was the environment he loved best, and where he excelled.

Part of Terence's broader education which he still cites as influential were the visits the school organized to stately homes and public buildings. He can remember visiting Montacute House in Somerset – an Elizabethan property with fine interiors and furniture – and Stourhead – a Palladian house built for the banker Henry Hoare. This had furniture designed by the younger Chippendale, and impressive gardens which had been laid out in an irregular,

11. Barty Phillips, *Conran and the Habitat Story* (Weidenfeld & Nicolson, 1984), p.6.

natural way rather than in the strict geometry favoured by the French. Although both Terence and his mother had an interest in gardening, which for him had begun with his Aunt Dorothy, he always talks about these stately-home visits as having influenced his attitude towards interiors – but not, as one might expect, through the grandeur of the family furnishings, but through the functional furniture of the below-stairs world (a preference he shared with William Morris). When, many years later, Terence came to write about his favourite influences, it was this artisan-made furniture he recalled: 'What they made had to be basic and functional; they stripped their furniture to its bare essentials.'[12]

The moral and aesthetic appeal of artisan-made furniture has remained with Terence. Partly this is a result of the influence of his mother, partly it is through the teaching of Don Potter, and partly it is through Terence's relationship to the things he saw. He knew he couldn't make the ornamental furniture of the upstairs world, but he could understand the construction of the servants' furniture and he knew how to reproduce it.

Although Terence now likes to play down his scholastic achievements, he did gain a School Certificate (the equivalent of 'O' levels/GCSE) with distinction in Metalwork. He also achieved passes in English Literature and Geography, and credits in General Science and Drawing. This wasn't the height of academic achievement, but neither was it disastrous. Indeed, although it welcomed academic success, the school was not especially concerned with results: Bryanston was about providing a boy with a rounded experience. With five Certificates, Terence could stay on at school and study for his Higher Certificate (the equivalent of 'A' levels), which would enable him to go on to university if he wanted. Although Terence doesn't remember having a clear idea of what he wanted to do next at this point, life at Bryanston was enjoyable and enriching. He could continue his pottery and metalwork with Don Potter, the school provided

12. Terence Conran, *Terence Conran's New House Book* (Conran Octopus, 1985), p. 14.

him with opportunities to see and do new things, and there were girls at a nearby school.

One of the properties which the Bryanston boys visited was Crichel House, which was eight miles east of Blandford. Apart from being a stately home with a lake and large grounds, it had the added attraction of eleven- to eighteen-year-old girls. A school called Cranborne Chase had been opened there after the war as a sister school to Bryanston, and it was run on similar lines – indeed its first headmistress, Miss Galton, had taught English and mathematics at Bryanston. Although the schools were some distance apart, they both encouraged the supervised intermingling of the boys and girls in such areas as music, drama and some sports. However, Terence was soon moving from supervised to unsupervised visits.

From an early age he had had a strong sex drive, and he discovered that girls found him attractive. Terence's sister, who was one of the first pupils at Cranborne Chase, soon learned that he was an object of interest: 'At school he had lots of affairs with girls. I used to hear girls whispering about him. They would come and say to me, "Your brother . . ." ' One girl in particular – a tall, vivacious redhead called Jane Howell – attracted his attention. (Her brother was David Howell, who went on to become a Conservative MP and Secretary of State for Energy in Mrs Thatcher's first government.) She had a Dior 'New Look' dress that she wore to parties, and Terence thought she was very glamorous. He would cycle from Bryanston to meet her in the countryside. (Terence remembers that the beauty of the school grounds wore rather thin when he had to cycle miles to his assignations.) Bryanston may have been a liberal school, but it was *in loco parentis*, and had also suffered from a wartime scandal when boys had been caught stealing munitions from the local barracks. Although that affair had been hushed up, the school was nervous about its position: it couldn't be seen to be tolerating the nocturnal excursions Terence had started making. When he was caught one night by a Blandford policeman as he returned from a rendezvous near the local Tarrant Rushton aerodrome, with no lights on his bicycle, the matter was referred to the school. Terence says that the headmaster, Coade, was quite nice about it, but nevertheless he was asked to leave. Terence doesn't remember being unduly worried that his school career had been terminated, because it was near the end of his last term and he had already determined what he was going to do next.

After his idea of becoming a potter had waned, he thought he would like to use his skill in metalwork and become a gunsmith. When he discovered that the apprenticeship lasted ten years, he dropped the idea and decided to ask Charles Handley-Read for advice. Although Terence could draw reasonably well, he was not committed to art in the way that such fellow pupils as Howard Hodgkin and Anthony Hill were. Handley-Read correctly saw that his skills were not in art *per se* but in the appreciation of pattern, form and colour. With his credit in General Science, he felt that Terence would be best suited to textile design.

At that time the best school for textiles was the Central School of Arts and Crafts in London. Terence applied and was asked to show his portfolio to the head of the textiles department, Dora Batty. He went for breadth, and showed her everything from his lepidoptery collection to his drawings, scraperboards, model-making and pottery. He remembers the interview going quite well: 'I think Miss Batty was interested more in the scope of what I had done, rather than the quality of the work, although I suppose it was reasonably good – certainly the pottery was.'

The Central School believed in encouraging its pupils to have a wide range of skills, so Terence's decision to show everything he'd done proved fortuitous. In the summer of 1948 he was offered a place there.

CHAPTER TWO
THE AGE OF AUSTERITY

> There were still many moments in the late forties – as there were to be other, very different moments in the fifties – when to many Englishmen this seemed to be an England they could scarcely recognize. Identity cards still had to be carried and shown at a policeman's demand. The streets were still drab, unpainted and dimly lit. In the West End, Oxford Street seemed to have become a succession of pin table arcades and garish side shows.[1]

The London which greeted Terence was a dowdy place. Bomb damage from the war was in evidence everywhere, rationing was still in place, materials were in short supply, the shops were half-empty, and there was little in the way of entertainment. The Labour government of Clement Attlee was effecting real social change in the development of the Welfare State, but intermittent financial crises limited its actions and created the need for wage restraint. Between 1945 and 1951, average weekly wages rose in real terms by only 6 per cent.

In spite of this modest increase, there was more disposable income than goods to buy. Manufacturers played safe, at least in the home market. There was no need to innovate with new ideas, because they could sell all they could produce of tried and tested products. Not surprisingly, there was little of note happening in the world of design. Many of the designers and architects who should have been coming to prominence at this time had been away fighting in the war and were now starting or resuming their education. Utility furniture, which had been introduced in 1942, was still the only type available. Although the idea of Utility – the production of sound furniture that was free of decorative detail –

1. Harry Hopkins on 1948 in *The New Look*, 1964.

appealed to the egalitarian principles of the Labour Party and the design establishment, it was not particularly popular with the public. Its necessity was recognized during wartime, but its continuation through the late forties met with resistance. When Utility was finally dropped at the end of the decade, consumers reverted to the type of furniture they had always bought: 'The same resilient British spirit that had "kept the home fires burning" also proved stubbornly resistant to well meaning attempts to change its taste for Jacobean sideboards.'[2]

A positive contribution of the Labour government was that it viewed design as an important ingredient in its reformist 'caring' strategy for Britain. Through the 'Britain Can Make It' exhibition, held at the Victoria & Albert Museum in 1946, the government tried to show the public that good design and new products were just around the corner. However, in spite of attracting one and a half million visitors, the exhibition was popularly known as 'Britain Can't Have it', for the balance-of-payments situation and the desperate dollar shortage meant that most of the things on display were for export only.

The design schools themselves were in a state of flux. The Royal College of Art occupied a collection of huts and buildings in South Kensington. Until 1948, when Robin Darwin became principal, the RCA was a bureaucratic institution which Darwin himself likened to a dodo. Its reputation was as a provider of secondary-school art teachers. Although the Central School in Holborn was in a large rambling building that had been bombed during the war, it was altogether in a better state academically. Founded in 1896 by the Arts and Crafts architect and educationalist William Lethaby (who had been chief assistant to Norman Shaw, who designed Bryanston's main building), it was firmly wedded to the practical. Whereas the RCA, where Lethaby was later Professor of Ornament and Design, had veered away from his belief in the importance of industrial design (the reconciliation of craftsmanship and technology) and towards

2. Harriet Dover, 'The War Cabinet', in *Design Review*, Summer 1992.

painting and sculpture, the Central remained true to many of his ideas.

Just as Bryanston was appropriate to Terence's abilities, so with its focus on craftsmanship was the Central School. The heritage of Lethaby was clearly influential on him in many ways: the emphasis on materials and function; the need to learn through direct experience; the importance in breadth of design education and the development of existing designs. Here Lethaby was not advocating being a slave to tradition, but rather, he sought to use earlier forms to achieve a new understanding: 'Usually the best method of designing has been to improve on an existing model by bettering it a point at a time; a perfect table or chair or book has to be well bred.'[3]

By the time Terence arrived, Lethaby had long departed, but one of his disciples, William Johnstone, had become principal in 1946. Like Lethaby, he believed in the marriage of art and industry and also in the importance of tradition. The prospectus for 1948 stated 'research and innovation are encouraged together with the study of the fine traditions of the past gathered from visits to the museums and from books available in the school library'.

Terence had signed up for a three-year course in textile design, along with, as he describes them, 'thirty-two young virgins from Surbiton'. This wasn't exactly true – the class was certainly largely young and female, but there were some mature students who had had their education interrupted by the war, and there were a few other men on the course. The head of the textiles department, Dora Batty, was newly arrived from Camberwell School of Art in south London. She was supported by Mary Kirby, who taught weaving and also the history of textiles. Once a week she took the class to see designs at the Victoria & Albert Museum. Whereas there had been a fairly relaxed teaching approach, Dora Batty was more disciplined. The timetable was filled from first thing in the morning through to the evening with classes not only in textiles

3. William R. Lethaby, 'Art & Workmanship', in *Form & Civilisation*, 1922, p. 211.

but, in keeping with the Central's belief in breadth of education, in the principles of design as well as drawing and painting. The teachers in these areas were either attached to other departments or were brought in as visiting lecturers. It created an exciting and challenging environment, and ensured that the students were in tune with the latest artistic and technical development. For example, Jesse Collins taught basic design along the lines of the Bauhaus – the German design school which has come to symbolize the modern movement in design – concentrating on the use of fundamental shapes and forms and colours to find design solutions. Among the part-time teachers were people from fine-art backgrounds, such as Naum Slutzki, who had worked with the painter Paul Klee at the Bauhaus, and the sculptor Eduardo Paolozzi.

Terence was only sixteen when he first started at the Central, and for the first year he lived at home and commuted up to London from Liphook by train with his father, whose gum-copal business had closed and who was now working as a salesman for Sir Bernard Docker's company Docker's Paints. Terence had acquired a slightly bohemian look, as befitted his status as a design student. He was very thin, had slightly long hair, and wore such things as a canary-yellow shirt with green trousers and a large beige gabardine jacket. He doesn't remember socializing with his fellow students very much, partly because he was having to commute and partly because he had little money. Occasionally he would go out with some of the girls on his course, but most of his spare time was devoted to his hobbies – in the evenings and at weekends he would rather be in his 'craft centre' at home, making pots and printing fabrics, than in a nightclub or bar.

The Central School made a strong impression on Terence. He acquired a good understanding of design history, learned screen-printing techniques, developed his design skills, and acquired a deeper sense of purpose. Whereas his pottery and model-making had been motivated primarily by the pleasure he found in craftsmanship, the Central and its influential teachers showed him the proselytizing power of design. Both the Arts and Crafts movement and the Bauhaus were egalitarian, leftward-leaning bodies that believed in design as a force for social betterment. However, whereas the Arts and Crafts movement was overtly anti-industrial and largely élitist, the Bauhaus came to embrace industry and realized that social change could only be effected by designing and producing for a mass market. Terence recalls:

> My whole attitude to life was really formed in those couple of years – about why shouldn't design be something that is available to the entire community? The mood in England in those postwar years was that we had an opportunity to reshape the world. I think we were all very much aware of what had been achieved at the Bauhaus, and we felt ourselves to be an extension of that – the ideals of the Bauhaus.

The 'whiff of the Bauhaus' that permeated the school came largely through the energy with which design was taught and the power it was seen to possess. Terence and the other earnest students believed in the importance of what they were doing and saw their ideals closely linked to the world of fine art.

For Terence the embodiment of the fine-art influence was the arrival of Eduardo Paolozzi. He started at the end of Terence's first year and taught a class with Robert Addington, who had just completed a degree in textiles at the Central School. Paolozzi, who was in his mid-twenties, had trained at the Edinburgh School of Art and at the Slade, and had just returned from two years in Paris. There, along with a fellow Scottish sculptor, William Turnbull, and the photographer Nigel Henderson, he had come into contact with new thinking about art. He had been influenced by Existentialism and Surrealism, and had met the Romanian Dada poet Tristram Tzara, the Alsatian artist Jean Arp, the sculptor Alberto Giacometti and the French painter Jean Dubuffet. Dubuffet, who rejected the idea of worthiness and expounded the idea of *art brut* – raw art – which endorsed such attributes as authenticity and spontaneity, was clearly influential on Paolozzi's sculpture at this time. Even more fundamental was Giacometti, who influenced both Paolozzi's sculpture and his collages.

During his years in Paris, Paolozzi had started to amass a vast collection of images from magazines and newspapers, which he used for collage. The juxtaposition of random images was intended to develop the students' awareness of colours, shape and form as well as a sense of the spontaneous – of art as chance. Paolozzi wrote of collage:

Divine ambiguity is possible with collage – flesh robots marred by object or object masquerading as flesh. There is nothing astonishing in that – witness the great portraits of Arcimboldo. We have learned to define collage as a process where dreams can be rejected and the victims exposed to ridicule. The word 'collage' is inadequate as a description because the concept should include 'damage, erase, destroy, deface and transform' – all parts of a metaphor for the creative act itself.

The images Paolozzi liked were those that best expressed popular culture – particularly American popular culture. Robert Addington remembers that Terence was very quick to pick up on everyone's ideas and 'soon did Eduardo's collages as well as Eduardo, if not better'.

Paolozzi's other interest that was to prove influential was in primitivism. Like the Dadaists and also Dubuffet, who looked to other cultures for spontaneity, he was interested in the two-way traffic between European and African culture. In Africa, discarded objects made by Europeans were put to new use, while in Europe the everyday artefacts of African culture were put in museums to be looked at and interpreted from a Western perspective. Paolozzi picked up on the themes of African art and began to use them in his two- and three-dimensional work. Notably in his early privately printed textile designs for the architect Jane Drew, there is a strong and rugged African influence in the shape and layout which is quite distinct from the obvious European influences of other textile designers from the period. His individuality was also emphasized by the method of application. His screen-printer and fellow lecturer Anton Ehrenzweig recalled that Paolozzi's silkscreens could 'be over-printed on top of each other in almost any position. Paolozzi printed rolls of ceiling paper in ever-varying overprints. He left it to the workmen who were papering the ceiling to put up the printed rolls according to chance.'[4]

Paolozzi's work may have possessed an obvious confidence, but personally he was diffident. He looked robust and possessed strong bear-like arms and hands, but Terence remembers that on his first day at the Central he went out in the lunch hour and used his sweet ration to buy toffee for the class – a way of breaking the ice. However, by the time he offered the toffee round it had been in his pocket and had bits of string and paper stuck to it. It broke the ice, but not in the way he intended. Sometimes he could also look quite unkempt and intimidating. Paolozzi – whom Terence once described as 'organic' – paid little attention to the way he dressed, and was frequently bespattered by clay and plaster. This was partly because his all-consuming interest was his work and partly because he had very little money – he had lived in Paris on virtually nothing. Robert Addington recalls being with his parents when he saw Paolozzi in the street looking very dishevelled. Rather than admitting their connection, he told them Paolozzi was a friend of his cousin Ian MacCallum, the editor of *Architectural Review*.

However, Terence was immediately drawn to Paolozzi and his originality, and can remember being 'very much under Eduardo's influence'. There is a sense in which Paolozzi was a father figure. He gave Terence the intellectual and emotional support that he couldn't get from Rupert. He challenged Terence's mind; he guided him and steered him. They would visit the Museum of Mankind together to look at ethnic art, and would visit scrapyards to collect pieces for Eduardo's sculptures. Thirty years later they were still doing the same thing – when in the eighties Paolozzi was commissioned to produce a sculpture of Sir Isaac Newton for the Science Museum, they went to a marine scrapyard in Portsmouth and scrambled round covered in grease and oil collecting enough pieces of metal to fill a large truck.

4. David Mellor, 'Existentialism and Post-War British Art,' in *Paris Post War* ed. Frances Morris (Tate Gallery, 1993).

At the Central, Paolozzi's classes were an inspiration because he showed Terence a world beyond the very insular milieu in which he had been studying. Paolozzi was never constrained by an English sense of compromise, and he demonstrated to Terence the importance of following one's own ideas, of challenging convention. Paolozzi introduced him to the mainstream of European art and to new ideas. The effect on Terence's work was very noticeable. While he had been a capable draughtsman before the Central, he had tended to look back to earlier influences such as Gill. Now, while his work could still sometimes be derivative, he was looking forward and 'bursting and bubbling with ideas'. Terence's textile designs from this time start to show a number of fine-art influences. There is the organic and African influence derived from Paolozzi, as well as the influence of painters such as Picasso, Wassily Kandinsky (who had taught at the Bauhaus), Paul Klee and Joan Miró. The work of Klee, in particular, is clearly evident as an inspiration in Terence's designs. Like Dubuffet, Klee was interested in the primitive – he tried to paint 'as though newborn'. The elements of his paintings, which often featured plants and flowers in rhythmic patterns, were particularly suited for adaptation to textile designs, and Terence's very organic textile designs feature both Klee-like motifs and the spidery lines that Klee used to link objects together.

Having learnt how to screen print at the Central, Terence set up his own equipment at home. However, fabric was not always easy to come by, and he would scour the markets to get pieces large enough to work with. He now started to print and sell his own textile designs. Anthony Hill remembers that people were often taken aback that Terence was selling designs while still a seventeen-year-old student. Anton Ehrenzweig noted his ability, and soon Terence was helping with his commissions. These included scarves and, for Ascher Ltd, a Matisse panel, which was some six feet high and sixteen feet wide.

In spite of the convenience of his home craft centre, Terence was fed up with commuting to the Central School by train every day and wanted more independence. At the end of his first year – summer 1949 – Terence came up to London with his mother to look for somewhere to rent. Eventually he found a room in a house in Paultons Square, just off the King's Road in Chelsea, which was owned by an actor – rent one pound ten shillings a week. The King's Road had long had a bohemian reputation because of the large number of painters and sculptors who lived in the area, but it wasn't the focal point it became in the fifties. The designer David Queensberry recalls:

> When I was a student at Chelsea Art College in the late forties, the King's Road wasn't a street that attracted any major retailers. There was a shop that sold artist's materials, a few grocery shops and chemists and the odd shoe shop, but it wasn't a street that anyone went to for shopping – that happened years later. Mary Quant started that.

Even if large parts of London were still drab, Chelsea had a vitality which Terence liked. At the time, he was living on a five pounds a month allowance from his father – plus the money he made from the occasional sale of a design. It was enough to enable him to start eating out in restaurants for the first time in his life. After the horrors of Bryanston food, this was a revelation. Although mostly he ate at home or went to Eduardo Paolozzi's flat, Terence can remember his first outing to a French restaurant in Soho called the Bagatelle with his father and a friend of his. He can't remember what he ate, but recalls that things such as asparagus and avocados seemed tremendously exotic then. The quality and variety of food in Britain at the time were strictly limited. There were some Chinese and Italian restaurants, but there was not a lot in between the mock grandeur of the Lyons Corner Houses and the restaurants in the big hotels like the Savoy and the Ritz. Many things were still rationed, including meat, and Mrs Beeton was still the cook's guide – Elizabeth David's first book, *A Book of Mediterranean Food*, didn't come out until 1950, and she didn't gain wide acceptance until later on.

One restaurant that Terence did enjoy and which was also affordable was a place on the King's Road called the Ox on the Roof. For about four shillings and sixpence there was egg mayonnaise, minute steak with ratatouille, strawberry tart and a glass of wine. Once a month Terence would go there with friends from the Central School. As for night life, there were pubs and clubs in Soho, but Terence was too serious to be part of the hedonistic, bohemian community of artists and writers such as Francis Bacon, John Minton, George Melly and Jeffrey Barnard that frequented the Caves de France and the Colony Club – although he does recall one visit to the latter with Eduardo Paolozzi when Francis Bacon bought them spring rolls from a local Chinese restaurant. However, he did occasionally spend an evening listening to records with his former schoolfriend Alexander Plunket-Greene, who was a great fan of modern jazz. Terence also remembers going with Alexander to a jazz club in Oxford Street run by Humphrey Lyttelton, called the 100 Club. As Alexander used to borrow his mother's trousers, which zipped at the side and were both too tight and too short, and Terence had invested in a pair of Black Watch trews, they must have looked a strange couple, even in the environment of a club.

On Saturdays Terence could be found playing rugby. Spurred on by his father, who thought his son should be doing something more physical than pottery and textile-designing, Terence turned out for his father's club, Rosslyn Park in East Sheen. He wasn't good enough to make the first team – perhaps not surprisingly, as Rosslyn Park was the pre-eminent team in England at the time, with an all-international back line – but he played for the A team as a hooker under the captaincy of Dick Storry-Deans, who had been with the club for a number of years and knew Rupert. Although Terence was relatively fit, he never had the physical power and bulk of his father, nor his enthusiasm – Priscilla remembers that her father would take her to Twickenham to see rugby internationals, rather than Terence. Also, Terence felt rather out of place in the socializing that went on after the games:

I don't think I was very gregarious at that time. For a very large part of my life I was very shy indeed. Even to this day I find it difficult until I've got to know somebody. When I used to play rugby I felt I had nothing in common with the others when they wanted to socialize in the bar and drink vast quantities of

beer after a game. I think they took a dim view of me when they discovered I
was an art student.

After he gave up rugby, Terence eschewed physical exercise. He
might garden with his mother, but team sports or diversions such as
'goff' – as Terence calls it – were an irrelevance. The environment
he felt most comfortable in was Chelsea and Fulham. Here the
people he would get to know would be writers, architects,
sculptors, artists and designers. They tended to be young men and
women who were concerned with their careers. The environment
was good for Terence in that it put him in contact with what was
going on culturally. Through Paolozzi he met people, like William
Turnbull and Nigel Henderson, who were at the forefront of
challenging the rather staid conventions of British art. He had his
own views, but he never stopped absorbing the ideas of others.
Terence was never an intellectual – he was always too commercially
oriented to be that – but he did share, for example, Paolozzi's
interest in American popular culture.

Terence's time at the Central was now to come to an end. In
their second year, students had to specialize 'depending on their
wishes to become either freelance weavers and printers or designers
to the industry'. Terence opted for the last, but says he began to
realize that 'the opportunity to become a textile designer when I
left the Central was very slight indeed'. Certainly the money that
could be earned by textile designers was limited. The average fee
for a textile design sold outright to a manufacturer was fifteen
pounds, plus two or three pounds extra for colour variations.
However, there was a developing, if still limited, market for
modern textile designers. Companies such as Cresta Silks,
Edinburgh Weavers, Ascher and David Whitehead were all
commissioning work from artists and designers, but the volume
market was in more traditional, floral designs: except for the
enlightened few, manufacturers were content to play safe and stick
with designs they knew would sell.

Given Terence's pessimism about his career prospects, it was
perhaps not surprising that he was susceptible to a job offer. The
architect and designer Dennis Lennon visited the Central School

and was struck by Terence's designs. He offered Terence four pounds a week to join him as a junior designer. Terence had learned a lot from people like Paolozzi, but he was keen to work in a commercial environment and was frustrated by doing designs for his teachers rather than real clients. He felt he would learn more from Lennon than he would by spending another eighteen months at the Central. Although Lennon's taste did not exactly match Terence's ideas, he was a Modernist and very strong on interior design. Whatever misgivings Terence had, it was too good an opportunity to miss.

CHAPTER THREE
GETTING ESTABLISHED

Terence's time with Dennis Lennon, which continued until 1952, represented an important phase in his development both as an individual and as a designer. There were some early achievements and a growing reputation, but there were also disappointments both in his personal life and professionally. The Terence Conran that emerged from these experiences was still young, but altogether tougher, more determined, and more aware of his own abilities.

The courage that Terence showed in his mid to late twenties when he started and developed a number of new businesses – in spite of little experience of the business world – was born out of determination. Whatever the vicissitudes he faced, his belief in the power of design to change people's lives remained unshakeable. The Bauhaus, which had been held up to him at the Central School as the way forward, demonstrated that modernity and the machine could change society. On a political level Terence was inspired by the Labour Party, and in particular by Aneurin Bevan, the Minister of Health. The appeal of Bevan, who was a man of strong Socialist convictions, was in the passionate and committed way in which he challenged the established order. Through the creation of the National Health Service and his attempts to improve housing, he seemed to be making Britain a better place for everyone. This process was extended into design by the Council of Industrial Design (later the Design Council), which was a creation of idealistic Socialism. The CoID believed that everyone would benefit from better-designed, mass-produced objects. For Terence, the idea that design should be élitist was anathema; he wanted design to be accessible.

Dennis Lennon was in his early thirties when he started practising architecture. He had studied at University College,

London, just before the war, but had then spent six years in the Army fighting in France, Italy and North Africa. His first job after the war was as an assistant to the Modernist architect Maxwell Fry, who ran a practice with his wife, Jane Drew. The architect Theo Crosby recalled those years in Dennis's obituary:

Lennon always had style – I remember him in the office of Maxwell Fry and Jane Drew in 1948. It was a place of great ebullience, packed with returned soldiers and avid colonials on the grand tour. He was broad, jolly, the possessor of an MC and a simply divine Triumph sports car. We could all see that he would go far.

One of Fry and Drew's early jobs was to design an exhibition stand at Earls Court for the developing rayon industry. Rayon was a man-made cellulose fibre, which had been manufactured by Courtaulds since 1905. It had long been used as a substitute for silk, but, although it hung well and was good for dyeing, it also creased easily. Given the postwar shortage of natural materials, however, consumption of rayon boomed – especially in overseas markets. Such was the success of the exhibition design that Fry and Drew were asked to work on a Rayon Design Centre for the industry in a large Georgian house in Upper Grosvenor Street. Lennon helped Jane Drew design the building and supervised the contract. As with much of his later work, there was meticulous attention to detail in the fusing of the new design with the Georgian architecture: 'the two were brought together by the sensitive colouring of the plasterwork, which was in turn related to the colours used for the furniture and furnishings.'

The Centre, which featured a design studio and an exhibition area, was opened in 1948 by the then President of the Board of Trade, Harold Wilson. In a newsreel from the time, Wilson named the £30 million a year rayon business as Britain's tenth largest export. Impressed by Lennon's work, the rayon industry offered him the job as the first director of the centre at a much larger salary than he was earning. He wasn't sure whether it was a good career move, but Fry and Drew suggested he took the post to earn some reasonable money and to gain experience.

Terence was delighted with his new job with Lennon. Lennon's view was that a designer should be able to turn his hand to anything, so Terence had a 'roving brief' and was not only given the opportunity to design textiles, but also to design the rayon industry magazine, *Rayon and Design*, and exhibition stands.

After Terence had been at the Rayon Design Centre a few months, Lennon decided to set up on his own and Terence went with him. Lennon found some premises in Manchester Square, and Dennis Lennon and Partners was formed as an architectural and design practice. However Lennon still retained his position at the design centre, and Terence continued to produce work for the magazine and to design textiles. The May 1951 issue of *Rayon and Design* features an abstract design on the cover by him as well as illustrations and photographs of his textiles. One of the textile designs has a very Festival of Britain look to it, while the others are more abstract. One of the amusing aspects of the magazine is

One of Terence's textile designs featured in *Rayon and Design*, 1951: 'a good design, for the upper classes.'

that it features comments from a panel which comprised Jane Drew, the fashion designers Hardy Amies and Michael Sherard, and a member of the public, called George Jones. Although the latter, with flat cap and thin lips, looks like a caricature of 'the man in the street', his comments on the class appeal of design are the most interesting. On one of Terence's designs, the comments were:

Jane Drew Very good design, but motifs a little too architectural and dispersed.

Hardy Amies Absolutely hideous; repellent. This reminds me of those terrible fan lights with alabaster bowls, upside down. I would not have it in my house. It has what I call hiccoughs, all the time.

Michael Sherard No real relationship between units, no real sequence.

George Jones This would not suit my house. I don't think it would suit the working class who want something more flowery. I think it is a good design, for the upper classes.

In addition to Terence, the other employees of the new practice included an architect newly arrived from South Africa called Bernard Wiehahn and an architectural graduate from Cambridge called Brenda Davison. At this time there wasn't much architectural work around, but the practice was still doing some design work for the rayon industry, and it soon started to pick up briefs for interior designs. Lennon was good at winning clients – not only was he outward-going and generous, he also understood design in a way that was rare for architects. He had a great concern for detail, for total design – that door handles should be consistent not only with the doors but with the overall structure of a building. The architect Sir Hugh Casson recalls that Lennon was 'a clever chap, who was one of the few architects who understood interior design', and Bernard Wiehahn says that 'Dennis had a very strong belief in integrated design – everything had to work together.' One has only to look at Terence's later creations, such as Quaglino's, to recognize that this was a view of design that he too came to believe in.

The first projects the practice won were an interior design for a US Officers' Club and a West End showroom for Partos Bras.

Dennis quickly saw Terence's skills as a 'chooser' of design, and set him to work selecting the materials and furniture for these jobs. Terence faced a problem that confronted all designers at this time: materials were in very short supply and permits had to be obtained for virtually everything. This meant that designers had to be creative in their choice of materials – and also adaptable, as it was quite likely that, having started an interior fit-out, the chosen material would suddenly no longer be available and would have to be replaced. Lennon also appreciated Terence's style of illustration and asked him on several occasions to paint murals for interiors. These were not always successful. When Lennon saw Terence's mural for Partos Bras, he thought it was inappropriate and had it painted over. Terence was furious.

Some of Lennon's ideas and Terence's were in tune. Lennon always liked to have the best of any particular material or product, and he had an affinity with strong primary colours – reds, yellows, strong blues. He was also interested in modern, especially Scandinavian, furniture. A Pathé newsreel from 1952 shows his home at Hamper Mill in Watford, featuring modern furniture, including some pieces by Terence. In a slightly sneering tone the newsreader says:

> Here's another curious chair with what is called a free-standing back, which like its attendant flowerpot [Conran-designed], implants the idea of a life without frills. Whether you could live with such furniture, you will be able to decide when you've looked round this room.

Where Terence and Lennon differed was in their appreciation of ornate furniture. Terence thought Lennon's taste was too glitzy; he preferred the plain and the simple. In an attempt to broaden his outlook, Lennon took Terence to the Wallace Collection, which was also in Manchester Square. The Collection includes famous paintings and a huge range of French eighteenth-century furniture, much of it from the royal palaces of France, by some of the great French craftsmen – Boulle, Oeben, Riesener and Carlin. Terence was nonplussed by it all. In a TV profile of Terence, Dennis Lennon recalled:

He [Terence] was bored to death. This great big desk with about fifty different marquetries in it – they are absolutely wonderful, really superb, but he didn't like it at all. It was another world, which he could not compete with and knew it was not possible to reproduce. But I think it was a good thing he saw it.[1]

What was important for Terence's development at this stage was that he had an employer who was able to guide him but who also gave him the latitude to develop his own ideas. He was always experimenting with new ways of doing things – with mixed results. When Terence was responsible for the design of the bar at the Institute of Contemporary Arts, he decided he would create a feature by cooking a lobster and then encasing it in plastic. Unfortunately, the plastic was not properly sealed, and it wasn't long before the lobster started to emit a horrible smell. However, his fabric designs for the ICA were more successful. He produced cotton curtains featuring organic shapes which show the influence of Klee in the leaf- and elliptical-shaped motifs that are the dominant element. The fabric design was subsequently sold by Liberty's and Dunn's of Bromley for ten shillings a yard.

Bernard Wiehahn remembers that, although small and occasionally short of work, the practice was a very exciting place. The people there all had strong personalities and were serious about their work, but when there wasn't much to do they would sit and drink, and Terence would cook some of the recipes he had learnt from his evenings spent with Eduardo Paolozzi. Paolozzi had learned to cook Italian recipes when he was growing up in Edinburgh, and had developed his skills in his impecunious days in Paris when he had had to be inventive to make a little money go a long way. He had shown Terence how to make some of his dishes, using such rarities as *calamare sue tinto* – squid in ink – to make risottos. When Terence produced these sort of dishes in the office, everyone was amazed. On Friday evenings after work Lennon, who was very much the *bon viveur*,

1. *The South Bank Show*, London Weekend Television, October 1987.

would take the staff out to a wine bar, and occasionally to a restaurant in Shepherds Place, in Mayfair, called the Café Boulevard. This was a favourite because Dennis Lennon and Partners had been responsible for its conversion from a tailor's shop. Dennis Lennon and Terence produced a dramatic interior by combining black with bright primary colours. Along the window frontage was a tubular-steel frame which contained a variety of house plants, and at head height running round the restaurant was a Conran mural. Like many of his later designs, it featured illustrations of food and drink.

In 1951 the practice was working on two major commissions, both of which Terence was involved with. The first was interiors for the Ridgeway Hotel in Lusaka, and the second was the Festival of Britain.

The Lusaka project had come about through some work Lennon had done for the Scottish Furniture Manufacturers' Association. Terence was asked to produce some chairs for the hotel. Although he had not studied furniture design at the Central, he had learned something about construction while at Bryanston and he knew how to weld. Also the Central had subscribed to many international design magazines, such as *Domus* and *Interiors*, and through the features in these magazines he was aware of the developments in furniture design, particularly on the West Coast of America. He recalls, 'I was very influenced by America and a magazine called *Arts and Architecture*. It had features on Knoll and Eames. They were my main influences.'

The influence of Charles Eames on British furniture design was considerable. The designer Robin Day says that 'Eames was a genius', and in her book *Mid-Century Modern* Cara Greenberg says, 'Charles Eames is the undisputed shining light of twentieth-century American furniture design.' Eames's furniture was pure, simple and functional. Trained as an architect, he saw design in terms of space and structure and it was the interplay of these that gave his furniture its impact. But, although designer furniture remained the choice of the few rather than the many, Eames's furniture was always created with a mass market in mind. His wife, Ray, said, 'We wanted to get as much quality as possible

Terence, 1951

into mass production so that more people could live with well-made things.'[2]

Terence liked the furniture and the ethos of Eames. However, the Ridgeway Hotel contract was not about mass production: Terence had to design and make the chairs.

He had at this time acquired a small lock-up garage in a railway arch in Bunsen Street in Bethnal Green, east London,

2. Quoted in Cara Greenberg, *Mid-Century Modern* (Thames and Hudson, 1984) p. 82.

Eduardo Paolozzi, 1951

which he shared with Eduardo Paolozzi, whom he was teaching
to weld. Brenda Davison remembers it as being most notable for
the cold. Terence would try to alleviate this by having a fire inside
the garage, but that created too much smoke for them to work.
At this time Paolozzi was experimenting with surreal sculptures
which fused images of machines and bodies, so his interest in
welding was in the creative effect rather than the technique. He
tended to get the gas torch too close to the metal, which would
then blister and explode leaving an uneven surface. It wasn't good
welding, but Paolozzi rather liked the blobs and barnacles

he achieved. In return for this tuition, Paolozzi was providing Terence with his Italian cooking lessons and aesthetic inspiration. Raymond Elston, who knew Terence from the Central School, remembers there was always a strong smell of garlic whenever Terence and Paolozzi were around.

Terence would also occasionally take the train to Hamper Mill, where Dennis Lennon had a workshop. Often he would be

Selection of Terence's designs, 1951

joined by Toby Jellinek, who had just left school and was helping Terence with his welding and furniture-making. Dennis's wife would pick them up from the station, and they would spend the day welding metal rods.

The chairs Terence produced for the Ridgeway Hotel were in wood and metal, with the spindly legs which were so typical of the furniture of the time. Their coverings featured a strong and brightly coloured design with a clear Paolozzi influence in its use of African motifs. Along with many of the other fabrics for the hotel, these were screen-printed by a Lancashire-based textiles company called David Whitehead, the managing director of which was an architect friend of Dennis Lennon's called John Murray.

The big event of 1951 was of course the Festival of Britain – 'A tonic to the nation'. This was the swansong of the Labour government. It had been suggested during the war as a festival to celebrate the centenary of the Great Exhibition of 1851; now it was to be an opportunity to show the world that Britain was back on her feet and to show the British people that austerity was a thing of the past. Herbert Morrison was the minister in charge, while Gerald Barry was in executive control. However, it was not a particularly popular event with either political party. Sir Hugh Casson, who was Director of Architecture for the Festival, remembers:

> The Conservatives were dead against it. Winston thought it was the advance guard of socialism – which of course it was. The left wing of the Labour party hated it because they saw it was controlled by the Hampstead wets, like Gerald Barry . . . There is a theory that in England nothing is taken seriously unless it comes from Hampstead.

However, for the designers and architects who were offered work on the Festival by Hugh Casson's architecture committee, it was a godsend. Many of the architects had been trained before the war and were now in an environment where there wasn't enough work around. Hugh Casson and his team chose the architects and allotted them sites:

All the architects were about my age – they were about forty – and they'd mostly never built anything because they'd left architectural school and then gone to war and hadn't been demobbed until 1946–7. They were producing mad ideas they'd designed in their fifth year at school. They were still learning their jobs.

The designers were selected by Misha Black, who was in charge of interior design on the committee. The problem he faced was that there weren't really such things as interior designers. The Royal College of Art started a school of interior design under Hugh Casson after the Festival, but most of those chosen to produce interiors were exhibition designers or architects.

With Dennis Lennon and Partners' growing reputation for interiors, it was not perhaps surprising that the practice was asked to contribute, by designing the interior of a quarter-scale model of a flying boat. Dennis Lennon determined the colours, and Terence painted a mural along the stairway that linked the upper and lower decks of the boat. Typically there was great attention to detail and both *Life* and *Vogue* produced quarter-scale magazines for it. Terence also produced furniture and a fabric design for David Whitehead, which was shown at the Festival in the Home and Garden Pavilion. Terence's mother thought the slightly phallic motifs looked like a series of signs for 'This Way to the Gents'.

Terence was caught up with the enthusiasm of the Festival. He slept at the South Bank site while he worked on the flying-boat, and got the chance to meet other designers and architects. It seemed as if design had arrived in Britain and that he was very much part of this brave new world.

In terms of public interest the Festival was a huge success – in five months it was visited by over 8 million people. Several designers and architects had their careers boosted by it, including Hugh Casson, the textiles designer Lucienne Day, the architect Basil Spence and the furniture designer Ernest Race. Design was being talked about not only by the Council of Industrial Design, whose job it was to promote good design, but in the press and in the street. For the first time, designers were news and were seen by some as marketable. Advertisements for Heal's textiles and furniture and later Midwinter ceramics gave prominence to the designer's name, and Lucienne and Robin Day appeared in vodka advertisements. There were articles in the specialist magazines and in national newspapers about design and a few high-profile designers. However, for most in the design industry there was no great leap forward. Materials were still rationed, manufacturers on the whole were pretty conservative, and the style of Festival design was rather backward-looking. It had elements of modernism, but it also tended to be fussy and whimsical. It was an attempt by many of the designers to create a style that drew on specifically English cultural antecedents. Looking back on the Festival, Misha Black wrote of it, 'it remains true that there was little real innovation, almost nothing on the South Bank which had not previously been illustrated in the architectural magazines.'[3]

The great breakthrough didn't happen. Rather than there being more work around, it actually dried up, and shortly after the end of the Festival Terence was laid off. Although Terence understood that Lennon couldn't keep him on and in retrospect thinks it made him more determined to develop his own ideas, he was profoundly disappointed. He had given up his course at the Central School to gain real experience, and here he was unemployed and unqualified. Lennon and Partners and then the Festival had raised his hopes only to dash them. Indeed, looking back, the whole Festival has the feeling of hype: 'the way in which the relative affluence of the fifties was used to delude the population into believing that Britain's health was sound, it might be more appropriate to describe the Festival as "A Narcotic to the nation".'[4]

3. Misha Black, 'Architecture, Art and Design in Unison', in *A Tonic to the Nation: The Festival of Britain*, eds M. Banham and B. Hillier (Thames and Hudson, 1976).

4. Adrian Forty, 'Festival Politics', in *A Tonic to the Nation: The Festival of Britain*, eds M. Banham and B. Hillier (Thames and Hudson, 1976).

Rather than look for another job, Terence was keen to emulate what furniture designers such as Robin Day were doing: producing modern furniture designs and getting them made. Unlike Day, whose work was manufactured by the modernist furniture company Hille, Terence couldn't find anyone to make his designs. So he determined to make them himself. He had already made furniture for the Ridgeway Hotel, and he started to pick up the odd private commission for furniture which, because of his limited funds, he had to use the London Underground to deliver. He also produced a fabric design for David Whitehead which was very successful and was sold on to the bedding company Myers, which used it for ticking. It was an abstract pattern which featured different coloured squares within a grid that was defined by wavy and dotted lines. Although the design shows the influence of Paolozzi, it does have a look which is distinctively Conran. From the scores of designs that Myers commissioned at this time, Conran's 'Chequers' was one of the few outstanding ones, selling over a million yards.

During his time with Lennon, Terence had earned enough money to get a new place to live. Through his colleague Brenda Davison, he had found a room in an elegant house in Warwick Gardens, just by Kensington High Street. There he could work as well as live – although he kept the Bethnal Green workshop for a time to do his welding. The house was owned by a young doctor called Ivan Storey, whom Brenda had started to go out with while at Cambridge. It had been in a poor state but Brenda and Ivan had renovated it together, and to help pay the bills they rented rooms out. Terence had a bedroom at the top of the house, as did Olive Sullivan who worked on *House & Garden*. Toby Jellinek moved in for a while, and so did the writer Den Newton. On the ground floor there was a dentist called Miller. In the basement there was a big kitchen with a table in the middle. Everyone used to have their meals there, including Paolozzi who was a frequent visitor because, Brenda recalls, 'where he lived was so horrid'. Eduardo and Terence also used the basement to work in, and Olive Sullivan remembers '. . . Terence and Eduardo filling rubber gloves with different colours of plaster of Paris in the kitchen to make an exhibit for a show at the Institute of Contemporary Arts, not realizing that plaster blocks sinks.'[5]

The atmosphere was very friendly and relaxed, although there would sometimes be scenes when Ivan, who was away doing his National Service, would come home and find that his wine stock had been seriously depleted. Somehow everyone's lives in Warwick Gardens seemed to interact, and they would continue to do so: Den Newton would write about Terence's textiles, Terence would build a close relationship with *House & Garden*, Ivan and Terence would go into business together and Terence and Brenda worked together and would later marry.

Terence's room was tiny, but he soon decorated it with his Paolozzi-like collages and some of his furniture. No one in the household had much money, but occasionally everyone would club together and there would be a party. Terence can remember one night in particular when there was a lot of strong cider to drink. Eduardo, who was 'large and unshaven', was persuaded by Terence that Olive Sullivan was secretly after him, and Terence and the others egged him on. Brenda recalls that Olive was 'very ladylike and proper. She and Eduardo were like chalk and cheese.' Eduardo screwed up his courage and went off to find Olive, only to appear a few minutes later with his tail between his legs. On another occasion Ivan, Terence and Toby had an evening out in the fish restaurant Wheelers, where they consumed large quantities of oysters and wine. When they got back to Warwick Gardens they all drank some gin, then went out to have races round the square at the back of the house. Toby can remember being so ill the next day that he had to go home to his parents – it was the first and last time he ate oysters. Terence, however, always seemed to have a large capacity for alcohol and a very robust constitution, and these drinking bouts never affected him unduly.

Terence's personal life was becoming complicated. He had

---

5. Ann Barr, '£150 million down and still smiling', in *Harpers & Queen*, July 1991.

started going out with Brenda, which caused some friction in the house, so Brenda decided to move out and got a flat in Ennismore Mews in South Kensington. Meanwhile Den Newton and his wife, the American writer Mary Lee Settle, who worked for Fleur Coles's magazine *Flair*, had moved into a house in Sloane Court West and Terence decided to rent a room from them. The sculptor William Turnbull and his wife also lived there.

Brenda was very bright and attractive. She was a few years older than Terence, and he felt that everyone thought he was her toy boy. Priscilla thinks Terence was 'mad about Brenda', but he wasn't faithful to her and continued to see other girlfriends. This would be a feature of Terence's long-term relationships: he was attracted to intelligent women who had careers and a sense of purpose, but he also found it hard to resist the temptation of casual relationships with girls whom he met socially or through his work. Not surprisingly, the relationship with Brenda broke down and she met a married man – an engineer called Leonard Bennett.

Brenda had been attracted by Terence's energy and enthusiasm, but Leonard seemed to offer a more serious relationship, which was something she was looking for – especially when she fell ill with tuberculosis and had to be hospitalized. Terence, whose mother suffered from arthritis for a number of years, found illness difficult to cope with. Not only was his and other people's mortality something he would rather not think about, he was also frightened of the emotions involved. He couldn't control the situation so his solution was to avoid it, and when Brenda fell ill he stayed away. In contrast, Leonard visited Brenda every day, and she became convinced that he would leave his wife and marry her. When she felt better, he took her to the Isle of Wight for a holiday. Once back in London, however, he started to have second thoughts about the affair. His friends and colleagues told him to leave Brenda and return to his wife, and he backed off.

After several months in hospital and the build-up of expectations, Brenda was both heartbroken and vulnerable.

Terence was still passionate about her and wanted her back. To keep her, he decided to propose. Although she had reservations, she accepted. Brenda now says, 'It was very irresponsible of me, and looking back you don't believe you did these things.' Priscilla believes her parents thought Brenda would be a good influence on Terence and says, 'I know that my mother was very fond of Brenda – she gave Terence her engagement ring to give to her.' Terence, however, isn't so sure: 'I think my family were a bit resigned about the marriage; they had the idea that it wasn't the best possible thing I could do.' Whatever the family view, the wedding in the summer of 1952 was a simple affair at Chelsea Register Office. The honeymoon was a visit to Lancashire, where the first night was spent with John Murray of David Whitehead.

Although Terence and Brenda had known each other for some time, the marriage was very short-lived – they were together for about five months. Leonard reappeared, promising to leave his wife. Brenda, who had believed the relationship was over and had married Terence on the rebound, thought she now had a second chance to make it work. She ran away with Leonard leaving Terence in Ennismore Mews. Terence says he 'was extremely upset and depressed', and there were reports of a scuffle between Terence and Leonard outside Dennis Lennon's office. His sister, Priscilla, thinks the breakdown of the marriage had a profound effect on his attitude towards women: that he was still very attracted to them, but that he was very cautious about making emotional commitments in the same way after this.

Although Terence's business was beginning to make some headway, he wasn't progressing as fast as he would have liked. He didn't have enough money to carry through his ideas, and sales of his furniture were spasmodic. This made him very frustrated and impatient. Even those who believed in him found that he could be aggressive and petulant. As with some of his other character traits, this was largely a protection for his own sense of self-worth, which had taken a hammering both personally and professionally. By bullying others and being assertive, he could hide and compensate for his fragility. Those who saw through this behaviour recognized it for what it was and accepted it. What was needed to help improve his humour was business success. Certainly the economic environment was improving. Rationing was still in place on many goods and materials, but the Conservative government which had taken office under Churchill in October 1951 was committed to its removal. But for a balance-of-payments crisis in 1951 and a resultant rise in interest rates – the first 'stop' of the fifties 'stop–go' era – there was real growth.

There was also the beginning of fifties consumerism; people had more money to spend. The problem for the designer – and indeed for the long-term success of the British economy – was the innate conservatism of manufacturers. The historian Martin Wiener believes this was a reflection of the cultural dominance of Whitehall:

The natural habitat of the gentleman-industrialist, of the industrialist as imitation civil servant, was a conservative one, where pervasive regulation and control (from government and from within) substituted for innovation . . . it was an environment in which lip service was paid to competition, enterprise, innovation, invention and salesmanship, while the disruptive and time-consuming consequences of these were feared.[6]

Terence believed passionately that design could provide industry with a competitive edge; that it could enable British manufacturers to make products that would succeed in world markets. Throughout his life he has continued to harangue both business and government about the difference that design could make to Britain's economic performance. Often his pleas have fallen on deaf ears, but he has never stopped trying to change attitudes. Indeed, when Mrs Thatcher was Prime Minister he sent her a copy of Martin Wiener's book on the decline of British industry.

6. Martin Wiener, *English Culture and the Decline of the Industrial Spirit 1850–1980* (Penguin, 1985) p. 151.

In spite of the general lack of attention paid to design, there were some manufacturers who were more enterprising. Although by the 1950s the textile industry in Britain was in decline, the quality of some textile designs was high. Lucienne Day won a gold medal at the Milan Triennale in 1951 for her 'Calyx' design, and artists such as Matisse, Henry Moore, Graham Sutherland and Ben Nicholson had all designed fabrics for Ascher. Another of the innovators was the textiles company David Whitehead, run by John Murray. He, like Zika Ascher, was committed to the idea of using distinctive designs for fabrics, and in his view that meant employing freelance designers and artists. He had seen some of Terence's work, which he liked, and offered him a retainer of £1,000 a year to produce designs. Other retainees included the Bauhaus-trained Marian Mahler and the artist John Barker.

Terence's work showed a variety of Paolozzi and fine-art influences, and Den Newton, writing on printed textiles in 1952, singled it out (while omitting to say that he was Terence's landlord):

> Terence Conran, who has worked under Paolozzi, has produced interiors, murals and distinguished furniture. More of his textile designs have been put into production than most other young designers'. In colours which range from the bold to the acidly delicious, they are extraordinarily sophisticated and elegant. Extremely receptive as he is, his work often has about it a lightness and a lack of any attempt at profundity which gives it all the great charm of the ephemeral.

John Murray remembers that Terence's work was not the most commercially successful in the Whitehead range, but that Terence 'had an intuitive appreciation for what was in vogue, for what was about to be fashionable. He was a very bright, derivative designer.' That ability to read the mood of the time was something that Terence would draw on again and again – as a designer, as a retailer and as a restaurateur. Looking forward ten years to Habitat, for example, it was his skill as a 'sensitive salesman' that would enable him to design and select a range which had an instantaneous appeal to the educated middle classes.

Terence also produced a range of designs for David White-head which could have had a very significant impact. White-head's had for some time produced denim cloth. In the USA denim jeans were quite a significant product – sales of Levi's in 1950 were worth about $200 million. However, denim was only just beginning to be a fashion item for young men and women: it really took off in around 1953, when Levi's introduced pre-shrunk denim. John Murray had the idea that denim could become a young fashion cloth and commissioned Terence and Raymond Elston, who had some knowledge of making clothes, to produce a range to be shown at the newly completed Royal Festival Hall. Terence and Raymond bor-rowed some space from a theatrical costumier and in the space of about six weeks produced seventy different garments. Raymond cut the cloth and Terence produced prints which featured abstract designs related to the shape of the garments. A photographic shoot, with some of Terence's furniture as props, was organized to show how the clothes would look when worn. However, when the clothes had been produced and the photographs had been taken, other directors of David White-head got cold feet about the idea, and the Festival Hall launch was cancelled. Terence and Raymond were very well paid for the efforts – about £400 each – but they were very disappointed that their hard work had come to nothing. Some of the material was subsequently displayed at an exhibition in Chester, for which Terence designed the stand, but the idea of printed denim disappeared almost without trace.

With the improvement in the economy, the furniture business began to enjoy more success. Gill Pickles, who had studied book illustration at the Central School while Terence was there, had started doing design work for him, and Raymond Elston was making the metal and wood furniture. It wasn't always easy to find buyers, but Gill remembers that Terence seemed to have such confidence in his ideas that it rubbed off on people; he could often persuade clients that he could do things better than anyone else.

Fashion designs by Terence, 1952

Before he left Sloane Court West Terence also had a piece of good luck which raised his profile. In the early 1950s *House & Garden* was *the* magazine for interior design. In the main it was fairly conservative and tended to like features on stately homes, but it was one of the few consumer magazines to talk about modern design. One of the ideas of the young design editor, Cynthia Blackburn, was to do a feature on sculpture in the house. As Den Newton was interested in primitive sculpture and had some of Paolozzi's African-inspired work at home, *House & Garden* arranged for Cynthia and the magazine's photographer, Michael Wickham, to call round. Having taken the photos of Newton's Paolozzi sculptures, they saw through an open door into what was Terence's room:

There was a bare floor sanded and waxed with button polish and a black ladder unit. There were those extraordinary chairs with the backs done up like corsets. Lots of nice tables in white and black marble. The ladder unit was full of beautiful objects. We shouted, 'Could we come in and take some photographs?'

Cynthia remembers that Terence was quite happy to have photographs of his furniture taken. She also recalls that they turned out better than the sculpture shots.

The corset-like chairs also achieved some celebrity recognition. After the oyster episode, Toby Jellinek had gone back to school for a year and then went to live in France with his fiancée, Sylvette David. Toby was painting and also making chairs to Terence's design next door to a pottery in Vallauris. Picasso, whose studio was across the road from the pottery, was quite taken by Sylvette David (who became his model) with her blond pony-tail and also with the design of the chairs. Toby gave Picasso a chair as a gift. Picasso was so delighted by its shape that he ordered two more. In her biography, *Life with Picasso*, Françoise Gilot wrote: 'It was such an abstraction of the idea of a chair that it reminded Pablo of certain paintings he had done during the 1930s in which Dora Maar is shown sitting in a chair made up of a skeleton framework much like this one . . .'

Cynthia got a full-colour full-page shot featuring Terence's chair and black ladder unit in the September 1951 issue of *House & Garden*. After that, if she wanted any furniture to prop a shoot, Cynthia would call up Terence, and throughout the fifties his furniture appeared in room sets in the magazine. It was the start of a long working relationship and friendship with both Cynthia and her husband-to-be Michael Wickham. Terence would inspire Michael to take up furniture-making, while whenever Terence was working on a new idea the Wickhams were there supporting

The chair Picasso bought

Terence at Simpson's, 1952

him. For his denim experiment, Cynthia and a designer called Heather Standring were the models, while Michael was the photographer.

Another piece of good fortune was that Terence's work was spotted by Natasha Kroll, the display manager of Simpson in Piccadilly. Natasha, who had been born in Russia and trained in

Display at Simpson's, 1952

Berlin, had been at Simpson since the early 1940s. She knew Dennis Lennon and through him saw some chairs Terence had designed for the Rayon Design Centre. She recalls, 'I saw Terence's work and I thought it was fresh. It was a student's work, but in the days when student work was exciting.' She offered Terence the chance to design and make some units for a

Christmas in-store display. These were in his familiar metal-rod style.

The units worked well, and Natasha offered Terence an exhibition of his work at the Jermyn Street entrance to the store. In the first few months of 1952 he busied himself putting together a range of his designs. A cabinet-maker's called Pegrams helped with some of the pieces, and a company called Tisserands, off the Euston Road, wove cane into the metal frames of the chairs and seats. Terence included some fabric designs and terracotta pots on metal stands, and his display cabinets featured some of his line drawings of such things as hot-air balloons – a very fifties motif. When the exhibition, called 'Ideas and Objects for the Home', opened in March that year, *Architectural Review* was on hand to take photographs of the exhibits and also of a very thin and boyish-looking twenty-year-old Conran.

Den Newton wrote up the event:

Apart from a very light and elegant chair in a traditional manner, Conran's work represents the same break with conventional craftsmanship in furniture that Turnbull's and Paolozzi's does with the tradition of stonecutting in sculpture.

Newton also liked Terence's 'careful opposition of line and mass' and his 'emphasis on economy'. Although he noted the influence of Charles Eames, Paolo Chesa and Eduardo Paolozzi, he concluded that:

The strict economy has an elegance which prevents it becoming arid, particularly since it is often combined with bright, glossy colours.[7]

The objectivity of the write-up is perhaps questionable, but the effect of the display was strong. While some of the individual items may have been derivative, Terence created a powerful and

7. Douglas Newton, 'Terence Conran at Simpson's' in *Architectural Review*, July 1952, pp. 55–7.

unified showpiece of modern design by treating the area he was given as a room set. He overcame the limitations of the high and poorly lit space by using directional lights and blinds and by creating a false ceiling made of bamboo – the chiaroscuro of the room made the products look desirable. The ability to create drama through design was a skill he would apply with considerable success in merchandizing the early designs of Habitat. Although he wasn't selling from the display, some terracotta pots and stands were commissioned from him, and Natasha Kroll asked him to produce some displays for the famous curved windows on the Piccadilly side of the store. She remembers that 'The colours were all primary – very Mondrian; there were no subtle autumn colours. There was some wit about it, without it being corny.'

His working relationship with Natasha Kroll and Simpson continued until she left to join the BBC as a set designer in 1954. During this time he did some more in-store work, and also provided illustrations for a book she was writing on window display. Although he was already very good at using shape and colour and texture in his designs when he met Natasha, she nurtured his skills and taught him how to use his creativity to produce interesting and effective displays and interiors. After they ceased working together, Natasha remained an admirer and supporter – she liked the spontaneity in his designs and his commitment and perseverance. Although the design establishment was for a long time deeply suspicious of him, she later recommended him for a Royal Designer for Industry medal and suggested he would be a good rector of the Royal College of Art.

Terence was encouraged by the response to his exhibition, but, although he was picking up the odd commission, the problem he had to confront was how to turn his amateur, almost hobbyist, approach into a business with a longer-term perspective. Even though modern furniture was being talked about in the wake of the Festival of Britain, traditional furniture was still the volume market. The designer David Queensberry says:

Design history is very selective, and people tend to imagine that everybody had what design historians write about. If you look at the fifties, someone will show you an early piece of Conran furniture as something that is important. It may be in terms of design, but it had absolutely bugger-all commercial importance in the High Street at this period. The mass of the UK market was as it had always been – traditional.

Neither retailers nor manufacturers were willing to take risks. It was the world so aptly satirized by the Ealing comedy *The Man in the White Suit*, in which a scientist who discovers a new material that never wears out or needs to be cleaned is pilloried by both management and unions. His invention is suppressed because it would upset the status quo. Of course the scientist's discovery would have been popular with the modernists, but less so with advocates of fifties consumerism. Philip Pollock, a friend of Terence's who had a furniture-manufacturing company in the fifties, says, 'trying to sell modern furniture to furniture buyers in those days was awful – they were culturally and aesthetically blind.'

Terence, like other young designers, continually had to face this reluctance to innovate. He believed that, if he could make and sell his own products, there was both a professional audience – designers and architects – and a consumer audience that would be willing to buy. All he needed was the capital to get started. His father helped him by providing him with the shell of the gum-copal business and its accumulated tax losses, and also by guaranteeing a £300 overdraft at the bank. Terence had some income from David Whitehead which would support him while developing the business. Even though he was taking a big step and was nervous about setting up on his own, he was courageous and believed in what he was doing. At twenty-one he launched 'Conran and Company'.

CHAPTER FOUR
FIRST SUCCESSES

If Terence was going to establish a professional business, he needed a workshop, a showroom and some staff. The workshop he found was a basement studio underneath the Ballet Rambert in Notting Hill Gate. Terence remembers that 'there were a lot of pounding feet and the rent was about thirty bob a week'. There was enough work coming in to employ four welders and furniture-makers. Raymond Elston came over from Sloane Court West, and Eric O'Leary, who had been introduced to Terence by Germano Facetti of Penguin Books, was also there. Eric O'Leary had originally asked for the introduction because he knew Terence owned a chair he wanted to copy. When Terence found out that Eric had made furniture for the designer F. H. K. Henrion for the Festival of Britain and done casting for Henry Moore and Jacob Epstein, he offered him a job. He was a few years older than Terence, and provided much-needed working experience to the new operation.

The subterranean existence continued with the showroom. Terence wanted a West End location, but couldn't afford a prime site. Underneath Balcons flower shop in the Piccadilly Arcade, Terence found another basement – even darker and danker than the workshop. However, the owner of Balcons was an architect called Richard Wright, and he agreed to make some improvements. It was a good site, because the Arcade linked the busy Piccadilly to the exclusive clothes and gift shops in Jermyn Street. Then, as now, the shops in the Arcade tended to be smart and slightly expensive. The flower shop was linked to Terence's basement by a spiral staircase. The renovated space was well lit, and it showed off his metal and wood furniture and his terracotta pots to good effect.

Initially Raymond Elston was brought over from Notting Hill to be manager of the showroom, but Terence felt he was better used in the workshop, and Brinsley Black – the 'deb's delight' – replaced him. Brinsley had been working for an estate agent's and had met Terence through Alexander Plunket-Greene. He had been looking for a job in an advertising agency, but like others he was infected by Terence's enthusiasm. His job was to sell the furniture range to retailers, such as Peter Jones, which he succeeded in doing. However, although Brinsley was very charming with customers, his working day tended to be punctuated with a long lunch at Fortnum & Mason. Terence, who has always had a somewhat puritanical work ethic, born out of his impatience to get things done, didn't approve, and eventually Brinsley was moved to manage a coffee bar that Terence opened in Chelsea.

Work wasn't flooding in, but Terence was just about breaking even – a combination of charm and luck got him through. There was a buyer at the John Lewis Partnership called Betty Horne. Raymond Elston remembers that she smoked Woodbines from a cigarette holder, was very thin, had a gravelly voice, and 'always looked as if she was off to a garden party at Buckingham Palace'. In her late fifties, she was one of the many older female patrons who were attracted by Terence's charm, and she was always pushing his furniture and putting in special orders, even when there weren't customers for it. She would explain this away by saying the customer had cancelled at the last minute. Another client was Robert Addington's cousin Ian MacCallum – the editor of *Architectural Review*. He commissioned Terence to produce some furniture both for his Chelsea flat and for his office. The American modernist architect Philip Johnson also visited and bought a chair. However, with trade orders Terence had to be careful that he was paid straight away: if he didn't get the money on delivery, his finances were such that he would be unable to buy the materials for the next batch. It was a precarious existence, but he was always able to carry those who worked with him by his determination.

In the country at large there was something of a boom going on. Between 1952 and 1955 there were no more 'stops' in the economy and the bank rate was cut in successive years, making borrowing cheaper. Shares on the Stock Exchange more than doubled in value in these three years. Materials began to be easier to obtain, and hire-purchase restrictions were eased. The Conservatives had also embarked on a major house-building programme: 327,000 houses were built in 1953, 354,000 in 1954. There were still reminders of wartime – especially in London, where bomb sites would still be in evidence until the early 1960s – but there was now much greater optimism about the future. There was also a gradual though noticeable move towards open-plan living and more modern furniture. This was less true of Britain than elsewhere in Europe – British furniture design tended to stay rooted in sideboards and three-piece suites: 'in general British furniture in the 1950s rarely rose above the level of the mediocre'.[1] However, Terence's range, displaying strong European and American influences, was among the best on offer.

When he had been with Brenda, they had put together a catalogue of his range, so that he could sell to designers and architects as well as to retailers. The range at this time featured his staple of the terracotta pot with metal stand – a device he has since echoed in the champagne buckets at his Quaglino's restaurant – thin-legged coffee-tables with wooden tops, cane-topped stools, storage units which showed a clear Eames influence, a woven basket chair on three legs, and the Tripolina – a version of the Hardoy chair, which was one of the most widely copied chairs in the 1950s. Jorge Ferrari Hardoy had taken the idea in the first place from a folding British officer's chair of the nineteenth century, and several designers then took it from him or from the original – there were many lawsuits about the source of the design.

---

1. Lesley Jackson, The *New Look: Design in the Fifties* (Thames and Hudson, 1991).

Many of the copyright disputes surrounding furniture design arose because architects and manufacturers were pressurizing designers to produce look-alikes. Terence liked to take existing or old designs and adapt them: he would draw out the essence of the design and use it in a new way – in Lethaby's terminology, Terence's designs were 'well bred'. Some, however, felt this was close to plagiarism. Terence hated the idea that people thought this about what he made, but he could also joke about it. Michael Wickham tells a story about his daughter Polly, when aged about ten, hearing the word 'plagiarist' mentioned. She asked what a plagiarist was. 'I am,' said Terence.

Both Robin and Lucienne Day, whom Terence met at a dinner party at Cynthia and Michael Wickham's around this time, felt some of his designs were very derivative – which may have made for an uncomfortable dinner. Robin Day says:

I remember him being an active, bright kind of designer. He had very good taste and judgement of design, so he was more than easily influenced by other people's design. If he saw something he thought was good, he wouldn't hesitate to do something like it. I personally suffered in that way, and a client of mine brought a lawsuit against him.

Lucienne adds:

He did a few quite nice textiles after he left the Central, but one of them was definitely a copy of mine. But a lot of people were doing that – I think manufacturers were pressurizing designers to do similar things. Terence was tremendously aware of the market.

In spite of criticisms about plagiarism, Terence got involved with an interesting venture which was at the heart of original ideas in British art and design at that time. In 1951 a number of leading artists who were interested in avant-garde abstraction formed a loose group to exhibit their work. Few of the major commercial galleries were willing to show their work, so one of their number, the abstract artist Adrian Heath, organized an exhibition at his studio in Fitzroy Street. The participants in this and the subsequent shows at the studio included several with Central School connections. There were paintings by Victor Pasmore and Robert Adams, who had both taught at the Central; photo murals by Nigel Henderson, who taught photography there; Paolozzi's collages; paintings and collages by Anthony Hill and Vera Spencer, who had been Central School students; and mobiles by Raymond Elston. Through Anthony Hill, Terence was invited to put some of his furniture into the show. He made a low table, a stool, a dining-chair and an upright chair – all in his familiar spindly-leg style.

Terence's furniture and the other works were all priced, but there is no record of any sales, even though the visitors' book for the show lists about a hundred and fifty people – including well-known patrons and critics such as Reyner Banham, Roland Penrose and Peter and Charles Gimpel. The most significant review of the event, by Tonio del Renzio in *Art News and Review*, was less than complimentary about Terence's furniture: 'Terence Conran makes his first appearance with this group, contributing some curiously dull furniture, a slick cushion cover in the Paolozzi manner, a smooth version of a Chiavari chair.' The negative comment is not surprising. Although Terence was making modern furniture, it could not be described as avant-garde or especially innovative. Tonio del Renzio, who was a fan of Dadaism, was unlikely to find anything iconoclastic about Terence.

After 1953 the exhibitions continued for a couple of years in other venues, but, with a poor review and a limited sales opportunity, Terence didn't contribute to subsequent shows. He enjoyed the milieu of the fine-art world, but except for the work of one or two artists, like Reg Butler and Paolozzi, he wasn't that interested in painting or sculpture – it was too élitist and individual for his taste at that time.

A more important influence on Terence was France. In 1953 he went there for the first time, on holiday with Cynthia and Michael Wickham and a new girlfriend, Patricia Lyttelton, the recently divorced wife of the jazz musician Humphrey. He says the experience changed his life.

Since he had first met Cynthia Blackburn and Michael Wickham in 1951, they had got married. Michael was a man of wide interests. In the twenties he had trained as an artist at the Royal Academy School, and had become interested in cubism and abstract painting. He had lived in Spain and France in the thirties, and had got to know Picasso and Georges Braque, with whom he shared a house in Cassis. Braque by this time had moved away from cubism and was concentrating on still lifes in which the objects were spread evenly across the painting. Braque influenced Wickham's painting, which is perhaps best described as 'romantic cubism', and the political maelstrom of thirties France influenced his politics, pushing him towards Communism. Wickham had often used his Leica camera to capture images when he was painting, and after he returned to England he found a job as a photographer with Condé Nast, working on *Vogue* and *House & Garden*. (One of his later assistants was David Bailey.)

If Paolozzi broadened Terence's awareness of fine art, Michael Wickham broadened his understanding of life. Michael taught Terence about food, about France, about culture, and about politics. The knowledge that Terence acquired would make him seem worldly and cultivated compared to his contemporaries. It was a knowledge that he would pass on to others. Maurice Libby, who went to work for Terence at the launch of the first Habitat some ten years later, says: 'In the shop we were the unwashed selling to the unwashed – only Terence knew. He would take us from the shop out to eat, and in the most gentle way he'd be teaching you.'

The trip to France started badly. They all set off in Michael's open-topped Lagonda for Lydd Airport in Kent. However, when they stopped in Ashford for lunch, Patricia realized she'd left her suitcases standing outside Ennismore Mews. Terence, who was trying to control his quick temper because he hadn't known Patricia long, stomped around and then got a taxi back to collect them. They finally set off in a car plane run by Silver City Airways. The interior of the plane, a Bristol 170, was essentially a large space which could hold three cars strapped to the floor and

Terence in France, as drawn by Patricia Lyttelton, 1953

a number of passengers who sat in wicker chairs for the half-hour journey to Le Touquet. The service had become extremely popular, despite two planes having been lost in the Channel only a couple of years before.

Although no one had a tent, the idea was to camp out, and various haylofts and fields provided beds for the night as they drove southwards to the Dordogne. Cynthia, who kept a diary of the trip, recalls that everyone spent a lot of the time drawing: they painted and drew each other, Terence and Michael drew still lifes on the beach, and Cynthia drew portraits. Patricia's drawing of Terence sitting in a village square shows a young man with spiky hair reading a book. The shirt he is wearing, which Cynthia remembers he was very proud of, was one of the range he had designed and made with Raymond Elston.

As they dawdled through France, they argued about politics, ate in simple restaurants, swam in the rivers, and looked at the shops. Michael recalls that they visited some French ironmongers: 'We said the way to run a shop is like those wonderful ironmongers you get in France, which have masses of things piled up everywhere. They gave a feeling of confidence and plenitude. Terence and I were beguiled by them.' The look and display methods of those ironmongers was something Terence would remember and be inspired by when he came to open Habitat.

After a week they reached La Mothe Fénélon in the Dordogne, where they were to stay in a cottage owned by the socialite writer Nancy Cunard. The Wickhams knew her through a friend of theirs, John Summerfield, but they were also connected by their mutual friendship with the Surrealist painter John Banting, who had known Nancy for nearly thirty years. She had been one of the bright young things of the twenties, and was photographed by Man Ray, who moved in the same Dadaist circles she frequented. His pictures make her look decadent, but she was no empty-headed hedonist: she was a friend of Tristram Tzara, who wrote a play for her titled *Mouchoir de Nuages*; she published poetry, campaigned for Negro rights in America, was a relief worker in the Spanish Civil War, and, when Terence met her, had just finished writing her portrait of the author Norman Douglas. Then in her mid–fifties, she still wore the big hats, white dresses and tennis shoes that had been her style thirty years earlier. Cynthia remembers that Nancy was very friendly, drank a lot of the 'awful' heavy local red wine, and was rather taken with Terence, talking to him about her great friend Norman Douglas and his book of aphrodisiac recipes, *Venus in the Kitchen*, which included such delights as lamb's ears and leopard marrow. Nancy, who was sexually assertive and over the years had had a large number of lovers, noted that Terence had lovely legs – just like the ballet dancer Nijinsky: not very long, but very shapely.

The Wickham party stayed at the cottage for about ten days and joined Nancy for meals in the main house, which was simply furnished, but full of interesting things:

> She would put vases of wild flowers and grasses on the shelves, as well as a collection of her latest *objets trouvés* – interestingly shaped stones, old bottles, curiously twisted pieces of wood covered with lichen or crystal-encrusted stones from the river. During the summer she kept a big table outside where she would work and eat. A woman came from the village to clean and cook. There was always a pile of big straw hats for guests.[2]

Terence and the others had lunch with Nancy by the river and went drinking with her at the railway inn at Souillac.

Terence enjoyed the environment and became more and more interested in the lifestyle of rural France: *'Terence aime la France. Il y découvre la vie.'*[3] He says:

> My thinking at the time – whether to do with furniture or food – was, why shouldn't good things be available at a price that ordinary people could afford? Anything that was good in England at that time was out of reach for ordinary people. In France, food and other everyday things – stoneware, terracotta, pottery, pots and pans – were affordable by all. France was a much more agriculturally based society; it hadn't been touched by the industrial revolution in the same way.

The pre-industrial feel of much of French life and the abundance of food in restaurants and markets were far removed from the austerity of industrialized England. Food was still rationed in Britain until 1954, and industrialization had largely destroyed the craft-based industries that William Morris and the other Arts and Crafts designers had tried to resurrect in Victorian times. There seemed to be a sensuality and robustness – a quality that Terence likes – in everything France had to offer. Things were well made, functional, unpretentious and generous. Rather than the artful displays of flowers that he had seen at home, flower stalls in France had great buckets of flowers. Similarly the fruit and

---

2. Anne Chisholm, *Nancy Cunard* (Sidgwick & Jackson, 1979), pp. 289–90.

3. Gilles de Bure, *Habitat – 20 ans de quotidien en France* (Michel Aveline Editeur, 1993).

vegetable markets had a great abundance of mouth-watering produce. It made a lasting impression.

Whatever the impact of the holiday aesthetically, it was less successful on a personal level. Michael Wickham remembers that Terence spent much of the trip in the back of the car reading Ellery Queen novels. Things hadn't really worked out with Patricia, and Terence was alternately cross and sulky. Cynthia says, 'There was some tension. Certain things hadn't been sorted out before they left London – like who was going to sleep where.' The relationship didn't last long beyond their return, but at this time there seems to have been a succession of short-lived girlfriends. After the failure of the marriage to Brenda, whom he divorced in 1954 (the writer and solicitor John Mortimer acted for him), Terence felt the need to have his ego boosted by sexual success. Philip Pollock says he was 'a great fornicator'. Terence was always very attracted to women, and they to him. He had enormous charisma and a self-confidence in his ideas combined with a shyness and fragility. Priscilla recalls that when she went to work for Terence, many years later, she was surprised to find that the people who worked for him adored him because he seemed to have 'an extraordinarily physical attraction'.

One of his long-term girlfriends at the time was an American called Betsy Scherman. Her father, who worked for *Time Life*, had sent her as a teenager to finishing-school in France. However, after spending some time in Paris, she decided to visit London. She had been given Anthony Hill's name by someone she knew, and she looked him up in Sloane Court West, where he and Raymond Elston had moved in after Terence moved out. Anthony remembers that they had never met anyone like Betsy before – she was supremely self-confident and precocious, and seemed to have lived an adventurous life. For a while she moved into Anthony's room, and then one day he introduced her to Terence. It wasn't long before she moved in with him.

Betsy and Terence were a good match for one another – they were both enormously energetic and driven people. Terence remembers that they had 'an amazing love affair'. They were not only attracted to each other's personalities, Betsy was also fascinated by the world of art and design that Terence moved in. She helped him with his showroom in Piccadilly, and made some kites which he used for displays. With her monthly cheque from her father she would go off to Paris and buy meat and bring it back, or would take Terence with her. They would stay in the cheap and bug-ridden Hôtel d'Alsace in the rue des Beaux Arts and go shopping and sightseeing, especially on the Left Bank, where Terence found the myriad of small streets and corner cafés particularly appealing. Betsy also helped him to find a job at the seafood restaurant La Méditerranée on the Place de L'Odéon, where, as a temporary dishwasher, he saw first hand how a professional kitchen worked. Betsy also worked in the first food venture of his career – The Soup Kitchen.

Almost as soon as Terence returned from his trip to the Dordogne he was involved with the opening of a restaurant in Chandos Place, near the old Charing Cross Hospital. The genesis of the idea was very casual. Some months earlier, one evening in the Warwick Arms pub, Terence, Ivan Storey and a friend of his, Jim Scott, had been discussing ways of making some money. The idea of a restaurant had come up, because they'd all experienced the problem of finding somewhere good but inexpensive to eat, especially at lunchtimes. Pubs at that time didn't serve food, and Lyons Corner Houses were uninspiring. The idea was to create a restaurant that they would like to eat at; the only drawback was that none of them knew much about food. Terence had learned something from Eduardo, but he had a very limited repertoire. If they kept the menu to something simple, like soup, they decided, they could probably muddle through. Gill Pickles can remember being told about the idea and thinking it was all just talk, but both Ivan and Terence were the sort of people who made things happen, and The Soup Kitchen moved from concept to reality quickly. Ivan found the premises and organized the funding, while Terence designed the interior.

In the design scheme, he applied the skills he had learned from Dennis Lennon and Natasha Kroll, using lighting and colour

The Soup Kitchen – sketch by Vivien Hislop, 1953

to create a modern and vibrant environment that would appeal to young and design-conscious people like himself. The innovation of The Soup Kitchen was the combination of quality and price – the food was inexpensive but good and simple. The traditional environment in which to sell such cheap fare would have been a 'greasy spoon', not a designer's 'kitchen', but what Terence understood, at this early stage in his restaurant career, was that people eating out want a total experience based on ambience, food and service. Dining, even at a basic level, could be much more than just sustenance – it could be enjoyable. Terence brought a marketer's eye to restaurants and treated them like shops – a parallel he has often drawn. He was guided by the principle of meeting people's wants, rather than following the precepts of others. He recognized that this made good business sense, but on a deeper level he was also driven by the egalitarian ideal which he had acquired at the Central School and in his trip to France, of making quality accessible. This would be an enduring feature of everything he would do in retailing and restaurants – from Habitat to Quaglino's.

The restaurant was made dramatic by means of large blow-ups of old engravings – an idea that had been developed by the Italian Surrealist designer Fornasetti, who had a theatrical background. Images of food and kitchen tools were suspended from the ceiling on boards, to mask the lighting and create areas of light and shade. The colours were vibrant: the boards were blue, grey and red, and there was a red wall at the back of the restaurant. The ceiling was black, and the floor was black and white tiles. The furniture comprised a long bench seat with zebra-striped cushions, cane-topped stools and light wood tables, both with Terence's familiar thin black metal legs. Ivan commissioned a large sign for the fascia. Tomato, pea or lentil soup was on offer at one shilling a bowl; minestrone, onion or scrambled egg soup were one shilling and sixpence. There was a Gaggia machine to make espresso and cappuccino coffee.

Betsy, Ivan and Terence were all there on the opening night in November 1953, as were Cynthia and Michael Wickham. The first customers were a group of tramps, who trudged in thinking it was a charity soup kitchen. The restaurant was an almost immediate success and got a small write-up in the *Evening News*. At lunchtime it appealed to young office workers who wanted something cheap and quick to eat in stylish surroundings, and in the evenings it attracted the theatre crowd, including Stubby Kaye and the cast of *Guys and Dolls*, who were performing at the Coliseum in St Martin's Lane, just round the corner. Betsy worked as a waitress, and Terence and Ivan would be there in the evenings after work. Betsy remembers that 'it became trendy very quickly'. Within a week of opening they were serving a hundred people a day. Six months later salads and omelettes were added to the menu and they were serving four hundred people a day between ten in the morning and midnight.

Ivan ploughed more money into the business, involved some other people, and the next year opened a second, bigger, restaurant in Wilton Place, Knightsbridge. Having been closely involved in the initial concept, Terence had now become marginalized. He wasn't cut out to be a follower – he had to be in charge – so he decided to take the money he had made from The Soup Kitchen and open his own restaurant. He found a site in a row of Georgian houses in the King's Road, near the World's End, and opened a new coffee bar. He says, 'I remember looking at the shop front and thinking, Either I can open it as a furniture showroom or I can do it as a café.'

Coffee bars aimed specifically at a young clientele, who were for the first time sufficiently affluent to enjoy an independent lifestyle, started appearing in the early fifties. They tended to have slightly exotic interiors, with modern furniture and an Italian espresso machine which would sit like a dominant piece of sculpture behind the counter. *Architectural Review* thought the style sufficiently interesting to run a feature on the phenomenon, including Terence's bar, which was called The Orrery – a mechanism which shows the movement of the planets. The Orrery was a bit more relaxed in design than The Soup Kitchen – less 'madly contemporary'. It featured black-and-white-topped tables, tongue-and-grooved walls, simple wooden-topped stools, more blow-ups of engravings, and a large orrery suspended from the ceiling. There was also a patio area at the back of the building, where Terence built a barbecue. The front of the coffee bar was all glass with an eye-level frieze featuring photographs by Priscilla, who was now a photography student. The overall look was very architectural in that it employed strong horizontal and vertical lines, which emphasized the planes in the design. The catering philosophy was the same as at The Soup Kitchen – good, simple food, mainly omelettes, served at reasonable prices in attractive surroundings – but the customers were of a different

type. Chelsea was populated with a lot of people like Terence – young people with artistic and design backgrounds – so The Orrery was less of a quick-lunch place and more of a talking-shop.

Though wanting to get the place up and running as quickly as possible, Terence faced his familiar problem of a shortage of funds. Eventually, however, he met a man called Victor Brewer, who worked for HM Customs & Excise and was interested in being a partner in a restaurant, and with his money and the proceeds from The Soup Kitchen, The Orrery opened in September 1954. Terence found a Polish chef who worked and lived in the restaurant – at night he slept on the deep-freezes – Philip Pollock helped out as a washer-up, Priscilla waitressed, their mother cleaned and helped out, and Terence cleared tables and served behind the bar in the evenings. Brinsley Black was briefly employed as manager, before he fulfilled his ambition to work in advertising. The timing was just right: The Orrery was a success, and even now it is surprising how many architects, designers and artists say, 'I first met Terence Conran when he had a coffee bar in the King's Road.'

One of his early customers was David Douglas, 12th Marquess of Queensberry – who called himself, more simply, David Queensberry – and his girlfriend, Shirley Pearce. David had studied fine art at Chelsea School of Art and pottery at the Central School, and was just beginning to get himself established as a ceramics designer. Shirley also had an artistic background: she had studied sculpture at Portsmouth Art College and had had a successful exhibition of her water-colours and oil paintings at the Architectural Association. With the money from her show, she was paying for a course in painting at Chelsea. The King's Road was their stamping-ground, so it was hardly surprising that they would notice a new restaurant. Also Shirley had read about Terence and seen his photograph in *House & Garden*. She recalls that she and David were looking into the restaurant, and talking about how it was important to promote yourself as a designer, when Terence appeared: 'This man with red braces leant out looking much younger than he was and said, "Why don't you criticize it from the inside?" I said, "I'm not criticizing it, I'm admiring it." '

David Queensberry can remember that once inside The Orrery it was stylish and charming. No one can remember what they talked about on that first occasion, but it wasn't long before David had moved to Stoke-on-Trent to work as a designer and Shirley was working in The Orrery as a waitress in the evenings: 'I got a few free meals, but he never paid me anything – he started as he meant to go on.' Terence would give her a lift home on the back of his Vespa scooter after work.

Shirley was twenty-two and from a wealthy background. Her father had a dry-cleaning business in Portsmouth and drove a Rolls-Royce. She had been educated at St Paul's Girls School in London and had been to finishing-school at La Chatelainie in Switzerland. Whereas her fellow art-school students were casually dressed, Shirley wore designer clothes. Looking at photographs from the mid-1950s, it is her aquamarine eyes that are striking – Wolf Mankowitz described them as 'magnificent' – and her mischievous grin. But she looked older than Terence, who still retained his rather boyish looks.

Shirley doesn't recall being immediately attracted to Terence, but he thought she was very beautiful. Once she started to get to know him, though, she found that she was attracted to his ideas and sense of purpose. Shirley says, 'He had a sense of mission; I was head acolyte – one of his first fans.' She decided to go to Stoke-on-Trent to tell David Queensberry what was going on. As with many things in Terence's life, things moved quickly – within six months Shirley and Terence were married.

In the meantime, David Queensberry's and Terence's paths had crossed again. Until 1952 ceramics came under the same Utility restrictions as furniture; there had been no decoration or ornament on pottery for over ten years. When released from these restrictions, the conservative potteries reverted back to the shapes and patterns they had always produced – as with furniture, demand exceeded supply, so the manufacturers didn't have to try too hard. David Queensberry says:

I remember in the early days, when I was doing work for Crown Staffordshire China, there was an extraordinarily angry lodgeman. He was the first point of contact for any visitor, and he would say, 'What do you want?' and you'd say, 'I'm a buyer,' and he'd say, 'I don't think they want to see any buyers, but you can sit down there and I'll see if anyone will talk to you.' In the immediate postwar period anything they made could be sold.

Despite this atmosphere there were a few pioneers. One of these was Roy Midwinter, whose family company, W. R. Midwinter, had been founded by his father in Burslem, Staffordshire, in 1910. Midwinter's had been a fairly traditional company, turning out mostly floral patterns. Roy Midwinter had joined the family firm from school, and by the early 1950s had become sales and design director. In this capacity he had been on a sales visit to North America, where he discovered not only that the Midwinter range was very dated, but that a design revolution had been taking place on the West Coast. People such as the packaging and product designer Raymond Loewy and the ceramics designer Eva Zeisel were developing new shapes and designs. Determined to bring modern design to British pottery, Roy Midwinter persuaded his father that there was a market for innovative products, and within six months Midwinter's created the 'Stylecraft' range. This had a rectangular shape and an abbreviated rim, and also featured several ergonomic innovations, such as stackability, jugs designed to prevent spillage, and teapots with bridges to stop overpouring. One year after its launch, the 'contemporary style' accounted for 60 per cent of Midwinter's sales.

With the success of Stylecraft assured, Midwinter's followed up with a new range called 'Fashion', which had a similar shape but discarded the rim. It was as streamlined and innovative as technical restrictions would allow.

To decorate these new plates, Roy Midwinter turned to his own resident artists, such as Jessie Tait, and also to outsiders. Hugh Casson produced a set of seven Riviera scenes for Stylecraft, and Terence was asked to work on designs for the Fashion range, as Roy Midwinter had seen the textile designs

Terence had done for David Whitehead. However, the first work Terence did for Midwinter's was not in ceramics but designing a showroom at the Midwinter factory to complement the contemporary pottery on display. The design he produced was simple and well lit, and featured cupboards with doors decorated with more of his photographic blow-ups of engravings.

The first ceramic decoration Terence produced was a series of black line illustrations called 'Nature Study', which was 'his interpretation of a page from a nature notebook' and picked up on his childhood interest in lepidoptery. Roy Midwinter was delighted with the work, describing it 'as a style that excited me . . . a lovely loose and free style . . . more abstract than Casson.'[4]

Nature Study was followed by 'Salad Ware' and 'Plant Life'. As with Nature Study, these designs coincided with Terence's interests. Salad Ware drew on his growing interest in food and cooking, and featured a series of coloured illustrations of vegetables. Although British awareness about food was strictly limited – a successful April Fool joke of 1957 was *Panorama*'s film of spaghetti being picked from trees – there was a growing interest in cooking, nurtured by Elizabeth David. Her books *French Country Cooking* and *Italian Food* (1954) and *Summer Cooking* (1955) had followed on from the earlier success of *Mediterranean Food*, and Terence had read them all avidly. Plant Life had indoor plants as its theme, and one of the references that Terence drew on was his conical pots on stands.

Terence continued working for Midwinter's throughout the fifties. He produced a collector's series of ceramic trays featuring line illustrations of vintage cars, early steam trains, bicycles and ships, and his last two series were 'Chequers' and 'Melody'. Chequers was an abstract design, similar to one of his earlier textile designs that had been sold to Myers. It was printed with black and sponged with grey, yellow and green; of all his designs for Midwinter, it is the most distinctive and durable. In contrast,

4. Alan Peat, *Midwinter: A Collector's Guide* (Cameron and Hollis, 1992).

Melody – a stylized representation of rosebuds – was more predictable.

After Melody (1958), Terence ceased working for Roy Midwinter, but they remained friends, and David Queensberry, whom Terence had introduced to Midwinter, worked with the company throughout the sixties. Looking back, Terence is rather embarrassed about the work he produced, but it helped to establish his name – especially as Midwinter's advertised heavily. Terence wrote of that time:

I cannot say that I have ever been particularly proud of anything that I did for Roy, but I helped him bridge that seemingly uncrossable gap between constipated conservatism and a better and more optimistic world beyond. He went on to do many more significant things in a continuously difficult commercial environment and he has left an indelible mark on the history of British pottery.[5]

His work for David Whitehead and Midwinter proved Terence's versatility as a designer. Another new business venture, called Basketweave, showed his versatility as an entrepreneur. The company was initially run out of the Piccadilly Arcade site, but it transferred to a mews house at 6 Cadogan Lane, just north of Pont Street, when Terence moved his furniture showroom there in 1954. His partners in the venture were Johnny Metcalf, who later went on to run the Dorlands advertising agency, the writer Wolf Mankowitz, and a Madeiran called Horace Zeno.

In addition to writing, Wolf Mankowitz also had a shop in the Piccadilly Arcade, which sold Wedgwood jasper-ware. Mankowitz had got to know Zeno, and it was through the latter that the idea for importing basketware from Madeira was developed. Terence teased Mankowitz that the basketware business was based on slave labour – however, when it looked like being a viable business opportunity, he joined in. A range of chairs and baskets was launched, and John Stephenson, who

5. Ibid., Foreword by Terence Conran.

continued working with Terence for many years, was taken on as a salesman – though he recalls that he not only did the selling, but also the administration, the invoicing and occasionally the deliveries.

Once the operation had moved to Cadogan Lane, a simple brochure featuring line drawings of work-baskets, hampers, jardinières and letter trays was produced by Gill Pickles and Shirley. Wolf Mankowitz wrote a rather effusive introduction:

> Instead of knitting, Madeiran peasants have continued weaving their baskets, always in the same patterns, giving meticulous attention to unvarying texture and unfailing high quality. Basketweave has changed nothing except the patterns. Basketweave's designer, Terence Conran, has adapted these into a range of furniture and accessories which bring the texture and atmosphere of Madeira into the contemporary settings they suit so well.

However, in spite of Mankowitz's praise, Lord Roberts Work-shops for the Blind took a dim view of the venture and campaigned against it, claiming it was undermining their basketware products. In response, the Board of Trade decided to impose quotas on the import of basketware, effectively putting an end to Terence's ambitions. The company was folded, and John Stephenson moved over to work with Terence on managing Conran and Company.

Basketweave and his work for Midwinter were in a sense sideshows: the real focus of Terence's activities was in trying to build his own company rather than being a freelance designer for others – much as he enjoyed it. After its shaky start, his furniture business was beginning to burgeon. At the end of 1953 Terence had moved the workshop from underneath the stomping feet of the Ballet Rambert – they had become worried that he might blow the building up with his welding equipment – and into a warehouse on three floors at 32 Donne Place, Chelsea. Gill Pickles, who was still designing for Terence, remembers it was like a big stable with a tiled floor. A woman called Margaret Bury was doing upholstery, and Raymond, Eric and the others were welding and making furniture. A year later Terence was employing six people. Shirley remembers that he was always busy: 'What was impressive when I first met him was that he could do five things at once. He moved around a lot and he always hurried, from the showroom in Cadogan Lane round to the factory near Ives Street and then back again.'

He had, however, reduced his commitments by one: after running The Orrery for a year, he had sold it on to someone he knew, and ploughed the money back into the furniture company. Design commissions were now coming in from lots of different sources – both retail and trade – and Terence was undoubtedly helped by the wide range of contacts he had acquired in the architectural and design profession, one of whom was his former wife, Brenda Davison. After leaving Dennis Lennon's practice, Brenda had set up an architectural partnership of her own, and, in spite of their marital falling out, she would use Terence to make furniture and fittings for the retail jobs she won. She recalls that things didn't always go smoothly and there used to be 'lovely rows'. Terence had very clear ideas about how things should be done, which didn't necessarily coincide with those of Brenda's business partner, who was equally forceful.

As well as producing furniture for other designers, Terence was increasingly being asked to provide complete designs. One was for a showroom for a lighting manufacturer in Knightsbridge called Troughton & Young, for whom Terence had also designed lights; another was the Chanterelle restaurant for Walter Baxter, who was one of the most professional restaurateurs of the 1950s. The Chanterelle was an interesting piece of work because it demonstrated many of Terence's earlier ideas but showed an increasing sophistication in their application. The colours were more muted than in his previous restaurants, and there was a sense of calm in the design. However, there was the continued extensive use of wood and the ubiquitous hanging panels suspended from the ceiling – this time featuring fungi. Terence's interior design was complemented by David Queensberry's designs for the crockery.

The *Architectural Review* said of the Chanterelle, 'The client wanted to give an instant impression of sophistication and solid comfort. This has been achieved by the use of natural woods and finishes combined with a warm but subdued colour theme.' The only failing it seemed was the illumination: when Vivien Leigh ate there, she thought the light was very unflattering. To correct this Walter Baxter insisted Terence paint the inside of the fittings pink.

By the mid-1950s Terence had begun to establish his name as a designer. Unlike his contemporaries, however, he was motivated much more by developing a design business than by creating innovative designs. The commercial impulse had been born out of necessity in his childhood, and in his adult life the idea of making a design which many people would buy would be far more exciting than the plaudits of his fellow designers. The argument that good design should enhance the lives of as many people as possible was something that Terence strongly believed in, and he used it to persuade Shirley to give up painting and concentrate on design. However, his business-like attitude didn't endear him to the Design Council or the Society of Industrial Artists. Shirley says:

> Right from the start I noticed there was a negative attitude towards Terence. I think it was professional jealousy – real envy and hatred towards this young man . . . Terence was very unpretentious; he just got on with it . . . I think Terence is a world-class design impresario – a sort of Diaghilev of design.

Habitat was still some way off, but the seeds of the thinking that would determine its look and its merchandise were already sown.

CHAPTER FIVE

YOU'VE NEVER HAD IT SO GOOD

The world that Terence was operating in in the late 1950s was altogether wealthier and more plentifully supplied with goods than that of the early fifties. Britain might still be lagging behind the rest of Europe in its rate of growth, but Prime Minister Macmillan's paean to consumerism, 'You've never had it so good', was largely true. In 1951, only 6 per cent of households owned a television set; by 1961 75 per cent did. In the same ten years car ownership increased by 250 per cent and, outside America, Britain was the biggest auto manufacturer in the world. Wages were rising rapidly, as was hire purchase. There was a degree of social mobility, especially among the newly educated young, who had benefited from the universal secondary education established by R. A. Butler's 1944 Education Act. Never before had the young enjoyed such spending power. A survey carried out in 1959 showed that 80 per cent of British teenagers were at work, 'but what's most significant was the disproportionate amount of money that teenagers had to spend on leisure and entertainment.'[1]

With money in their pocket, people had become largely uncritical in their view of society: compared to the results of the 1943 Mass Observation Study, the British public was now much more interested in its own well-being. A 1959 Civic Culture Study revealed a highly satisfied citizenry, more concerned with personal issues than with national ones. Fifty-five per cent felt their family's economic situation was satisfactory, and 70 per cent expected their economic situation to stay the same or improve. 'The results showed a belief in democracy, respect for British

---

1. Nigel Whiteley, *Pop Design: Modernism to Mod* (The Design Council, 1987).

institutions and confidence in official fairness.' However, there were some who expressed their irritation with Britain, including Terence. Although not especially politically concerned, he was appalled at the British government's bowing to jingoism over Suez. He saw the 1956 invasion of the Canal Zone as outmoded, backward-looking imperialism and he was sufficiently moved – as he would be later over the invasion of the Falklands under Margaret Thatcher's government – to register his protest. In this case he wrote letters to his MP and got his colleagues to do likewise.

The other notable protests in the country at large were both political and cultural. In 1957, the Campaign for Nuclear Disarmament was formed, and by 1960 the annual Aldermaston marches were drawing an estimated 100,000 people. There was also a newly critical theatre, with John Osborne's *Look Back in Anger* (1956) and Harold Pinter's *The Dumb Waiter* (1960), as well as some dissenting voices among fiction writers, such as Kingsley Amis, Colin Wilson, John Braine and Alan Sillitoe. But to see this activity as mainstream would be mistaken: it was minority criticism of the sentiments and opinions still held by the majority.

What did this all mean for Terence? With increased affluence and a significant achievement in home-building during the fifties there was an increased demand for furniture and furnishings. Whereas sales through furniture shops in 1950 were £275 million, by 1957 they were £342 million. There were also 500 more furniture shops, and the average annual turnover per shop had risen from £14,947 to £18,078. However, the great majority of shops remained small – with an average of five employees – and concentrated on the mass market, offering traditional three-piece suites. In addition to Heal's, Liberty's and Dunn's of Bromley, there were one or two new retailers who did stock modern furniture, but they tended to be at the exclusive end of the market – reasonably priced modern design was almost impossible to obtain. This meant that the consumer market was still difficult to penetrate for a designer and manufacturer like Terence. Not that it stopped him trying, and Conran and

Terence in one of his chairs, mid-1950s

Company was a regular advertiser in *House & Garden* — something that upset the rather non-commercial design establishment. However, there were better opportunities among designers and architects. Major building projects were under way — the whole area around St Paul's was being reconstructed in the mid-1950s and there was much refurbishment and rebuilding of schools, public buildings and office blocks — and there was also a growth in transport work, both in aviation and in cruise liners. This professional market was generally more receptive to Terence's work, in that architects and designers had been brought up on the Modernist canon and were interested in using modern design. Terence recalls, 'We were selling to a few shops, but it was mainly contract work. We sold to architects who were specifying for schools, offices, hotels and hospitals. There was quite a flurry of new building going on in the public sector at that time.'

Terence was still operating out of Donne Place. The furniture he was creating was still typically modern, but its quality of finish was now much higher. Whereas in his earlier work the proportion was sometimes uncomfortable, a precise human scale was evident in the range from the mid-1950s onwards. The style was not flamboyant; rather, it showed a strong simplicity of line which would have worked well in modern office environments. With help from Philip Pollock, who had a company called Aerofoam, Terence had also started to produce sofas and armchairs. Philip remembers that Terence would draw a design on the back of an envelope and say, 'Why don't we do something like this?' Philip would then prototype it, and it would eventually become a part of the range. Terence was also importing some chairs. Shirley Conran can remember that for their honeymoon, in 1955, they drove to Italy and spent their time looking round furniture factories. They came back laden with chair samples, and seven Italian chairs were added to the Conran range, including Gio Ponti's classic Leggera chair. Terence still carried some early staples, however: the conical cane chair was still a feature, as was the ubiquitous plant pot on a three-legged frame.

Apart from the interest created in his products through advertising, there was a huge amount of press coverage during the fifties. Shirley had briefly worked as a press officer for the jewellers Asprey Suchy, and knew something about the media and the way they operated. Terence already had excellent connections at *House & Garden* through Cynthia and Michael Wickham and Olive Sullivan, but Shirley wanted to extend the coverage into other media. Terence says, 'I'd never really bothered to publicize what we did until Shirley suggested it. She was extremely good at getting the press involved.' Where they disagreed was in the nature of the press coverage. Shirley felt that the best way to reach a larger audience was through personal profiles which would focus on their private lives but would also make a point about their design interests. Terence was very keen to grow and to broaden his profile as a designer, but he was very reluctant to take the route Shirley suggested – he had always been uncomfortable talking about his relationships to people he knew, let alone to journalists. However, the limited circulation of magazines dealing with modern design – essentially *House & Garden* plus the specialist magazines *Design* and *Architectural Review* – meant that Shirley's approach was probably the only effective way of heightening the awareness of the company – something that Terence now recognizes.

Something we used to have terrific rows about was personal publicity. I loathed it and still do. I don't mind publicity about my work – I'm happy talking about that – but my private life is private. She felt personal publicity was important, and at the time she was undoubtedly right.

Shirley's first success was to get a double-page feature in *Queen*, one of the most influential style magazines of the late 1950s. It featured their new home at 11 Regent's Park Terrace, with photographs by Priscilla Conran. Terence had acquired the property with a mortgage of £4,000 before he and Shirley had met. However, to afford the house Terence had to rent out rooms. Gill Pickles, who had recently married, had the basement flat, the first floor had a design studio at the front, where Gill worked, and a room at the back which was occupied by the then penniless poet Christopher Logue, whom Terence had met on one of his trips to Paris with Betsy Scherman. Logue remembers that, although Terence had a tendency to pomposity, he was very supportive and a good friend. Together they would go and look at antique shops in the Portobello Road, and Terence would talk about the objects they saw – 'gesturing with his hands the way he still does'. After a brief stay in Regent's Park Terrace, Logue did a midnight flit while Terence was away. He recalls, 'I left owing Terence fourteen pounds in rent. When I see him he sometimes mentions it, but he never really cared about it.'

Terence and Shirley lived on the top floor. The living-area featured an expanse of space which had been achieved by converting three small rooms into one large one, and the whole effect strongly prefigured the Habitat look. This clearly reflected Terence's taste rather than Shirley's – in fact, Michael Wickham recalls, 'Eric O'Leary, who worked for Terence, moved Shirley's

Terence and Shirley out on the town, 1955

furniture into the house, and I can remember Terence persuading Eric to break a few of her things.'

The *Queen* photographs show built-in shelves, an Eames chair, Gio Ponti Leggera dining-chairs, a Noguchi lamp, a kilim rug, a Conran-designed sofa, and collections of copper saucepans and eighteenth-century glasses displayed in the kitchen. The article noted:

Although this is not everyone's design for living, it is not extravagantly modern: old furniture is mixed with new, paintings range from Reynolds to Reg Butler, and the unit furniture is cleverly designed and not, as it often tends to be, too clinical looking . . . From the tongue-and-grooved boarding and teak working surface in the kitchen, to the polished slate in front of the fireplace, natural surfaces have been used where possible.[2]

A similar feature entitled 'Setting up house the hard way' – this time with photographs by Michael Wickham – appeared the following year in *House & Garden*. There was also a 1955 feature, in the now defunct *Picture Post*, of Terence and Shirley at home and out on the town – she in a white dress with fur jacket, and Terence in double-breasted dinner-suit. In addition to these home features there were articles about Conran furniture and textiles in *Architectural Review* and in a magazine called *Art and Industry*. Having been shown the way by Shirley, Terence thrived on this type of coverage. Once he was known to the media he didn't seek them out, but he always made himself available if they wanted furniture for a photographic shoot or a quote for an article.

Although things were going well with the furniture business, it wasn't all plain sailing. Terence was committed to his business to virtually the exclusion of all else, but he had no real business training and the company was undercapitalized. He knew how to design and he knew how to market what he made, but he had a

2. '11 Regent's Park Terrace. The Home of Mr and Mrs Conran' in *Queen*, 5 October 1955.

Terence and Shirley at home in Regent's Park Terrace, 1955

certain naïvety about the mechanics of running a company. He was not alone in this: Mary Quant and her husband Alexander Plunket-Greene experienced the same problem when getting their business going. Terence now realizes that his mark-ups tended to be too low and didn't fully take into account mistakes or wastage. The administration side of the business – never his strong point – was also weak. Christina Smith, who worked for Terence, recalls that more than once on Friday afternoons she had to race round to customers to get enough money to pay the staff. Terence, looking back from the success of Habitat, thought, 'Perhaps if I had been trained as a businessman I would have been able to manage the expanding firm, but I was a designer and it got to the stage where my bank used to say, "OK, this week we'll pay the wages, but nothing else".[3]

Terence found it difficult to confide in people, so the financial situation tended to weigh heavily on him. It would make him irascible and bad-tempered. He bullied those around him and became impatient. He would get infuriated because he could see a design clearly in his head from the beginning and couldn't understand why no one else could. To get the job right, he would take over the making himself. At one point the staff had had enough of him and there was a walk-out from Donne Place, including Eric O'Leary. This caused Terence considerable anxiety, but internal dissent was in fact rare, because Terence tended to command tremendous loyalty in people. Although he didn't have many close personal friends – people found him too competitive – in his business life he was very good at sustaining relationships with those he trusted. He could still be difficult, and he rather enjoyed provoking people, but because most of his colleagues accepted his vision and enthusiasm he engendered a sense of excitement in everything he did.

As the business grew, Terence recognized that it had outgrown Donne Place, so a new workshop was found in Fulham. The premises had been an old forage merchants called Lavenders in the North End Road. The building was run down, but it had sufficient space for metalwork, woodwork and a design office, and in time it also housed Terence's new fabrics business and a curtain-making service on the top floor. When the necessary renovation work was completed, the office was decorated with some style. To support him on the design side, Terence took on some new designers. He didn't always have enough work to keep them busy, but when times were tough he got them to think up new ideas.

In addition to the contract work, Terence had started to

3. Polly Devlin, 'The furniture designer who became a reluctant businessman' in *House & Garden* November 1964, p. 78.

design exhibition stands and retail outlets. He had had some experience of exhibition design when with Dennis Lennon, and he had started to get work referred to him by the graphic designer Ian Bradbery, who had taught exhibition design at the Central School. Bradbery would design the stands and Terence would make them. However, Terence wasn't keen to do just the manufacturing if he could help it, so with Bradbery's encouragement he started offering clients a design service as well, which led to the creation of the Conran Design Group in 1956. There was some early work for the Atomic Energy Authority, which was exhibiting across Europe at the time and was about the only free-spending client that Terence had. (John Stephenson recalls that after he and Terence had set up an exhibition stand for the Authority in Spain they rushed off to St Tropez to sit on the beach and make out the invoices.) There was also an exhibition design for a pharmaceuticals company called Smith-Kline & French, which left its samples of Purple Hearts and the barbiturate Drinamyl behind after the exhibition. There was no real drug culture then and everyone was naïve about what Purple Hearts would do, but Terence remembers that he and the designers soon discovered they could work all night when they needed to with the aid of these stimulants.

From the late fifties onwards the Conran Design Group was working in a variety of areas – graphics, exhibitions, furniture and interiors. Where it could it would charge for its work, but even when it offered design as part of a package there were considerable benefits to the other parts of the group and also considerable opportunities for cross-selling. When the Conran Design Group designed a shop, it could also specify Conran furniture and fabrics. Similarly, although many of the fabrics and furniture sales were through architects, there were occasional opportunities to sell them the services of the design company. In time the design side of the company would move wholly on to a fee-based service, which would separate it out from the shopfitters who offered retail clients designs for free.

Following on from the coffee bars and restaurants that Terence had designed earlier in the 1950s, his first high-profile shop design was in 1957 for Mary Quant. She had opened her first shop, called Bazaar, on the King's Road in 1955, selling her own fashion designs. Originally she thought she was aiming at a strictly limited market – 'the people we knew and who lived in Chelsea and Fulham' – but she soon realized the market was larger. Her shop seemed to divide people: some would look in horror at the window displays, while others were very enthusiastic. The success of the first Bazaar encouraged Mary and her partners Archie McNair and Alexander Plunket-Greene to open a second shop. In her book *Quant on Quant*, Mary recalls how it happened. They were all having lunch in Alexander's – the restaurant they owned underneath the Chelsea Bazaar – when 'Shirley came rushing in rather late with the news that there was a shop going in Knightsbridge.' The site on Knightsbridge Green was almost opposite Harrods, so it would have a lot of passing traffic. It was important that the store should stand out and entice people in, and Mary asked Terence to design the interior:

I remember we had great bales of materials hung on the wall – the material we used in the clothes. There was a great feeling of excitement, and he designed an open staircase leading to the mezzanine above, which also gave a tremendous life to the place. The window was open so that you could see right into the shop, which wasn't the way things were normally done . . . We discussed the design quite a lot. We had similar ideas – as soon as Terence put them forward they gelled.

Terence's design gave the new shop an atmosphere and personality without it dominating the merchandise. He achieved this by using muted colours such as white and greys with light timbers. It was significantly different from his early restaurant designs, where the colours and design were more strident. The glass front was also a departure, as most retail outlets liked to fill their windows with merchandise to entice the customer. Terence believed that part of the appeal of Bazaar was to be able to see the atmosphere and bustle in the shop. Shirley described what the first shop was like in her novel *Lace* (1982):

Bazaar was a sort of nonstop, free-drinks cocktail party, to which the prettiest girls in London dragged their husbands and lovers. As Bazaar had only one minuscule dressing room, the girls all had to try their clothes on in the middle of the shop, where every passer-by could gaze through the plate glass and enjoy the view.

While Terence designed the interior his new contracts division, Conran Contracts, made the fittings and helped install them. Mary Quant recalls that Terence was passionate about getting the design just right and paid great attention to the detail of the scheme. Although others complained of his bullying, Mary feels that he was very good at motivating people and getting the best out of them. On the night before the opening, Terence was there hoovering the carpet and making minor adjustments. The shop opened with a great fanfare and achieved a lot of press coverage. Like much of Terence's design work it was done on a tiny budget, but it undoubtedly raised his profile.

Although Terence was not involved with the design of subsequent shops for Mary Quant, they remained close friends. Terence found a lot to admire in the way in which Mary had taken the plunge and started designing, making and retailing, and when Habitat opened he would draw parallels with her experience. Mary also found Terence good company. Through Alexander, they had got to know each other at the time of The Soup Kitchen; they were very much part of the same milieu. When Mary opened the first Bazaar and Alexander's, a restaurant, below it, Terence had just opened The Orrery further down the King's Road. They had many common friends in the art and design world and would eat at each other's restaurants. Although Terence could be very earnest, Alexander was a great practical joker, and occasionally Terence would let his hair down and get involved with his pranks. Once Shirley arrived on the scene, the four were frequent companions.

Mary can remember all of them going down to Bryanston with Shirley's younger brother, who wanted to go to the school. Terence and Alexander briefed 'the poor boy' on how to behave and what to say. Given that Terence had been expelled and

Alexander had frequently been in trouble with the headmaster, they weren't the best coaches, and when they got to the school they 'collapsed into small schoolboys'. The headmaster mistakenly believed that the boy was Alexander and Shirley's son, and they continued with this charade all afternoon. On another occasion, the four went down to the Hamble river in Hampshire for lunch. There was a lot to drink, and Terence ended up either falling or being pushed into the river. Everyone thought it was a great joke except Terence, who was wearing his one and only suit. He squelched his way back to London.

Outside work, Terence could relax and have fun. Mary says, 'I never feel Terence has changed at all. He's got a marvellous great laugh and a naughty Cheshire-cat gurgle, which is hugely attractive. There's an enormous feeling of appetite about the man in every way.' Most of his appetite, however, was directed towards his work. Even when the foursome were out lunching, work was most often the subject of conversation. In her book, Mary relates that many of their endless lunches at Alexander's were spent discussing 'Plunket's Proposition' – a joint venture in which Terence and Shirley would make fabrics which Mary and Alexander would use in their clothes. Although this came to nothing, Terence and Shirley did start Conran Fabrics.

While Shirley was pregnant with their first child, Sebastian, who was born a year after they had got married, Terence met a man in Manchester called Cyril Winer, who bought and sold textiles. He had acquired a mill and was looking for someone to design upholstery fabrics for him. After Shirley had come out of hospital, she met Winer and his wife. They discovered their mutual ambition to produce and market really good fabrics at a reasonable price and decided to form a company.

Initially Conran Fabrics supplied most of its work to Terence's furniture business and there was only one weave made in about ten different colours with one stripy version; however, once the company got going, it expanded its horizons quite rapidly, and Shirley and Terence started to develop the range. At first Shirley designed from home, and there is a photograph of her 'Zuleika' design in the 'Setting up house the hard way' feature in the April 1956 issue of *House & Garden*, but as soon as Sebastian was old enough, she moved into Cadogan Lane and used the furniture showroom as her base. The initial collection of screen-print designs for furnishing fabrics featured five by Terence and three by Shirley. The designs, which were intended for architects and interior designers, were colourful and abstract. For example, 'Zuleika' featured a design of stylized falling leaves (created by torn tissue-paper) in contrasting light and dark colours, while 'Leaf' was an enlargement of a steel engraving of an ogee pattern.

Weaving was done at Cyril Winer's mill, and at first they used a printer in Manchester to do the printed designs. This wasn't particularly convenient, however, so they decided to use an eccentric lady they had met who had a basement in Powys Square in Notting Hill. She did hand printing, so they could produce short runs, which was ideal in the early days. However, the quality tended to be variable. With hand printing, she used white spirit with the pigment. Once the pigment had been applied, the cloth had to be put through a gas oven and baked very quickly. Sometimes the baking process wasn't quick enough and the machine would explode, singeing the cloth.

Shirley was learning about these things as she went along. She had good tutors in Terence and also in Laura Ashley's husband, Bernard, whom Terence had met when he opened The Soup Kitchen and who now showed Shirley how to print and where to get materials. (Although Terence's and the Ashleys' view of design was very different, they would remain friends for many years.) Whatever the benefit of Bernard's tutoring, Shirley still lacked a formal education in textiles, but this was remedied when, along with her assistant Jeremy Smith and Terence's secretary Dinah Herbert, she took a course in textiles at the Central School. There she was taught by Margaret Leischner, who had been a student at the Bauhaus and also head of weaving at the Royal College of Art, and Marianne Straub, who had produced designs for the Festival Pattern Group at the Festival of Britain.

To expand their range, so that they had enough to interest architects and designers, Shirley and Terence also brought in fabrics from Scandinavia. Shirley remembers that at first she was petrified at having to call up architects and make appointments. However, once she got in to see an architect, she found that the range was so unusual and extensive that she would almost always get some business.

The first big contract Conran Fabrics won was the interiors of British European Airways' fleet of Viscount airliners. Shirley got the job through an architect who worked with Hugh Casson. She took Margaret Leischner with her, and promised that she would keep designing until something was approved, and that they would beat the competition on price. Luckily the second set of designs – a honeycomb weave in shades of grey – was accepted. However, making the fabric was a nightmare. The fabric had to be sound absorbent and flame-resistant, which meant it had to be 100 per cent wool, treated with a special solution, and then certificated. A mill in Dumfries was found that could do the job, but it left very little profit margin in the project. The Viscount contract did help to get the business going though, and later there were further orders from BEA.

Projects for two Orient Line ships followed. The first was the 2,200-berth *Oriana*, and then came the 2,300-berth *Canberra*. They were both large vessels – the *Oriana* was the largest passenger ship launched in Britain since the *Queen Elizabeth* some twenty years earlier – and ten nautical miles of fabric was specified. Coordinating the *Oriana* design was a consultancy called Design Research Unit (DRU), which worked with a naval architect to try to ensure continuity of style and quality. In addition to DRU a large number of designers and consultancies undertook specific tasks, including Conran Fabrics. For the even larger *Canberra*, where design was under the control of Hugh Casson, Shirley's Zuleika fabric was chosen in a variety of colour ways for bedspreads, curtains and seat covers. However, Orient line soon found that the design's olive-green, mustard and cornflower colours and shimmering shapes made people feel seasick, and tried to make Conran Fabrics take the fabric back.

Although Terence wasn't involved with Conran Fabrics on a day-to-day basis, he was involved with all the major decisions. Shirley remembers that, although the business was winning some contracts, neither she nor Terence knew enough about the commercial side of textiles. Terence had always worked for other textile companies before, and they had determined the operations and the mark-ups. Conran Fabrics would put on small mark-ups to make sure it won jobs. What Shirley and Terence didn't realize for quite a long time was that the textiles they produced were not being stretched properly and their small profit was disappearing before the order was delivered. Also, in a desire to have a strong range, a large amount of stock was being held by the company. Shirley says, 'I was interested in offering a complete selection, so that when an architect said "I want something in sky blue and pink," I would have it.' The fabrics side could make money when the specifier was the Conran Design Group, but there wasn't enough volume in this alone.

With neither the fabrics side nor the furniture company making much money, Terence was still living the hand-to-mouth existence that had prevailed since his earliest days. Everything was run on a shoestring, and Terence and Shirley's personal life was always constrained. As Shirley says, 'in the fifties we were always short of money, but we put on a glamorous exterior. We lived in Regent's Park Terrace and we used to invite people round, but then we gave them egg mayonnaise followed by lemon soufflé. Terence was very thin and gangly.'

Their house guests were mainly the people that Terence had got to know through his work, although occasionally there were new people whom Terence admired and wanted to know. Elizabeth David fell into this category, but having invited her for dinner he and Shirley felt intimidated by the prospect of cooking for Britain's foremost food writer. In her early forties, Elizabeth was Terence's hero. She represented in her cooking and recipes all the sensuality of French and Italian cuisine that Terence loved, but on a personal level he found her more difficult. She was a witty and amusing writer, but she could also be very acerbic and was deeply critical of others. Terence felt she 'lacked generosity'. Nevertheless, her interest in simple, well-cooked Mediterranean food was very influential on him and later helped to define his approach as a restaurateur.

To help improve his and Shirley's financial position, Terence decided to embark on some extra work. The first project was to publish his first book, which was to be called *Printed Textile Design*. He had agreed the idea, soon after starting Conran Fabrics, with Studio Publications, which published a range of practical design and art books – including the book on window display that he had worked on with Natasha Kroll. As Sebastian was still a baby and Shirley was spending most of her time at home, she did the research for the book and helped with its structure. It is interesting from many perspectives. Not only does it present Terence's views on design and profiles of designers that he admired – such as Eduardo Paolozzi, Alexander Giraud, Astrid Sampe, Tibor Reich and Lucienne Day – it also includes practical information on marketing fabrics and on contracts. Two of the more heartfelt views that are put across in the book are his belief in abstract design and his disgust at the failure of British manufacturers to seize the design opportunity created by the Festival of Britain. His criticisms were shared by many of his contemporaries, but his strength of feeling six years after the event does suggest the depth of disappointment Terence must have felt when nothing happened after the Festival and he was laid off by Dennis Lennon:

Consciously abstract design had been produced as early as 1913, but this was the first time [after the Second World War] that quite complicated abstract patterns had proved a popular commercial success. This movement was also directly influenced by modern art but it also owed a great deal to the Bauhaus group in Germany who reawakened interest in the slumbering concept of design . . .

. . . Exhibitions which theoretically exert a good influence on design often do just the opposite. Manufacturers quickly realized the success of the 1951 Festival of Britain without understanding its essence: their interpretations

which were aesthetically worthless but financially remunerative bore no
legitimate relation to that which they aped and domestic design, especially
printed fabric design, became increasingly decadent.[4]

The writing is perhaps a bit tortuous, but Terence's views are not
surprising. He demonstrates his belief in the importance of design
and of a sound commercial attitude towards it – something he
damns William Morris for lacking, in the book.

The book does not seem to have been widely reviewed, but
such reviews as there were were generally positive. Wyndham
Goodden in *Art and Industry* thought Terence was almost
'uniquely qualified to tell us how to set about every stage of
work' and that he had a 'thoroughly professional approach'. In
fact, whatever its literary merits, the book was a useful marketing
device for Conran Fabrics – some of Terence's and Shirley's
designs were featured in the book, and the impression it created
was of someone who had intimate knowledge of his subject, both
aesthetically and commercially.

Terence's other method of supplementing his income was
lecturing, both at the Royal College of Art and at the Central
School. By the late fifties Robin Darwin had transformed the
RCA, and, as part of the change, Hugh Casson had taken over
the running of an interior-design department. Although Terence
had never qualified as a designer, Casson liked his work and
invited him to lecture one day a week. Terence was a born
teacher: he taught the people who worked with him, and he
taught the people who later came to shop at Habitat. Terence
always wanted to show people a better way of doing things – of
enhancing their lives through well-designed objects. But
lecturing, which he did at the RCA for five years from 1957
to 1962, was not quite the same – even though Hugh Casson
thought he did it very well. Terence was always trying to slot his
teaching in between all his other commitments and he thought

4. Terence Conran, *Printed Textile Design* (Studio Publications, 1957).

the full-time staff never took teaching seriously enough and were too busy pursuing their own interests. Nevertheless, the RCA did put him in touch with the work of many students and teachers who would later interact with his life. These included David Hockney, and the clothes designers Marion Foale and Sally Tuffin.

Even though he was still in his twenties, Terence came over as being experienced. Hugh Casson says:

I think Terence was a very self-confident fellow, which the students rather liked. Most people think being a student is a time when you don't have to be too serious. If you're designing a hospital, you don't have to design stairs that work, you just write 'Staircase'. He didn't do that. He said, 'The stairs need to be big enough to carry a coffin down.' He knew these things . . . He had a streak of being frightfully sensible – he made sure the mistakes were ironed out.

He didn't necessarily encourage students to be highly creative, as Eduardo Paolozzi had tried to do at the Central, but he did create an awareness among them of the commercial realities of design. Most would argue that this comes to students all too soon when they start work, but it is difficult to imagine him approaching the teaching of design in any other way.

The students' more interesting work also gave him inspiration – although Terence's reputation for deriving ideas from others also encouraged some of the students to joke, 'Hide your work, Terence Conran is around.' A quote by Terence in an article by Wolf Mankowitz in *Everybody's Weekly* in August 1957 contrasts his work with that of students and almost suggests a sense of longing for freedom from the compromise necessary in a world largely populated with myopic design buyers:

'Every day', he [Terence] says, 'brings a problem with personnel, or delivery dates, new tools or more space – or suddenly finding that someone else is doing something better than we do it. I just saw a students' design exhibition.

To see all that magnificent work makes me feel old. That's what we have to keep up with.'[5]

At the Central School, Terence was teaching in the evenings. Min Hogg, who later became the editor of *The World of Interiors* magazine, recorded her thoughts on Terence's first few lectures:

> *25 September 1957*
> Had an incredible man to teach us, looks around 23 but has a string of wives and children already. We had to design a kitchen unit. Quite fun – mine could have been worse. Terence Conran was his name and he seemed nice.
>
> *9 October 1957*
> Had a beastly evening class with Terence Conran, couldn't do a thing and left early.
>
> *30 October 1957*
> Managed to bring myself to go to Terence Conran's lecture which wasn't too bad and he quite liked something I did which makes a change.
>
> *19 November 1957*
> Went back to Terence Conran's class. I designed rather a good cheese shop which he liked in some miraculous way.

Lecturing wasn't particularly well paid but was quite time-consuming, and with manufacturing and designing work as well it meant he had little time for home life – and neither did Shirley. In the photograph of Terence that accompanied the Wolf Mankowitz article in *Everybody's Weekly*, he looks very baggy-eyed and worn-out. It was a point Mankowitz stressed:

> Terence Conran is a slim, pallid, poker-faced tycoon of twenty-five . . . Conran's slightly Edwardian appearance is seedy, the suede shoes are battered

5. Wolf Mankowitz, 'He'd Redesign the World . . . if you gave him a Chance' in *Everybody's Weekly*, 17 August 1957, p. 15.

and worn, the close-fitting trousers are going at the knees, his fingers are stained and his nails broken.[6]

Although the Conrans' lifestyle was exciting, it was also exhausting. In addition to a fast-paced working life, their relationship was also intense. Both Terence and Shirley had strong personalities and liked to get their own way. In business they complemented each other: Shirley taught Terence something about public relations and running a business, while Terence taught Shirley about design. She showed the same sort of enthusiasm and commitment to getting things right that Terence did. Even Terence's temper was sometimes held in check with Shirley. She can recall making a mistake in promising a client an exact match in a piece of design, which then couldn't be delivered. The client sued and the Conrans lost. Although Shirley was mortified about the money it had cost them, Terence never complained. Home life, however, was more trying. Terence's recollection is that, once Shirley started at him about something, she would continue until he would lose his temper. Occasionally she would drive him into a complete fury. When Terence was irritable he could be quite cruel and critical of her, but he nevertheless found her criticisms of him deeply uncomfortable.

Shirley's relationship with her in-laws was also strained, which in turn created tension between her and Terence. Terence was devoted to his mother, and whenever time allowed he would visit and help her in the garden. Shirley could see that Christina adored Terence and lived her life vicariously through him. Shirley felt that she couldn't live up to her mother-in-law's expectations – that she wasn't good enough for Terence – so she found the visits to Liphook uncomfortable and intimidating. Whereas others saw Christina as warm and welcoming, Shirley felt rejected. She also upset the family dynamic by being more at ease with Terence's father. She recalls, 'Rupert was very nice and very agreeable, but he had a weak head – by which I mean he used to like to drink: not to great excess, but the lack of control was seen as a great sin in the family.'

6. Ibid., p. 14.

The idea of not being able to control his own life or emotions was particularly worrying for Terence. Terence wouldn't express his emotions – what he once called his 'simplicity in that area' – and would put up barriers to prevent Shirley and others getting close to him. This meant that Shirley felt she didn't get the support she needed, and it led to confrontations between them. Philip Pollock remembers that occasionally the arguments would prove too much for her and she would run away.

The 'famous rows' and their devotion to their careers also tended to impact on the children – Sebastian and their second son, Jasper, who had been born in 1959. Although the idea of both parents working is commonplace now, it was much less so in the fifties and Terence and Shirley had to juggle the requirements of trying to build a business, about which they were both passionate, with bringing up two young children. Compromises were made. Even though Terence came to develop a good relationship with his children when they were older, he doesn't believe he was a very good father to his eldest two – he was never there when they were very young, and Sebastian thinks that his father's later animosity towards Shirley, following their divorce, made his own relationship with Terence strained. He found it difficult to break down Terence's barriers and gain his approval. With his parents busy working, Sebastian spent a lot of time with both his maternal and paternal grandparents. Christina, in particular, doted on him and told him about Terence's boyhood and she also encouraged him – as she had Terence – to make things. However, Sebastian cannot recall he ever did anything with his father when he was young.

Although Terence and Shirley were to become friends again later on, the failure of the marriage was acrimonious. Shirley eventually found that her personality was being eroded by Terence's need to lead and dominate in both their business and private lives. Terence found the emotional battering unbearable and sought solace in affairs with other women – most notably his assistant, Christina Smith.

By the time they separated, in 1960, their lives had diverged completely. Terence would argue that it was Shirley's intense ambition that drove them apart. Initially her ambition was devoted to developing Terence's business – she was good at making connections, and Terence says that 'She pushed me more than anyone else' – but as their marriage progressed Shirley discovered her talent for journalism and became more ambitious to develop her own career. Priscilla, probably with greater objectivity, thinks that the problem was that in many ways they were very alike and both intensely ambitious.

Although the problems at home affected Terence's work, the business as a whole continued to thrive. By the late fifties, Terence was employing about a hundred people and had run out of space again. Jeremy Smith had read about Terence in the *Everybody's Weekly* article and applied for a job with him. When he was taken on as an assistant, he recalls, one of his first jobs was to help move the furniture-making side of the company into a site at Cock Yard, behind a bus garage in Camberwell, in south London. The new building had been a jam factory and, like North End Road, it was in a parlous state. John Mawer, who went on to run the furniture side of the company and had met Terence when he was selling Hille furniture to Conran Contracts, remembers that there was no real control over Cock Yard – for example, he was horrified when he saw that some furniture that had been finished and was ready for packing was covered in coffee-cup marks.

The furniture range by this time was quite extensive. The 1958 catalogue, which was art-directed by the graphic designer Ian Bradbery and featured line drawings by Shirley, ran to sixteen pages. The price list covered over a hundred different items, both for home and office, including old staples like the Tripolina chair, the conical cane chair and those plant pots. The furniture had a very cohesive look with its black metal legs and African-walnut tops. It was confident and distinctively modernist: there were no concessions to British whimsy or to the Victorian style that the poet John Betjeman was campaigning for at the time. These were versions of modern classics, with strong lines and with little reference to the organic shapes that had been popular earlier in the decade. There was no flamboyance or extravagance – just the simplicity that Terence had always loved. It was furniture that demonstrated that sense of rightness that modern designers possessed in the fifties, before sixties pluralism set in. Robin Day says, 'In the forties and fifties there was a much greater certainty as to what was good and bad . . . a curious confidence that we knew what was right.' For someone who was never popular with the design establishment, it is notable that one of the pieces – a sideboard in walnut with French cane doors – had been selected by the Society of Industrial Designers the previous year.

The range was to prove more popular on the contract side than with consumers. Partly this may have been due to the lack of suitable outlets, as Terence was later to discover, but the range was probably too clinically modern for most British tastes at the time. Apart from those aware of design, people generally liked their modernism toned down – if they liked it at all – a factor that Terence recognized when he launched Habitat. This was the constant problem faced by the Council of Industrial Design, which in a rather paternalistic way had been trying to give the British good taste since before the end of the war.

In fact while the Council had been trying to impose a sense of taste from above, a newly emergent young, well-off, educated middle class – Habitat's future customer base – was beginning to develop its own standards. In part this constituted an act of rebellion against the style of their parents, but to a greater extent it seems to have been a search for an identity that reflected their own aspirations. Art colleges – and in particular the RCA – led the way. Artists such as David Hockney, R. B. Kitaj, Derek Boshier and William Green began to challenge artistic shibboleths, while Marion Foale and Sally Tuffin carried on the fashion campaign that Mary Quant had begun.

The success of many of the iconoclasts was made possible by changes in the media. Television started to take an interest in art and design. There was a new arts series called *Monitor*, and William Green's experiments with bicycling over splashed paint were filmed by Ken Russell for *Tonight*. The late fifties also saw the revitalization of two magazines that would prove influential, *Town* and *Queen*. *Queen* – an old-fashioned, rather dull monthly that had been around for almost a hundred years – had been bought by Jocelyn Stevens in 1957. Under Stevens's ownership and the art direction of Mark Boxer, it was transformed into a stylish magazine aimed at the Chelsea and Fulham readership for whom Mary Quant had opened her first shop. *Town* (originally *Man about Town*) was an arts-biased publication, owned by Michael Heseltine and art-directed by Tom Wolsey. Now 'these magazines geared themselves to a new audience of affluent knowing consumers, "pacey" individuals who were "aware" of trends'.[7]

Together with the colour supplements introduced in the early sixties, these magazines responded to and helped fuel the interests of a specific audience who were increasingly aware of design. New styles of photography, typography and indeed printing methods not only stimulated a greater awareness of how things looked, they also provided the means of promoting the work of designers to a wider audience. The new 'promotional culture' was a vital component in enabling Terence to develop the scale of his business, not only because it impinged on his consumer audience, but also because it affected the attitude of his professional clients. Even some conservative retailers and manufacturers started to recognize the importance of their image. Austin Reed, for example, a rather traditional men's outfitters, had asked the artist Robyn Denny to paint a mural for its Regent Street store that would show its commitment to fashion:

Denny's mural was completed in May 1959 and it epitomizes the euphoria of London in the process of redevelopment – at the height of the office-building explosion which had begun the previous year. It spoke the language of the new promotional culture that stood on every hand in the consumer boom

7. David Mellor, *The Sixties Art Scene in London* (Phaidon Press, 1993).

during the run-up to the election victory of Eden's successor, Harold Macmillan, on 8 October.[8]

The Conran Design Group was given similar opportunities. Back in 1955, Terence had been asked to design an invitation for a show at Woollands, the department store that stood next to Harvey Nichols in Knightsbridge. Martin Moss, who was running Woollands, recalls, 'Terence seemed very young . . . I wasn't sure about him . . . He was overly assertive and came across too strongly.' However, the invitation led to other things. Elgin Anderson, who ran the furniture department, bought some Conran furniture, and Terence was asked to design a new shop within a shop specifically aimed at a young market.

Woollands was a high-profile job. The store, which, like Harvey Nichols, was owned by Debenhams, was about 55,000 square feet. Although it had been in existence since the middle of the nineteenth century and had got rather staid, Martin Moss had created some lifestyle departments:

> It had an amazing reputation. We had a floor that was empty, and I decided to create something that was entirely modern design – more modern than Heal's. We brought the other departments up to date by using the best designers of the time. It became a cult place. As things became interesting, we opened a department for them.

The youth shop, which typified the early sixties, was called The 21 Shop, and was designed by Terence in conjunction with two final-year students from the RCA, Rita Allen and John Wildbur. Although the shop design featured wood both on the floor and on the walls, it wasn't typical of Terence's style – it lacked contrast of texture and colour. None the less, it was both influential and successful, but it also had a design fault that was probably due to Terence's relative inexperience in designing shops. Martin Moss says:

8. Ibid.

It had a major error, in that it had a raised stage in the middle of the shop. There were too many blind spots. Right from day one the shop was a phenomenon, but so was the shoplifting. They came in droves and pinched. The stage had to be taken down.

In spite of this problem, Terence went on to design the men's shop in Woollands.

By 1961, the Conran Design Group was about twelve strong and was taking on a wide range of projects, including packaging, literature and interior design. Along with Allied International Design, it represented the first of the British multi-disciplinary practices that would thrive in the sixties, seventies and eighties. It was based on the American model that had been pioneered by Raymond Loewy, although it also owed something to the Central School belief that a designer should be able to work in a variety of media – as the designer Misha Black said, 'a jack of all trades and master of one'. Terence's diverse experience and his strong belief in a commercial approach to design was ideally suited to such an approach, and he was also willing to challenge the accepted way of doing things. Whereas shops in the fifties tended to be designed and built by shopfitters from a kit of parts, he treated every job individually. Although there was a typical Conran style – pared-down interiors; natural materials and colours; the modern juxtaposed with the old; a robust and raw feel, and great attention to detail – it wasn't formulaic design.

Terence's allies in the retail-design revolution were his designers. As Rodney Fitch says, 'One of Terence's great strengths was having the knack of choosing the right person to do the job – not always, but more often than not.' Rodney himself was one of the right people. Trained as a graphic designer at the Central School and at Hornsey School of Art, he had been working at a design practice called Charles Kenrick Associates before he joined Terence at the end of 1961. He was young and ambitious, but his career with the Conran Design Group almost ended before it started. He had been interviewed and offered a job by John Stephenson, who had moved on from the Basketweave days to run the design company, but before he could start work he was put in prison. Rodney was a socialist and an activist in the Campaign for Nuclear Disarmament.

He was involved in illegal broadcasting and in demonstrations against the siting of American nuclear bombers in Britain. When he was leading a sit-in at an American base in Ruislip he was arrested. As part of the process of passive resistance, Rodney and his fellow detainees refused to give any details about themselves to the authorities; consequently they were put in prison until they did. After about three weeks, during which time he should have started work at Conran's, Rodney wrote to his mother, and the authorities found out who he was. His mother contacted John Stephenson, who was appalled at the idea of employing someone with a prison record, but Rodney says, 'Terence, on the other hand, was hugely sympathetic and supportive about it and kept the job for me.'

Working for Terence, however, was not to prove easy. One of the first projects that Rodney was put to work on was an exhibition stand for Reed Paper. He developed a design in his own style, only to overhear Terence say to John Stephenson, 'What on earth does that young man think he's doing? That's absolutely not what we want.' Rodney quickly came to realize that working at Conran's meant designing in the Conran style: Terence had the ideas and provided the direction which the designers followed. Rodney says, 'My job was to design what I thought Terence would design if he were doing it.' Although this could have dampened some designers' enthusiasm, Rodney enjoyed the work, because he came to identify with Terence's approach:

> There was always this sort of roughness around the edges, which gave his work a very human scale. It's like Vuitton luggage – because it's handmade the screws don't line up exactly. Terence's interiors always had that feeling of being human, which I liked a lot. It created robust interiors – healthy. It was never fey or self-indulgent.

One of the big projects of the early sixties that was typically Conran and which contained elements of the future Habitat style was for Harveys of Bristol. Harveys was a long-established sherry company which was being modernized by its chairman, George McWatters. Part of the programme of change involved a complete corporate-identity review. In the days when most client briefs were simplistic and in turn proposals were equally concise, the Harveys project was remarkably sophisticated. It took three years to complete, and included the design of retail shops and off-licences, vehicle liveries, bottles, packaging, the London head office and a restaurant in Bristol. It showed remarkable attention to detail, and provided a cohesive scheme that encompassed all aspects of the company's visual presentation. To help ensure the consistency was maintained, Conran's developed a design manual to guide Harveys' executives on the use of the logo, typography and colours. Shirley worked on the development of the identity programme, and it was through George McWatters's wife, Joy, that she was introduced to journalism, which she pursued full-time from 1962 onwards, when she became home editor of the *Daily Mail*.

Of all the work that Conran did for Harveys, it was the restaurant, more than the off-licences and shops, that now looks like a forerunner of Habitat. The restaurant was some 7,000 square feet underneath Harveys' Bristol offices, in cellars that had once been part of a medieval monastery and contained Romanesque archways. Rather than fundamentally altering the interior Terence, being true to his materials, simply painted the bricks and masonry white. The result had that roughness and scale that Rodney Fitch so liked, and created an unfussy, simple backdrop to the details of the restaurant, which featured classic modern chairs by the Danish designer Hans Wegner, oak tables, modern lamps and deep olive-green upholstery. The walls were decorated with old prints and a collection of paintings of flowering bulbs. A large eighteenth-century ship's figurehead was used as a dramatic focal point, and there was a big open charcoal grill where customers could see their food being cooked. Although the details of the design have now been altered, what is striking is that the original elements of the design that remain today have not dated and are as strong and as successful as they must have been in 1963.

The late fifties and early sixties were a time of growth for Terence's businesses. In addition to Harveys, the Conran Design

Group was doing exhibition work for ICI, a reception area and offices for the British section at the International Labour Exhibition, and a major project for Gillette, which involved developing designs for three factory canteens. The canteen designs were utilitarian, but the spaces were broken up by the use of partitions, for flexibility in use, and again there was great attention to detail. Plates, cutlery, cups and table-cloths were all specified by Terence, while all the furniture was made by Conran Furniture. Also, one of the canteens featured an idea Terence had been using since the design of The Soup Kitchen ten years earlier – the photographically enlarged engraving. The success of the canteens led to Conran Design Group being asked to produce the interiors for a new complex featuring a theatre, cinema and refreshment areas as well as the reworking of the main entrance hall.

With the development of his various businesses, the previous showrooms and factories had become inadequate, and in the early sixties Terence moved both.

In March 1961 the design group and the contracts business moved out of Cadogan Lane and into a Victorian warehouse in Hanway Place, just off Tottenham Court Road, which most recently had been a Jewish charity school. Although initially the company didn't take the ground floor, the space was much larger than the Cadogan Lane mews. The main showroom on the first floor was a hundred feet long by thirty feet wide and used simple finishes, a louvred pine ceiling and white-painted brickwork. The furniture was ranged along the length of the room in groups. Space was also made for offices, workrooms and storage areas. Conran Fabrics, which was now selling Finnish textiles from Marimekko and fabrics by Timo Sarpaneva with large woven designs, had created a display of samples down a corridor. The extra space and the impressive interiors excited everyone – the move seemed to symbolize that the Conran group was really going places.

It was a lively time, with lunches out at Bertorelli's in Charlotte Street and the ground floor at Bianchi's. John Mawer remembers there was a terrific bustle about the place and a real commitment to what they were doing: 'Everyone used to work late. There was a tremendous loyalty to Terence – a dedication and a belief in what he was trying to do. He got people to believe in what he believed in, not only in the office, but in the factory as well.'

It seemed the only dissenting voice was the Society of Industrial Artists (SIA), which was responsible for defining the code of professional conduct for the design industry. Terence had always taken a commercial approach to design, and when the office moved he sent a number of companies a newsletter detailing the design group's achievements. For this he was hauled up before the SIA, which told him that he was not allowed to solicit business from companies who might be the clients of other SIA members. Terence asked how he was meant to promote his company. The SIA's solution was that he should get to know clients by joining a few gentlemen's clubs. Terence, who hated the Establishment ethos and conservatism of clubland, recalls, 'I said, "It's not my style. I think the rules need changing." The secretary said, "Will you give me your word that you won't do this sort of thing again?" I said, "No, I won't." Eventually it went before the committee of the SIA and I was thrown out.'

Following the success of the office move, planning began on a move for the factory. Terence had long dreamed of emulating people like Hille and such American manufacturers as Knoll and Herman Miller, who were able to produce well-designed furniture in volume in modern surroundings. He wanted to create the sort of environment where there was a strong shared corporate ideal based on design excellence. The new location that Terence found was in Thetford, Norfolk. Under the Expanding Town Scheme, the London County Council was encouraging businesses to move out of London, and the site at Cock Yard was due for redevelopment anyway. The LCC agreed to build a new factory to Conran's specifications and rent it to him. Houses would be provided for staff. Although, as John Mawer says, they really had no idea how to plan the factory space, the idea of a new purpose-built factory after the make-do-and-mend situation at Cock Yard seemed perfect. The staff were all taken to see the new site and a model of the factory was built to show how it would work. Terence was keen to keep as many people as possible, and he spent much time persuading families, many of whom had lived in London all their lives, that a rural life could be enjoyable. In the end he helped about eighty families make the move northwards, and he himself found a weekend home at Dalham, on the Suffolk/Norfolk border.

In 1963 the new factory was opened by Paul Reilly, head of the Council of Industrial Design, and John Mawer was sent up to run it. Set in three acres, it had 40,000 square feet in a single-storey building with panels of timber and brick cladding on a steel frame. It wasn't quite the high design of Herman Miller's Michigan headquarters, but Terence was euphoric about the building and the new machinery that would enable the company to produce better and more varied furniture. In an interview with Fiona MacCarthy, he later described it as 'the most exciting thing I ever did'.[9]

Although the Conran empire was still making money one year and losing it the next, Terence had seen tremendous growth during the decade he had been making furniture, and he had moved a long way from the days of welding in an unheated garage in Bethnal Green. However, he was never one to rest on his laurels. Thetford was the fulfilment of his youthful goals, but it ultimately proved to be merely a stepping-stone on the way to his next business idea – a shop called Habitat.

9. Fiona MacCarthy, *Modern Painters*, Summer 1989, p. 67.

CHAPTER SIX
CREATING HABITAT

By the early 1960s the Conran organization had become more sophisticated and professional. It had a purpose-built factory and a stylish showroom, and it was able to offer a comprehensive service in design, fabrics and furniture. As part of its development, a domestic range of furniture was developed. Known as Summa, it was designed to be versatile and portable. This was important in several respects. First, furniture retailers were never willing to carry stocks of a product – in their view, this took up too much room and was too costly. Inevitably this led to consumer frustration at having to wait six or seven weeks for the sofa or chair which would then be delivered on a weekday – something that was inconvenient to the growing number of households where both partners worked. By providing furniture which could be assembled from a kit of parts, Terence's Summa range overcame the storage and delivery problem. Second, in the 1950s, there had been enormous growth in flat-building. This created a demand for furniture that could easily be transported in lifts and would work in small spaces. Last, there had been a move to a more relaxed, flexible, informal way of life within the home, reflecting the overall change in attitudes that emerged at the beginning of the sixties.

The 1962 Summa brochure was well designed, and instead of the rather sterile product shots of earlier brochures it featured room-set photography that juxtaposed new furniture with antique accessories. The idea of presenting furniture within the context of homes to be lived in was an important development, and one that would be re-created in Habitat. Rather than just selling furniture, the new brochure was trying to suggest a lifestyle that people could aspire to. The furniture was modern,

Room set from the second Summa furniture brochure

comfortable and robust without being avant-garde or challenging, but for less confident consumers – probably the majority at the time – the brochure offered style with security. For those who found it difficult to imagine how a chair or a table would look in their home, the brochure showed them before they bought. Later, some journalists would criticize Habitat for imposing a taste on people. However, this seems to miss the point: Terence's success was derived from an intuitive understanding that customers wanted suggestions and guidance and reassurance.

The lifestyle theme was continued in the second Summa brochure. On the cover there was a busy kitchen table in the background, lit by one of the round paper lampshades that would become synonymous with Habitat, with a radio and a set of early-eighteenth-century beer mugs that Terence owned. Other room sets featured enamel coffee-cups and mugs, bowls of fruit, books and dried flowers. The introduction to the brochure set out Terence's aim:

Conran furniture is designed to match the mood of present day living. What people want now for their homes is lively practical furniture in good basic shapes and warm unspoilt materials – natural timbers, leather, canvas – set off by bright fabrics.

With some prescience the brochure goes on to say, 'The whole range will look at home anywhere – today and for years to come.'

The strong linearity of earlier ranges had been softened, and the thin metal legs that typified Terence's furniture in the 1950s had disappeared. The furniture was rarely organic in its form, but there were some softer lines and much greater use of wood. Typical of the softer style was the Carimate chair produced by the Italian designer Vico Magistretti. Magistretti had designed the chair for the Carimate Golf Club restaurant in Italy. Its shape was based on a traditional country chair, but it had curving, down-ward-sloping arms and was finished in red gloss paint. It was forward-looking and clearly reflected the influence of Scandinavian design, but it also had a sense of comfort. Originally the chair had been 'discovered' by Christina Smith when she was on holiday in Italy, and she had ordered some samples for Terence to see. As a joke Terence had told her that she would have to pay for the samples if the chair didn't sell, but it turned out to be an inspired choice and was produced under licence in a variety of finishes.

The kitchen furniture on offer was a variant of a pine showroom fitting that Terence and John Mawer had seen at the Copenhagen store Illum's Bolighus. Pine furniture was seen as innovative, and Terence got the Conran Design Group to develop a version as a way of getting a foot in the door at Heal's, which was interested in a Swedish pine kitchen system. It was 'bang on the trend for cosy countrified living'.

The kitchen wasn't the only derivative design: a range of unit seating called Abacus was very similar to part of the Hille range, and the canvas and wood Tiffin chair was similar to a British Army campaign chair. However, the notable shift in the whole range was away from a purely modernist approach towards a more Scandinavian, Arts-and-Crafts-influenced range. There was greater use of natural materials, an emphasis on space-saving and versatility, an unpretentious simplicity of design, and a sense of craftsmanship. Indeed part of the range had been manufactured by Dancer & Hearne, a traditional High Wycombe furniture workshop. Terence's favourite piece in the range was the SU12 – a solid craftsman-looking dining-table offered in oak or ash.

Much would be written about the stripped-pine look of Habitat furniture in the 1960s. The reality was that there were light woods, there was cane seating, and there were bentwood chairs, but there was no stripped pine. The Habitat look was inspired by Terence's visits to Scandinavia, both to the furniture fairs at Copenhagen and to Den Permanente, a store-cum-exhibition which showed the best of Danish design. However, there had always been a strong Arts and Crafts feel to Terence's work right from his days at the Central School. In his *Printed Textile Design* he might have criticized William Morris for trying to hold back the inevitable, but there were strong similarities to Morris in other respects. They shared beliefs in the importance of simplicity – they both loved white – authenticity and craftsmanship in design, and both adhered to the idea of good design being both beautiful and functional. Jeremy Myerson, in his biography of the furniture designer and retailer Gordon Russell, believes that Conran and Morris shared common interests that were linked by what Terence called the 'peculiarly English' genius of Russell.

The other factor behind the development of the Conran style

was the move to create furniture for a consumer rather than a contract market. Cold linear design may have worked well in an office context, but, even if they were looking for modernism, British consumers wanted a sense of comfort. It was a point of view with which Terence empathized. As Fiona MacCarthy says:

I think Terence likes the simplicity of the Bauhaus and its vision of improving society, but he also has an English sense of comfort. There is a generosity and a feel for the Mediterranean in him, just as much as there is a Northern European Bauhaus influence. That taste is expressed in his own homes.

Designing furniture and presenting it was only half the task. Terence's belief that people would buy well-designed objects if they were offered them at a price they could afford depended on him getting the range into retailers. Some small modern home furnishing shops had emerged in the fifties, but to reach a volume market he needed to get his furniture into some large mainstream stores. In 1962 there had been a harsh recession, which made things difficult, but his overriding problem was the continuing con-servatism of retailers: 'too few of them [furniture retailers] make any attempt to guide the manufacturer by gauging public taste or forecasting demand, while too many act merely as ordering agencies, keeping samples rather than stock.'[1]

Furniture-making continued to be a highly fragmented craft-based industry. There were some 1,500 manufacturers, of whom 45 per cent employed fewer than ten people. It was impossible for manufacturers to dictate to retailers, who 'underestimate the taste and intelligence of the public'. Although 1963 and 1964 saw an increase in furniture sales, this was primarily at the bottom end of the market, where furniture supermarkets were selling from stock rather than by order. Terence believed that there was a pent-up demand for good furniture at reasonable prices, but people weren't offered it: what they were shown was traditional furniture in uninspiring surroundings. Rarely was there any attempt to inspire

1. Leslie Adrian, *Spectator*, 12 February 1965, p. 211.

the consumer by creating room sets and dressing them appropriately – most shops simply presented a sea of merchandise from which items had to be ordered.

The Summa range was well received by some buyers, but most retailers would only buy a small amount or sell direct from the catalogue. With the factory at Thetford geared up to produce in volume, there was considerable excess capacity. Having set up his dream – which cost more than anticipated – it was already under-utilized. Terence decided to make a tour of retailers to find out if there was any way of boosting sales. He visited some eighty shops and found an almost universally negative attitude. His furniture, when it was displayed, was simply put in with other ranges. There was no attempt to merchandise it effectively, and retailers were not prepared to put it in the context of a room set unless Terence paid for the space – which he could ill afford to do.

The one real exception to this mediocrity was Woollands. Elgin Anderson and Martin Moss had created a small modern-furniture department within the store. Primarily this sold Scandinavian furniture, and even before Terence had produced the Summa range it used to take some of his more consumer-looking contract furniture. Not only was the display cohesive, it was also well presented and sold by experienced sales staff. Maurice Libby was a Woollands furniture salesman:

> We saw Terence standing round and someone waylaid him and he said, 'I've come to see how you're selling so much of my furniture.' He started telling us about his research, and then he said he could see why we were doing so well: 'Because you've bought it, you're displaying it beautifully, and you're good sales people.' After that he used to come into the store quite often.

Woollands proved to Terence that he could sell his furniture if it was presented in the right context. However, one department store was unlikely to generate the sort of turnover he needed, and it seemed akin to pushing water uphill to instil Woollands' attitude into more retailers. The long-held idea of starting his own shop – harboured ever since the trip to France with Michael

Wickham a decade earlier – now began to take a real shape. He had watched Mary Quant make a very successful move into retailing in the mid-fifties, and in the late fifties there had been the development of Carnaby Street, led by menswear retailer John Stephens. In Denmark, Terence had seen good modern designer furniture and housewares being sold through Illum's Bolighus and Den Permanente; yet in Britain there was still no one trying to sell affordable modern furniture and furnishings. He believed that the same people who were shopping at Mary Quant's Bazaar and buying fashions from new RCA graduates such as Sally Tuffin and Marion Foale would like to express their lifestyle through their homes as well as the clothes they were wearing. They were simply not being given the opportunity to do so. Largely they were being offered the same sort of furniture as their parents.

The desire for a new home lifestyle was being nurtured at the time by the media. In addition to *Town* and *Queen*, the early sixties saw the emergence of the colour supplement. The first, in the *Sunday Times*, appeared on 4 February 1962 with a range of fashion and lifestyle features on such people as pop artist Peter Blake, Mary Quant and David Bailey. It was clearly aimed at a young, affluent and largely urban audience. In April the supplement carried a 'Design for Living' feature which was critical of the functionalism that the Council of Industrial Design promoted, arguing instead for 'an unexpected touch of salt; something not off the conveyor belt'. The success of the *Sunday Times* led to the *Sunday Telegraph* and the *Observer* following suit with their own supplements.

The general iconoclasm against established values was also evident in entertainment and on television. The Establishment, a satire club, was set up in Soho in 1961; *Beyond the Fringe*, starring Dudley Moore, Alan Bennett, Peter Cook and Jonathan Miller, transferred to the West End stage in May of the same year; and in October the new satirical magazine *Private Eye* was launched. In 1962 the satirical television programme *That Was the Week that Was* began broadcasting with viewing figures of roughly 3 million (rising to 12 million by the next year). The

Conservative government provided the satirists with rich material. Macmillan looked like an anachronism, and his successor, Sir Alec Douglas-Home, also sounded like one. The Profumo affair of 1963, when the Minister of War was found to be having an affair with Christine Keeler, who also seemed to be sleeping with a Soviet agent, seriously dented the government's credibility. The iconic photograph of Keeler posing naked in a copy of Arne Jacobsen's modern classic 3107 chair which appeared in the world media demonstrated the power of the new promotional culture. The photograph was in turn satirized in *Private Eye*, when Gerald Scarfe substituted a tired-looking Macmillan for Keeler.

It seemed like a time of change and opportunity: 'The sixties era didn't really start until 1963 – the liberated sixties, the Beatles sixties, the mini-skirt sixties, the flower-power sixties.'[2] The era, which the women's magazine *Nova* came to epitomize, was liberated and optimistic. People were encouraged to express their individuality. There was nearly full employment, real incomes were rising fast, and an ever-growing range of consumer goods was meeting the change from fifties 'needs' to sixties 'wants'. The reality of economic performance was of course somewhat different. The writer Arthur Koestler had been the editor of a series of essays entitled 'Suicide of a Nation?' in which it had been pointed out that Britain's share of world trade had shrunk in the previous ten years by as much as it had in the previous half-century. However, none of this affected the view of Britain being the centre of a new, irreverent world:

> The fashion was progressive in the sense of being questioning and irreverent and against the authority of Church, school, social hierarchy and government. It affected attitudes not just to sex, censorship and popular music, but also to privilege, social class and opportunity.[3]

2. David Gibbs, ed., *Nova 1965–1975* (Pavilion Books, 1993), p. 38.

3. Ben Pimlott, *Harold Wilson* (HarperCollins, 1992), p. 268.

The timing seemed perfect for Terence to open his own shop, but he was beset by a familiar problem – shortage of funds. The Conran group of companies might have grown significantly, and was now employing over two hundred people, but it was still under-capitalized. Even tiling the showroom floor at Hanway Place was a big issue. When the contracts showroom was moved from the top to the bottom floor, Terence had hexagonal matt tiles laid. John Mawer remembers that John Beevor, the financial director, complained to Terence, 'We can't afford these.' Terence's reply was typically curt: 'If I want to put fucking hexagonal tiles on the floor, I will. It's got nothing to do with you.'

Terence, John Mawer and John Beevor – in spite of the latter's reservation about the Habitat idea – went to see their bank manager about borrowing some money to get the project off the ground, but he couldn't or wouldn't advance a loan. For a while Terence discussed setting up the new company with David Bishop, who had worked at Woollands and for Terence, and Christina Smith, but they decided they would be better off on their own and set up a company called Goods and Chattels which imported items for the home from around the world. They would be an early and important supplier of enamelware, Japanese lampshades and Indian fabrics to Habitat. Eventually Terence found two allies in Philip Pollock and the model Pagan Taylor, who had been introduced to him by her husband's partner, the architect Bob Chapman. Along with Terence and his new wife, Caroline (whom he married in 1963), each put in a lump sum to form the new organization, Habitat Designs Ltd. Additionally, with the security of his foam company, Aerofoam, behind him, Philip gave guarantees to the bank for a working overdraft.

Although many of the businesses in Terence's life had been set up – mostly successfully – with indecent haste, Habitat took some time to put together. Getting finance was only one of the problems: a site had to be found, the interior designed, stock purchased and displayed, and staff taken on. Terence's life was as frantic as ever. Not only was he trying to run the furniture business, he also had the Conran Design Group, Conran Contracts and Conran Fabrics to oversee. And home life was equally disruptive for a time.

Terence had met Caroline through her sister, his former secretary Dinah Herbert. After he had separated from Shirley, Caroline rented a room in Terence's house at Regent's Park Terrace. She and Terence would bump into each other on the stairs, and they started going out. Caroline had been Olive Sullivan's assistant at *House & Garden*, but was now home editor for *Queen*, which gave her the opportunity to write about interior design and cooking. She was less ambitious than Shirley – supportive rather than competitive – so her relationship with Terence was less confrontational. Terence says, 'Caroline put up with my ambitiousness, but she never supported it or subscribed to it.'

Caroline was tall, red-headed and thin. In contrast, Terence, having looked gaunt in fifties photographs, began to look fuller by the early sixties. Caroline says, 'He was beginning to be plump – but I've found I rather like plump people, so that was a plus.' Although Caroline would work in the business for a while, she was always happier pursuing her own interests and family life. The immediate problem Terence soon had to face was that he and Caroline had nowhere to live. As part of his divorce settlement in 1962, Shirley had moved back into Regent's Park Terrace and Terence was staying with various friends. Somewhat ironically, he asked John Stephenson if he and Caroline could come and stay in his flat in Campden Towers in Notting Hill Gate, little knowing that John Stephenson had started going out with Shirley. Eventually they found a maisonette at the top of a Georgian house in Fitzroy Square. It had no plumbing or gas, the ceilings had caved in, and the walls were crumbling, but Terence and Caroline spent the early months of their marriage putting it back together again.

Meanwhile Terence was looking for a suitable location for his new shop. He'd decided that the ideal site was somewhere in Fulham or Chelsea. Although he had done no formal research, he had had showrooms and a workshop in the area before and his restaurant had been on the King's Road. It was an area for what

Terence liked to call, in sixties vernacular, 'switched-on people' – the sort of customers who shopped at Mary Quant and read *Queen*. The site he eventually found was about 6,000 square feet on the Fulham Road in what is now known as Brompton Cross. Although today the area is full of shops – not least of which is The Conran Shop – in the early sixties the area was largely residential. There were some small shops in Walton Street and some restaurants in the Fulham Road, but there were no retailers of any size. In fact the site that Terence found was still being developed – what had been a pub, the Admiral Keppel, was being replaced by a shop with a tower block above it.

People advised him against the location: 'Although there was a general buzz in the area, everybody who knew anything about retailing said it was a daft area for a shop, because there was no foot traffic. It was breaking all the rules.' However, the rent was cheap – about thirty shillings a square foot – and the basement was thrown in for free, as the landlords didn't believe anyone could sell from it. To save money, Terence didn't take the whole site; there was a section of the shop on Draycott Avenue that was being offered as separate units which remained unlet. He had a staircase put in so that the basement could be used as retailing space, and a glass frontage was designed so that the ground-floor interior, which featured the furniture range, could be seen from all sides. The interior was designed by Terence and Oliver Gregory, who had joined the Conran Design Group in 1960.

Oliver had originally been a cabinet-maker, but during a sabbatical in Australia he became interested in design and became a partner in a firm of architects. He continued his new profession with a firm in Richmond, Surrey, when he returned to England at the end of the fifties, and he started going out with a girl in the office who also knew Terence. She told him that she knew someone else who made furniture: 'He's just like you – a real shit.' In time Oliver became known as the 'shit man', not because of this connotation but because he ended up doing the shitty jobs, like firing people, that Terence hated doing. It wasn't that Terence was a coward; he simply couldn't cope with the emotions involved.

As designers, Terence and Oliver Gregory were alike. They both had grown up as makers and knew how to construct things, they both had an intuitive feel for the right materials, and they both believed in a simple, practical approach to design. Terence says, 'Oliver was wonderful; he was entirely practical. He raised your spirits. He knew how things were put together, and he would take responsibility for making things happen.' To this, Terence could add his eye for detail and breadth of vision.

The first Habitat they designed was the model from which all the subsequent variants were derived. It had a certain similarity to the design for the Harveys restaurant in its use of natural materials: there were quarry tiles on the floor, whitewashed brick walls, white-painted wooden-slatted ceilings, and spotlights. The design created a feeling of space, and also focused the customer's attention on the product. There was no sense in which the design dominated the merchandise – the personality of the shop would be derived primarily from the products it sold.

Getting the merchandise together took the best part of a year. Although the majority of the products were made in Britain, Terence went on a tour of Scandinavia, France and Italy to look at furniture and cookware. He had realized early on that he couldn't just sell furniture and fabrics: both to generate foot traffic and to offer a complete lifestyle range, he had to sell everything for the home. Furniture shops tended to be staid – partly because furniture was a large, infrequently made purchase and customers were few and far between – but Terence liked shops full of people. It helped to overcome customers' inhibitions and make life more enjoyable for the staff. To create a sense of excitement, busyness and fun Terence needed more frequently purchased items. For cookware, Terence turned to France for his inspiration. He had long been fascinated by a small shop in Soho called Madame Cadec, which sold French-made professional cookware. It was where the best restaurateurs shopped. Pagan Taylor also knew a place in Les Halles in Paris, called Dehillerin, which wholesaled *matériel de cuisine*, so Terence, Caroline and Pagan went off and bought pepper-mills, pâté moulds, copper pans, pots, salad bowls and shakers, cook's knives, carafes and

legumes sieves. From Scandinavia Terence bought crockery and wooden furniture, and from Italy, chairs. There were also fabrics from the Conran range, Philip Pollock's Aerofoam-made sofas, and some of Christina Smith's Far Eastern imports.

Most of the furniture range had a strong rustic, crafts feel, which would have appealed to British city-dwellers' attachment to the myth of the British countryside. As Fiona MacCarthy says, 'The British have always had a craving for a somewhat spurious peasant style of living – a tradition one can follow through from Heal in 1900 to Habitat much later.'[4] However, there were some modern classics: the Magistretti chair, Harry Bertoia's sculptural birdcage chair and the Le Corbusier bentwood chair were all included.

Although Pagan Taylor and Caroline both contributed to selecting the merchandise, it was chosen, as Terence says, 'with one pair of eyes': Terence had the ultimate say over product, and Habitat was very much his collection. What unified the merchandise were his talent for product selection – for getting the form, function, colour and texture of products right – and the accessibility of the range in terms of both price and style. The furniture was modern and comfortable without ever being avant-garde, while the china and glass were simple and sturdy. Although not every product was unique to Habitat, the combination of everything under one roof and the way in which it was presented provided a unique experience, and the environment in which the goods were sold provided added value in the customers' eyes – a wooden spoon bought in Woolworths was not the same as a wooden spoon from Habitat, whatever the physical similarities in the product. Terence was one of the pioneers of the retailer as a brand. Fashion retailers such as Mary Quant had already gone down this route, but no one had applied the idea to housewares. Terence says, 'Habitat had a fashion connection. It was never devised as a static business: it was designed to be constantly changing, with new looks and new

4. Fiona MacCarthy, *British Design since 1880 – A Visual History* (Lund, 1982), p. 82.

ideas. However, classic cookware and furniture was the permanent base of it all.'

To staff the new shop, Terence turned first to Woollands. He
had spent some time in the store watching the way the sales staff
sold furniture to customers. Although it wasn't aggressive selling,
it was a world away from the Heal's selling style, which was very
old-fashioned and formal to the extent that the salesperson had to
be introduced to the customer by a receptionist. At Woollands,
selling was informal and theatrical – at least as it was practised by
Maurice Libby, who had come from Heal's, and by Kate Currie,
who had worked at Liberty and for the designer David Hicks.
They were both intrigued by what Terence was up to. Maurice
Libby remembers:

Terence told us that he was so fed up with retailers using his finance and his
catalogue to sell his furniture that he was thinking of opening a shop. He said,
'Don't tell anyone, because I'll be opening in direct competition with my
customers.' Gradually he fed us bits of information, but he wouldn't tell us
where it was. When we knew he'd found a site, both Kate and I asked him if
we could have jobs.

Terence employed them both, and afterwards a third member of
the Woollands team joined them. However, Maurice Libby says
he almost changed his mind when he found out where the shop
was: 'I thought, I'm Knightsbridge – I can't go all the way down
there. There won't be any customers.' Although they were
reassured by the concept once Terence explained it in detail,
Maurice says he thought at the time the whole thing was a real
risk.

The other two key members of staff were Sonja Jarman and
Zimmie Sasson. Sonja Jarman, an Australian, had had some retail
experience as a buyer at Liberty's and had then worked at
Conran and Company on the sales side. Zimmie Sasson, who
went on to work at Habitat for a number of years, had trained as
a designer but was working for a travel agency. She was a
girlfriend of Oliver Gregory's, and through him she met

Terence. She can remember cooking osso bucco for Terence and Caroline at Oliver's Abingdon Road flat, and, thinking his idea for Habitat sounded exciting, asking him for a job. Terence told her that he had already filled all the jobs except for the bookkeeper. In spite of having no training in bookkeeping, she volunteered and Terence took her on. She learned the job as she went along, filling in the gaps in her knowledge from her father, who was an accountant.

By early 1964 Terence's idea had a name. While in Scandinavia, Terence and John Mawer had racked their brains for a name for the shop; back in London, Pagan Taylor had looked up 'house' in Roget's *Thesaurus* and found 'habitat' – 'the usual natural surroundings and conditions of animals and plants'. Terence knew straight away that this was right – it was both appropriate and distinctive. From the outset the shop name was presented in lower case. Typographically this was an idea that had been generated by Herbert Bayer at the Bauhaus. His view was that when presented entirely in lower case, words became more legible and economic – 'Why have two symbols for one sound.' The type itself was a distinctive classic but simple face called Baskerville that reflected the personality of the shop.

In the months leading up to the opening, the merchandise that Terence had ordered started to appear. He had involved the staff in buying-meetings to show the products he was thinking of ordering, but most of them had little idea what the non-furniture products were for. As things arrived, however, Terence would show everyone what each product did and get them to experiment with it. Maurice Libby recalls: 'We didn't know what half of it was meant for. We all scalded ourselves with coffee-pots trying to learn how they worked.'

If the staff were often surprised by what products did, they were equally so by the quantities involved. Terence remembered the joy he had experienced at the plenty of those ironmonger's shops in France back in the early 1950s, and also of the French warehouses he had visited in his search for products; he wanted to try to re-create that feeling in Habitat. Rather than wasting valuable selling-space on a stockroom, the site was to be both shop and warehouse. Maurice Libby describes how the shop was merchandised:

None of us could understand why there were these enormously deep shelves that were eighteen inches deep and three feet wide. Terence would go into a kind of trance trying to convey to us the unbelievable thrill he'd had in the big French wholesalers. We didn't know what he was talking about. He said, 'I want this whole shelf full of glasses,' and I realized he meant all the same. Everything had to be on show. He'd just used gut feeling to judge how much to buy.

The shop wasn't cluttered, but presenting the kitchen products in large quantities created a feeling that the shop was bursting with merchandise.

To get as much product in as possible and to convey the texture of such things as terracotta bowls, wooden spoons and copper pans, Terence had all packaging removed – the sculptural shapes and the natural materials of housewares were not only to be seen, but also to be touched. Terence always recognized the emotive value of handling a product, of feeling the surface, and he wanted his customers to experience that availability when they were shopping.

The same sculptural quality was to be conveyed in the in-store displays. Maurice Libby had been in charge of display in the furniture department at Woollands, and Terence had asked him to take on the same role with Habitat. To begin with, Maurice produced the artful displays that he had always done – two glasses draped with a piece of silk – but Terence hated them. He wanted to see fifty pots stacked to create an interesting form – the sort of design that in a museum context would be conceptual art.

Part of the power of Habitat was its sensuality: the combination of touch, sight, sound and smell. In addition to the tactile displays, there were the pervasive odour of herbs and spices and the sound of modern jazz playing. The shop itself was spacious, and the use of spotlights created drama by highlighting

Habitat, Fulham Road, 1964

specific products. The neutral backgrounds made the products the
focus of attention – they almost demanded reverence.

Terence also paid attention to product juxtaposition. Just as he
had done in the Summa catalogue, he inspired people to buy looks
or combinations of products by displaying appropriate items
together. David Phillips, who later joined Habitat from Woollands
as its first professional buyer, says:

> Terence got people to look afresh at things they had been seeing for years and
> years. The interesting thing was that he took basketware and tea towels and
> dish mops and simply by putting them together in a mass he made them
> interesting. Terence's great talent is that he gets people to use their eyes – if
> they have the eyes to see.

Pagan Taylor remembers that Terence was very excited in the
months leading up to the opening. Everyone was infected by his

enthusiasm, and the initial scepticisms were replaced by an almost euphoric belief in the concept. Terence believed wholeheartedly in the idea of Habitat, but he was extremely nervous about it. The gamble of the venture was stimulating, but there was a lot at stake – if it failed, the consequences for the factory and for his other companies would be dire. He says, 'It was a dangerous thing to do at that time. I was absolutely terrified about Habitat – especially as none of us had any real experience of retailing.' However, Terence always kept his emotions to himself: he wasn't going to show his partners or anyone else his anxiety, and he wouldn't allow his uncertainty to be a barrier to action. Although he might ruminate on an idea for a long time, when the decision to act was made – usually on the basis of his gut feeling – the commitment was complete. He was so often successful precisely because of this. Caroline says:

I think one of the things that has made Terence very successful is that he doesn't question himself. Having a tremendous belief in your ideas is a quality that major painters have – they know they're right. I think Terence is like that, and very often he has been right. He works from his guts, not his head.

In spite of the collective retailing inexperience, Terence was inspirational at motivating people and bringing their talents to the surface. (This also often gave him a good excuse not to pay them very much.) Many of the original employees of Habitat and the design group would stay with him for the next twenty-five years. Imbued as they were with the original thinking of Habitat, they would be the guardians of its ethos.

For the opening of the shop, there was an evening reception between 6 p.m. and 8 p.m. on Monday 11 May 1964. The staff had Vidal Sassoon haircuts and were dressed by Mary Quant, with striped butcher's aprons to protect their outfits. The press releases – which gave prominence to Pagan Taylor, because Terence was worried about how the existing stockists of Conran furniture would react – stressed that the range was aimed specifically at 'young moderns with lively tastes'. The press picked up on the story, and the *Sunday Times* ran a small preview the day before the opening with a photograph by Terence Donovan – the only person who has persisted in calling Terence 'Terry'. The text, by Liz Good, stressed the fashion positioning of the shop and was clearly aimed at a female readership:

> 'The bright young chicks have got to have a red Magistretti chair the way they've got to have a Sally Tuffin and Marion Foale dress,' says Terence Conran with a blissfully happy smile.
>
> Say 'Sally Tuffin and Marion Foale' to the average furniture man and he'll say 'Who?' But to furniture designer and manufacturer Terence Conran who makes and sells Magistretti chairs, the world of fashion and furnishing do equate. He has a happy knack of knowing what the 'smart chicks', and the simply smart, want next in furniture and is doing his best to make sure his is the firm that's selling it . . .
>
> If you don't shop in London don't make the mistake of thinking Habitat or its campaign to make shopping fun is not eventually going to affect you. The staff scream in anguish if you call it 'that shop in Chelsea'. And with good reason. That shop in Chelsea is just the first link of a plan for a chain of sixteen more stretching all over the country.[5]

Whereas Terence as a fifties furniture designer could seem quite serious – even if he did occasionally do something mischievous, like send all the architects on his mailing list a backscratcher – Terence as a retailer conveyed a sense of humour. There was a wit about some of the products, such as the bright enamelware, and there was a jokiness about their presentation. For example, the captions in the opening leaflet were full of puns: 'Shell out for this special white snaildish' and 'What a grind – pepper-mills from France' typified the style. The idea of shopping as an enjoyable, light-hearted experience to be savoured rather than endured was entirely new in home furnishings – far removed from the po-faced approach of most retailers.

5. Elizabeth Good, 'What the smart chicks are buying' in the *Sunday Times*, 10 May 1964, p. 43.

Unlike other retailers, Terence Conran understood the great change that had taken place in households from keeping up appearances to emphasizing and *enjoying* the chores – fun follows domestic function. He understood it because that is the way he liked to live. Servants had gone, working wives come and Habitat provided cutlery that wasn't silver and tables that didn't expect cloths or polishing, stackable chairs, non-heirloom plates and jolly kitchen equipment.[6]

Terence was absolutely clear about who his target market was – partly because he was part of it – and how it lived. Like Terence, his customer base included a large number of people who were buying up old houses cheaply and renovating them. This was the idea of 'Conspicuous Thrift' that had been formulated the year before the opening of Habitat in *Town* magazine by the Old Bryanstonian and Terence's next-door neighbour Nicholas Tomalin. He suggested that a section of the population was interested in simplicity and taking good old things and converting them for modern lifestyles. This idea was developed further by the opening of a shop in Kensington Church Street, which Terence was much taken with, called The Lacquer Chest. Its owners, the Andersons, were selling 'downstairs' artefacts as antiques. The idea that there was value in Victorian kitchen equipment, for example, was entirely novel. When a television programme was made by the BBC after the opening of the third Habitat, the presenter described The Lacquer Chest as 'the first antique shop in London to switch from mahogany and porcelain to pine and earthenware; and not only to tables and pots but even old advertising signs. Here the art of the Victorian common people, long since relegated to attic and junk shop, was made desirable.'

Simultaneously the attitudes of women were changing. More women were going out to work and enjoying greater levels of independence. Shortly after Habitat opened *Nova* – which had the

6. Ann Barr, '£150 million down and still smiling', in *Harpers & Queen*, July 1991, p. 89.

subtitle of 'A new kind of magazine for the new kind of woman' – was launched. It carried articles which suggested that women had interests beyond the cooking, knitting and looking after the home features in other magazines. The *Nova* woman was interested in these things, but in *Nova* they were represented as enjoyable and self-fulfilling, rather than as the means to be a better housewife. At home, and especially in the kitchen, the new woman wanted to express her personality. For Habitat, the timing was perfect.

Terence spent no money on advertising – he was always loath to do so if it meant spending less on getting the shop right – but he learned how to handle his press relations well, and he could turn on the charm for the mostly female home editors, so word of mouth and favourable press reports made Habitat an immediate success. Commenting on the opening, *The Times* said, 'Many of Habitat's first visitors thought they must have gone to heaven. It was a revelation to the customers and a revolution in the home furnishing trade.' And a week later the *Financial Times* reported,

> By the time I came back to Europe this week, so much had already been said about London's new shop, Habitat, that I felt any further mention of it would be stale news. But after visiting it, I find I must bring it to the attention of anybody who may have missed out on earlier announcements. . . . It really does have the most tempting range of merchandise for any and every corner of a tasteful home, ancient or modern.

The shop soon attracted a high-profile clientele, including George Harrison, John Lennon, Lord Snowdon, Julie Christie, Margot Fonteyn and David Niven. On Saturdays people would use the shop as a meeting-place and would come to browse and listen to the music. Customers were intrigued by the novelty of the kitchen goods and enjoyed the idea of buying things such as saveloy kettles which, even if used only once, they could show to their friends. The previously insular British were beginning to travel abroad for their holidays more and more, and were becoming aware of other cultures. Habitat appealed to their growing cosmopolitanism and sense of self-discovery. Terence was teaching a whole generation about how life could be lived.

However, not everything was running smoothly. Terence had originally had the idea that Habitat would be self-service, just as supermarkets had started to be, but initially people didn't understand what they should do – and no one had thought to provide them with shopping-baskets. That was easily remedied, but soon a larger problem loomed. Habitat was such a runaway success that the stock which should have lasted for six months started running out. Terence was desperate to get the shelves restocked, not only because of the potential missed sales but also because empty shelves would destroy the whole ambience of the shop. It wasn't too difficult to replace the furniture, much of which was made by Conran Furniture, but many of the smaller suppliers of china and glass weren't geared up for large production runs and couldn't provide new stock quickly. Pagan Taylor remembers that Terence got very worried about the situation as he tried to find alternative suppliers at short notice. In the end, however, the shop muddled through, and Terence felt confident enough to take the remaining part of the site in Draycott Avenue shortly afterwards.

Whatever the early vicissitudes, everyone who was involved with the early days of Habitat remembers them as being hard work and a lot of fun. The staff felt they were involved in creating something new and worthwhile. Terence could be volatile – frightening and aggressive one moment and charming the next – but it was always exciting working with him. Once people got to know him they could see his changes of mood coming, but some can also recall the looks of perplexity on others as they tried to fathom his personality. Terence expected and largely got total commitment from his employees. This often meant long hours, because during the day Terence would be working on the furniture business or on contracts or with the design group and would arrive at the shop only around closing time and expect the staff to stay while he looked around inspecting every detail. Maurice Libby says:

> Just when we wanted to go home, he would arrive. We could then be there to all hours. He would be so angry if anyone wished to get away or was absent from work. I can remember a girl in the shop left early one evening and called a taxi. I've never forgotten his outrage, and he said, 'Watch her – she's got her hand in the till.' In his eyes she was both imprudent and disloyal.

Although Terence could sometimes be generous, the long years of scraping through had made him prudent. He lived in a nice house and enjoyed driving fast cars, but he was never profligate and, rather than take money out of the company, he would always prefer to plough it back in to expand. His work was the focus of his life. He might indulge himself by occasionally buying a nice painting or an antique, but his clothes were always basic and his lifestyle simple. He had – still has – a hatred of waste, and would go to great lengths to impress this on those around him.

Although many of the shop staff stayed with Terence for several years, the original investors soon departed. Philip Pollock was indiscreet with another member of staff and Terence suggested he should resign, while Pagan Taylor – who later married Oliver Gregory and came back to run The Café in the King's Road Habitat – decided that she didn't know enough about retailing. Terence bought both their shares and so became the main shareholder. Caroline had had a baby – Tom – and was spending more time at home. Although she would remain involved with the shop until 1968, she wasn't a full-time employee. Peter Hope, who had worked with Maurice Libby at Heal's, was brought in to run a toys and accessories department, and Terence subsequently made him manager. Zimmie Sasson, whom Terence used to refer to as 'the lady in black bombazine', started helping with the buying.

At the end of the first year, Habitat's turnover was £62,000 – about £10 per square foot. The margins were variable. On some items, such as wooden spoons, the percentage mark-up was huge, but on furniture it was tighter. The first net profit was £1,649.

The shop was successful for a variety of reasons: Terence's vision and drive and eye for products, the quality of the staff, the cohesiveness of the stock and the marketing of the concept.

Habitat was never a 'designer' shop – something which design commentators could occasionally get sniffy about. It appealed to a very specific and aware group of people, who were willing to question accepted values but were still imbued with an English sense of restraint. Although Terence was bringing good design to people at affordable prices, Habitat was not so much a design triumph as a marketing one. Terence understood the aspirations of the market he was selling to, and he was sufficiently confident in his intuition as to what that market would buy that he was able to challenge the conventional wisdom of how a home-furnishing retail business should be run.

The year 1964 was a real marker in Terence's life. At the age of thirty-two he had fulfilled his long-cherished ambition to open a shop and had launched his mission to change attitudes to shopping and design. In retrospect his timing seems perfect. After 'thirteen years of Tory misrule', in October a new Labour government was elected, committed to changing Britain to a more technocratic and egalitarian society; there was a booming economy; and there was the start of a retail revolution, with both Barbara Hulanicki's Biba fashion store and the upmarket shop Quorum, run by ex-RCA students Ossie Clark and Alice Pollock, opening that year. *Time* magazine's eulogy of 'London – the Swinging City' was still two years away, but when Terence opened Habitat he was right at the beginning of the movement that would make London for a few years the most fashionable place in the world.

CHAPTER SEVEN
THE SIXTIES

For Terence the sixties was a period of growth. Having struggled for ten years to establish himself as a furniture designer and maker, the development of Habitat from a shop into the beginnings of a chain launched him on a new path which would make him a key figure in British retailing. The problem that confronted him along the way was a familiar one – insufficient funds. He solved it first by borrowing, then by merging and finally, fortuitously, by de-merging. Thanks to Habitat, by the end of the decade Terence's businesses were in better shape than they ever had been. The furniture-making company and the design consultancy also performed well, benefiting either by their direct involvement with supplying or designing for Habitat or indirectly through an enhanced reputation by association.

One of the interesting aspects of Terence's growing reputation was that it coincided with the high point of a pop culture whose focus on the disposable and the ephemeral was the antithesis of everything he believed in. Terence's view – 'I like to design simple things, everyday objects that don't shout at you, that slip quietly but efficiently and elegantly into your house or garden. I like to design the ordinary' – was at odds with the icons of pop: Union Jack symbols and bull's-eyes. Michael Wolff's notion that 'it will be a great day when cutlery and furniture designs (to name but two) swing like the Supremes,'[1] didn't accord with Terence's. Terence would have been quite happy to have the shopping environment of Habitat 'swing like the Supremes', but not the cutlery. However, there were some elements of pop styling in Habitat's range – especially in the use

1. Michael Wolff, *Society of Industrial Artists Journal*, January 1965, p. 10.

Terence and Caroline with Tom, 1964

of bright primary colours in cookware, fabrics and furniture. Nevertheless, Terence never compromised his belief in functional design: products had to be right for the job. Pop may have only touched Habitat merchandise at the edges, but it was important in creating an iconoclastic atmosphere and a youth culture that was determined to define its own values. Terence was creating a market for Habitat, where none seemed to exist before:

> Still only months old, Habitat is the result of Conran's shrewd observation that, while today's young newly-weds will spend money on making themselves look 'absolutely super' they often neglect the surroundings in which they live. The reason, he maintains, is that until now it has been difficult to create a lively, spanking-bright home without spending a mint of money, or undertaking the perpetual burden of hire purchase payments.[2]

Habitat gave people the opportunity to define their lives through the furnishing of their homes, and gave them the reassurance that they were doing the right thing. Sixties pluralism created an uncertainty about what constituted good taste – despite the attempts of the Sunday papers, with their 'Look' and 'Ego' columns, to redefine this. Through its strong visual appeal and considered combination of elements, Habitat tried to create a style for the less confident consumer.

> In a society where there was, in the 1960s, an unprecedented degree of mobility within social classes, and to a much more limited degree across classes, this social uncertainty became focused on lifestyles and upon the objects that constituted them. In this commodity world where you were what you bought, the problem was knowing what to buy. Habitat resolved this problem. It took the guessing out of good taste.[3]

Although Terence claimed in the initial press releases that the first Habitat was to be part of a chain of shops across the country – an idea that was picked up by the media – he says that in reality he had never seen the Fulham Road shop as anything but a one-off. The idea of a chain was really wishful thinking, but Habitat was so immediately successful that Terence decided 'this is a bigger opportunity than one small shop'. To achieve this, he knew he would need additional funds.

2. Anne Barrie, *House Beautiful*, December 1964, p. 57.

3. John Hewitt, 'Grand Design in the Market Place: the Rise of Habitat Man', in *Oxford Art Journal*, 10 February 1987, p. 40.

Terence always had a dislike of bankers. He had found it difficult to get funds for expansion during the fifties, and no one had been willing to lend money for the start-up of Habitat. To Terence, bankers were the antithesis of everything he was. Whereas he made decisions largely by intuition, he found bankers wanted to analyse everything; whereas he was always positive and wanting to try out ideas, he believed bankers found reasons for not doing things; whereas he thought long term, bankers wanted an immediate return; and whereas he always wanted to seize an opportunity, he discovered bankers were bereft of the imagination even to see it. Nevertheless the success of Fulham Road and his integrated company structure, which provided design, manufacturing and retailing, demonstrated the potential inherent in the Conran group, and when Terence was introduced to the merchant bank Morgan Grenfell he found, almost to his surprise, that it was willing to lend him the £150,000 he was seeking. Philip Chappell of Morgan Grenfell remembers his first impressions of Terence: 'He struck me at once as immensely shrewd – very lively when he knew about something, prepared to shut up and listen when he didn't.'

Armed with sufficient funds, Terence set about finding a new site: 'You look, you drive around, you sniff the atmosphere, you look at the car traffic.' Having seen the sort of people who were shopping at Fulham Road, he wanted to find another location with a good catchment of young 'switched-on' people. The site he found in Tottenham Court Road was near both his home in Fitzroy Square and his office in Hanway Place and well positioned for north-London shoppers coming from Camden and Hampstead. At the time, Tottenham Court Road was notable for two famous furniture shops – Heal's, which had pioneered the introduction of Scandinavian furniture in the fifties and had been in Tottenham Court Road since 1818, and Maples, which had been there since 1841. In Victorian times the Road had been the centre of the furniture trade. That was no longer the case in the 1960s, but in addition to the two famous shops there were also some contract-furniture showrooms which made the street a shopping destination for anyone interested in buying furnishings.

The only negative factor, compared to the Fulham Road, was that the much larger scale of buildings and shops took away the human dimension which had made the first Habitat seem cosy and comfortable. Caroline Conran always found Tottenham Court Road dreary and grey, whereas in the Fulham Road 'it was all very matey and friendly – people came in and chatted. That didn't happen with the second shop.' However, Tottenham Court Road was not the locational risk that Fulham Road had seemed: it had a good passing trade, and was well served by buses and trains.

The new Habitat was an 8,000-square-foot former furniture store owned by Great Universal Stores. The going rate in Tottenham Court Road at the time was £3 a square foot, but Terence was never willing to pay prime retail rates if he could avoid it and he managed to negotiate the rate down to 22s 6d – which was hardly surprising given the state of the building. Terence said, 'The premises were indescribably depressing when we took them over. There were at least twenty layers of brocade wallpaper, wrought iron fittings everywhere, and most of the woodwork was rotten.'[4] Tottenham Court Road was one in a series of buildings, from North End Road to Cock Yard to Hanway Place, in which the skills of the Conran Design Group made unlikely or rundown interiors viable. However, it was Terence's vision in the first instance that saw the potential of these and also later locations.

The design and fitting-out of the new shop, which took over six months, mirrored that of Fulham Road. There were floor-to-ceiling windows, white-painted walls, an open-plan furniture showroom lit by spotlights, and a black-and-white-tiled floor. The overall effect, aided by the extra space, was of a light and airy shop – at least on the ground floor, which carried the furniture and textiles. The basement contained cookware, herbs and toys, and there was also a mezzanine containing a new product area: hi-fi and television.

4. Hilary Gelson, *The Times*, 5 October 1966, p. 15.

To launch the new shop a seafaring theme was created with the slogan 'Heel over to Habitat'. Caroline remembers that Heal's was incensed about this, but the campaign appealed to Terence's sense of mischief. He liked Anthony Heal and he admired the Heal's building, which had been extended and modernized in the early sixties, but Terence thought that Heal's had become very uncommercial and conservative. For example, the self-assembly furniture (KD or knock down) that Conran Furniture pioneered was rejected by Heal's, in spite of its popularity. They insisted that the furniture be fully assembled for inspection on their loading dock. Given the opportunity Terence felt he could run Heal's much more efficiently:

They [Heal's] were a company with a terrific reputation, but they weren't prepared to grasp the modern world in any sort of positive way. If something didn't fit in with their rather genteel attitudes, that was that.[5]

After the shop opened on 11 October 1966, the press reaction to the second store was a bit more muted – perhaps not surprisingly, as it could never have had the impact of the first. The most interesting media comment was from a small publication called *Peace News*, which ran the headline 'It's War between Habitat and Heal's.' The mainstream press was more circumspect. The *Observer* was positive, as was *The Times*, which talked about Habitat turning shopping from a chore into a pleasurable pastime. In the *Guardian*, however, Fiona MacCarthy was more critical:

Conran has perceptively exploited urban restlessness. In Habitat, things happen almost anywhere you look. . . . The merchandise is ordinary really, fairly cheap. But its setting and its build-up, the frenzy all around it, makes it seem more covetable, gives it its mystique.[6]

5. Susanna Goodden, *A History of Heal's* (Heal & Son, 1984), p. 134.

6. Fiona MacCarthy, 'In Habitat', the *Guardian*, 5 October 1966.

Terence was always irritated by what he saw as unfair criticism, but he also understood the press and would not be diverted from his chosen path:

> If the image of urbanized shoppers buying a rustic way of life makes amusing reading in the *Guardian*, I really prefer to take the sneer than not to have done anything at all.

Although the Habitat product range had been expanded, its core remained. The Magistretti chair still featured, as did the Chesterfield sofa and Scandinavian wooden furniture. Kitchen-ware still had a predominantly French feel, but there were some additions in the form of brown glazed-earthenware cooking-pots and the chicken brick – a hollow earthenware container made in two halves, in which a chicken could be cooked. Recommended by the master chef Escoffier for producing *Poularde en conserve*, it was an example of Habitat meeting the growing desire of people to be more adventurous in the kitchen, and in time became almost synonymous with Habitat. The fabrics had also been adapted to meet changing consumer demands, and the bright and sometimes jarring colours now on offer were clearly influenced by pop and quite different from the more muted ranges that had been sold two years earlier.

The choice of stock was at this time still largely undertaken by committee, but with Terence still the dominant influence. The furniture designer Rodney Kinsman, who had just left the Central School and had set up a company called OMK with two friends, remembers trying to get a chair he had designed into Habitat. Initially he had approached Maurice Libby at Fulham Road, who had suggested that he talk to Terence. An appointment was made, and Rodney turned up at Hanway Place with a sample of a metal-framed chair with a slung leather back and seat. Rather than being introduced to Terence, he was asked to send the chair up in the lift. Rodney wasn't sure he should let the chair go, but a few minutes later a call came down and he was invited up. Terence loved the chair and agreed to buy it for Habitat. The order was the making of

OMK, and Habitat continued to buy from the company for many years.

Terence's taste and belief in simplicity were the company's point of continuity. Maurice Libby says:

Terence loved tradition and loved interpreting it and modernizing it. In textiles, for example, he could take an old fabric and modernize it by knocking out three-quarters of the design while still retaining its essence. Everything he's ever done has been to simplify, to prune away, to find the truth.

Terence's ability as a chooser of designs seems to have been born out of his early influences in the form of his mother and Don Potter, coupled with his eye for detail. The ability to focus on the things that mattered was a skill he used both with products and with the stores themselves. He was intensely aware of visual imperfection, and he tried to encourage the Habitat staff to share his pride in the way things looked. Often the encouragement was of the blustering kind, and when people knew Terence was going to pay a visit there would be much scurrying around to make sure the shop was perfectly presented. Maurice Libby recalls that, when the staff at Fulham Road knew Terence was coming, everything that was damaged or broken or simply out of place would be thrown out of the back of the store – until one day Terence went 'truffling' in the wreckage and discovered what they'd been up to. By turns he would inspire and then bully, but he was never cynical. His aim was always to deliver to the customer his view of what was right. He would never sell something he didn't think was good, and largely he sold what he personally liked. There was a sincerity and honesty in this that most of the staff whole-heartedly shared.

This personalization of his business would represent both the greatest strength and the greatest weakness of everything that Terence has ever done. From Habitat to Mothercare to The Conran Shop to his restaurants, Terence's personal vision and taste have been the key determinant. Success would require two things: that sufficient customers shared his view and that the people who worked with him shared his ethos. As Habitat grew and developed both would become harder to sustain. In the early days, Terence was sufficiently close to everyone who worked for him for the Habitat ethos to be clearly disseminated. Employees quickly got to understand his ideas on products and presentation and, because they were appealingly humanistic, adopted them as their own. David Phillips, who became the company's first buyer, says:

> The strength of Habitat was that you had a single eye looking at everything, which gave a consistency and sense of style. That can only happen when there's one person in charge. I occasionally found it frustrating, but not often, because I was very much on the same wavelength as Terence. On the whole, I knew what Habitat and Terence needed.

In display, Maurice Libby also became adept at knowing what was right. The displays that worked and that Terence liked were those where the combination of objects added value to each other. This required simplicity – clutter would detract from the intended meaning. For example, a simple array of Elizabeth David books on French provincial cooking allied with French cookware made all the items more appealing because the juxtaposition stirred the customer's imagination. Terence recognized that people were interested in fulfilling their desires rather than in meeting their needs.

Terence loved the simplicity and charm of Maurice's memorial window display when Sir Winston Churchill died in 1965. It consisted of a newspaper containing the announcement alongside a cigar in an ashtray and a vase with white Madonna lilies. He also liked the humour of an Easter display Maurice produced, with a children's steamroller set in the window with a row of flattened Easter eggs behind it. However, sometimes Maurice could misread the situation. He remembers producing a display for some fabrics, for which he hired a huge stuffed peacock. When he knew Terence was coming to the store he retired to the basement, 'preening myself in anticipation of praise'. However, one look from Terence, who beckoned him upstairs, told him it wasn't right. Maurice says he watched in horror as Terence took a long run and 'booted the peacock up the arse and across the store'. In business, Terence always made it clear what he thought, even if the statement was occasionally silent. Maurice says, 'I've never known him not to speak his mind – you know you're going to get the truth. In business, he's incredibly honest and up-front.'

Terence moulded the early Habitat into a family, which thrived on the excitement and stimulation he created. It was friendly and intimate, but it was absolutely clear who was in control.

In many ways, Terence's home life mirrored that of the workplace. Indeed the borders between home and work were very blurred, and always had been. Given his almost total commitment to work, this was perhaps not surprising: most of his friends were people he had met through work, and those he knew from elsewhere almost invariably got drawn into his work projects. This was also true of his relationships with wives and girlfriends. Even his three honeymoons had revolved around work. Later on he would involve his children and his sister in his projects. Priscilla thinks, 'He loves having people on the hook. And he does it through work. He doesn't seem to want to have a relationship that's not connected through work.'

In the early days of Habitat, Terence found the time to have at least part of the weekend off. He still liked to check up on the shops, and he would work on design projects at home, but after the Conrans moved from the maisonette in Fitzroy Square and into a house in St Andrew's Place, overlooking Regent's Park, he started gardening at weekends. He had been interested in plants and gardens ever since his youthful visits to his Devonian great-aunt. Also his mother was a keen gardener, and he would still go and help her occasionally. For Terence, gardening – like cooking, which he also enjoys – has all the attributes of a perfect hobby. It is creative, involves working with one's hands and requires an understanding of shape, texture and colour. Terence finds it relaxing, and working in the garden a good time for contemplation. However, before he could start working on the new garden it had to be cleared. The new Conran home was no different from his other houses: it was in a beautiful location, and the building itself was a stunning 1820s Regency house designed by Decimus Burton – who was the architect for many of the buildings at Kew Gardens – but it was cold, crumbling and rotting. On one side there were derelict houses where rats roamed – Caroline remembers her housekeeper leaving her baby on a rug in the garden and coming back to find a rat attached to the baby's arm. On the other side was an eccentric purple-clad lady who frightened the children. Terence and Caroline had the house renovated, but Caroline remembers it as 'really only a surface job.'

The interior was in typical Conran style. There was extensive use of white, floors were natural wood, and modern furniture classics were mixed in with antiques. The kitchen, which was always a focal point of any Conran house, featured the Summa units in Swedish pine. Although there was some clutter in the house – mainly because Caroline and the children liked it that way – the overall look was clean, spare and Terence's taste. He never went to the extent of Gordon Russell, who forbade his children toys because of the mess, but he could be irritated by the flotsam of family life. He could be offended by the way butter was cut, and annoyed by plastic bottles on the table. Just as he needed to control the look of Habitat and the products it sold, so he needed to impose his vision on his houses and on those around him. This included the way Caroline dressed:

> Caroline agrees that Terence influences her dressing. He brings the same sharp eye to the cut of her clothes as he does to the line of a design for furniture. 'I may bring something home and like it,' she said, 'and he makes me take it back. By that time I hate it so much that I do.'[7]

Although Terence was often absent because of his work commitments, the house was invariably busy. Sebastian and Jasper lived up the road in Regent's Park Terrace with Shirley

7. Polly Devlin, *House & Garden*, November 1964, p. 79.

and were frequent visitors. Before the birth of her second child, Sophie, Caroline was fully involved with Habitat, but by 1967, when the third shop opened, she cut back to three days a week and was spending more time at home. Although she was also writing for *Nova* and creating the Habitat Cook's Diary each year, she became more interested in the children and enjoyed their company. Jasper remembers, 'Caroline was always fantastic – she made a huge effort to look after us, but he [Terence] would be at work, so I wouldn't really see him. We had quite a sparse relationship.'

Terence really only began to develop relationships with his children when they became adults. Working weekends meant he preferred quiet and the company of his work colleagues rather than noisy children. Jasper says that his father 'always had his own thoughts and didn't like them interrupted'. The effect on his two elder children was to make them rather withdrawn. They were in awe of Terence, and desperate to have his approval.

Sebastian had his own workroom, where he made things and where he kept an 'incredible' train set that was out of bounds to the other children. In the absence of his father, Sebastian became close to Eduardo Paolozzi, who helped him with his constructions. The lack of a relationship with his father made life complicated – something that has continued. Sebastian says, 'All my life I've wanted my father's approval.' For his part, Jasper wanted to be close to his father but thinks that Terence's difficult relationship with Shirley meant that he was categorized as his mother's son. Until his late teens, Jasper was quiet and uncommunicative. He was rather a chubby boy, who spent much of his time drawing. Although both children would go on to become very good designers, neither of them remembers Terence nurturing their interest in design – or, indeed, in other things. Terence says, 'I don't think I was a bad father, but I was an absent one. I wasn't the kind of person to take them to a football match on a Saturday afternoon.'

The one place where family life did exist for Terence was around the dining-table. Sometimes he would be the chef and would take great pleasure in preparing and making a meal that both looked and tasted good. Although he wasn't a chatty person, around the table he would express his views and to a certain extent his emotions. He found cooking and eating relaxing, and they made him more accessible. Jasper says:

> He would never cry or say 'I love you,' but he comes closest to expressing emotion in this context [around the table]. It is there, but he can't express it — it makes it very difficult for the people around him. That's not to say he's cold — you can see when he is happy to see you, or annoyed.

In the late sixties, Terence's emotional balance was badly upset by the death of his mother. She had long suffered from arthritis, and had now developed cancer. Terence, who always found illness very difficult to bear, was devastated. His commitment to Habitat meant that he hadn't spent as much time with his mother as he felt he should have. She had been the guiding light and motivator in his life, and when she died, in October 1968, Caroline remembers Terence was profoundly shocked:

> His mother's death affected him very deeply — he was shattered. He really felt that everything he'd ever done was for her. I'm not sure he went out to seek her approval, but the way he was in her eyes was very important to him.

Unable to confide properly in others, and with no religious beliefs from which to draw comfort, Terence had to find his own method of handling the pain. His ability to cope made him seem strong, but those who knew him well could see the impact the death had had on him.

At work, his seeming toughness and lack of emotion were to his advantage. He was the rock of stability around which people's emotions swirled. Even long-serving employees found it very difficult to get to know Terence, but, provided they didn't assume too much familiarity, he was always loyal to them and keen to nurture their abilities. He had high expectations of himself and also of others, and he encouraged people to achieve their potential. Terence was rarely jealous and he got great satisfaction from the individual successes of his protégés.

One of his early disciples, who was becoming increasingly successful in the Conran Design Group, was Rodney Fitch, whom Terence thought was extremely good at both selling and managing design. The design group had a clear ethic and style, both of which were defined by Terence and which revolved around the need for design to be commercially accountable. All his companies had been built up on this basis, and he applied the same principles to the work he did for others. In 1964, when Conran and Company won the first Royal Society of Arts Presidential Medal for Design Management, alongside the long admired Hille, Terence said:

We're very lucky in that at the core of the whole thing there is a design group of about thirty people. Making design work all the way through a firm is very much a matter of internal conviction – people think of us as an amalgam of marketing and design from the start and this is a very big advantage.'[8]

He also had the advantage that Habitat was living proof of the effectiveness of his approach.

The first Habitat had been designed by Terence and Oliver Gregory, while Rodney worked with Terence on the second. The Tottenham Court Road store was much more modern, and Rodney thinks that it sat less comfortably with the Habitat style than Fulham Road. Rodney was also responsible for the development of Hanway Place. In 1963 the contract business had been doing well enough to expand, and Terence acquired the ground floor of the building. Rodney converted the warren of small offices into a spacious showroom with a steel-supported mezzanine with a spiral staircase. However, although internal projects were a good showcase for the design group's work, they also created tension by tending to take precedence over the work for external clients. In time this would be resolved by splitting the design group into two.

8. Dennis Cheetham, 'Design Management', in *Design*, June 1965.

Most of the high-profile work the design group was doing at the time was three-dimensional: exhibition stands and shops. Rodney remembers that one of the most outstanding designs from the period was an exhibition stand in Moscow showing the best of British industrial design. Exhibition work for Wates & Co. and the Atomic Energy Authority followed. Two retail projects, which showed the clear influence of Habitat, were a shop for the women's wear company Peter Robinson and an extension to the Cambridge department store Joshua Taylor. Peter Robinson had a wooden-slatted ceiling with spotlights, white walls and a sense of space – not entirely divorced from a later Conran project, Next. For Joshua Taylor, Rodney converted a garage next door to the main shop into an interiors department. Several of the old elements of the garage were retained – the car turntable, the ceiling joists and a spiral staircase – but were offset by a clean modern feel created by painting ceilings and walls white and laying the floor with brown quarry tiles. In both cases the design was a backdrop to the merchandise, and there was a lightness derived from the use of white paint and light woods.

Rodney's ability to interpret the Conran style earned him the role of creative director and a seat on the board of the design group in 1965. Although Terence had some personal projects that he was involved with, he didn't have enough time to devote to the design group and he needed people like Rodney, Oliver Gregory and also John Stephenson to carry on the Conran ethos. Rodney says:

> Terence's creative direction was unnecessary, because the Conran design ethic ran through the firm very, very strongly. We had our gods. We would never use anything other than pine or beech. We would never dream of using mahogany. We all bought into a collective aesthetic.

The collective aesthetic was vitally important when it came to major projects, and in the late sixties the Conran Design Group was involved with the largest job it had yet undertaken, the interior design of Terminal One at Heathrow Airport. The architects for the project were Frederick Gibberd & Partners. As well as designing the structure they had put forward proposals for the interior, but the design coordinator, Philip Gordon-Marshall, hadn't liked them. Gordon-Marshall had seen Habitat and the excitement it generated, so he called Terence and asked if the Conran Design Group would like to put forward proposals. One of the designers, David Wrenn, developed some ideas which were accepted. The airport design was very unlike the retail interiors that the design group had been doing, but there was a coherence to the work, from the telephone booths to the terminal seating to the graphics and signs. The design was functional, long-lasting and well received by the public and the press, and Terence was very proud of it.

The Conran Design Group seemed to be at the forefront of changing the face of three-dimensional design in Britain. There were other strong design groups around – such as DRU, Wolff Olins, Fletcher, Forbes, Gill and AID – but their focus was on graphics and the emergent discipline of corporate identity. In environments, and especially in retail design, Conran was pre-eminent. Apart from Conran, before 1968 shop refits were carried out either by shopfitters – who provided very little design input and tended to work from a kit of parts – or by architects, such as Yorke, Rosenberg & Mardall. Uniquely, Terence offered his clients individual and consumer-oriented design that helped to create a clear identity for the retailer. As well as producing distinctive forms, he also had the advantage of an in-depth understanding of function and the detail of retailing gained from Habitat. Until the American Raymond Loewy won the contract to redesign John Lewis, there was no serious competition. The overriding problem was retailers' lack of design awareness – for the most part they didn't recognize the value of design. Terence's irritation with them was forcibly expressed at a 1966 international design congress:

Sack all the retailers . . . It is no good a manufacturer collaborating with a designer and producing a magnificent article if it cannot be sold properly. Retailing in this country, and throughout the world, is at an appallingly low level.

Terence would obviously not have included Habitat in his condemnation, and indeed the success of the Tottenham Court Road store led him into ideas of further expansion. He acquired two new sites, which opened in 1967.

The first was in Manchester. Although the opening of a northern shop would stretch the company logistically, Terence was keen to see how well Habitat would work outside London. Although London was *the* swinging city, celebrated in such films as *Darling* (1965) and *Blow Up* (1966), the sixties style was not confined to the capital. In Manchester it might already have been possible to buy brown earthenware cooking pots – a Habitat staple – on ordinary market stalls, but there was a strong interest in style and good design amongst the young, and the Manchester store, with its typical Habitat interior and a standard product range, was as immediate a success as its predecessors. The BBC's report about the opening said more about the London orientation of the BBC than about that of Habitat – the presenter opened with:

> Take a city like Manchester: the public surroundings are certainly grim enough. It doesn't look like a place where fashion could take hold. Mancunians are still close to the traditions of Victorian England: the muck, the commercialism, the money-counting.

The second new store, which opened in November 1967, only two months after Manchester, was at Kingston upon Thames, in Surrey. Situated in a shopping precinct, with 13,000 square feet, the store was even larger than the one in Manchester. It had a narrow frontage, but the design created a series of focal points within the store. There was nothing radically different about the look, but the range was supplemented by a do-it-yourself section. Terence had seen the growth of DIY, alongside the increase in home ownership, and he thought there was an opportunity to sell hand tools in Habitat. However, the DIY range did not sit comfortably with the other products and the experiment was never extended.

The addition of the two new shops added substantially to Habitat's turnover, and by March 1968 sales for the preceding nine months (the company was changing to a different year end) was up to £512,057 – effectively ten times what it had been at the end of the first year.

Habitat had by this time become the focus of the group's activity. It was the driving force, and the other parts of the company fed off it. But growth also required adequate business systems. These had never been Terence's strong point, but he was astute enough to recognize the need and brought in people to provide the necessary discipline. The first of these was Michael Tyson, who had joined in 1965 to run production at Thetford. The furniture division, having grown up as a workshop-based enterprise, was ill-equipped to make the transfer to a factory, but Michael reworked the production systems and also acquired a new building at Thetford to help sustain its growth. On the buying side, Terence had brought in David Phillips, whose role was 'chief truffle-hound', searching out new ideas and putting them before the selection committee, which was chaired by Terence, who in spite of all his commitments remained the guiding light in product choice. David says, 'I think a successful shop has to have a house style – otherwise you dilute the offer. Habitat said to people, "This is a way you could live." For the first ten years the Habitat image was very clear.'

Even if the image was clear, there were other problems. Habitat remained short of cash, which soured relationships with suppliers, who were rarely paid as quickly as they would have liked. Similarly, Terence's expansion programme was constrained by the lack of funds. He added a new shop in Bromley, and there were some successes overseas with a contract from Macy's in New York, a franchise in Toronto, and furniture design for Prisunic in France, but for Terence the pace of change was too slow. He needed a partner. When he received an approach from the paper group Reed International, it looked as if the opportunity had arrived.

Reed proposed a merger subject to a review of the business to be undertaken by David Abbott (now of Abbott Mead Vickers) at its advertising agency, Doyle Dane Bernbach. Terence and Abbott presented the results of the review to the Reed board of directors and came away feeling very optimistic. 'We got terribly excited,' Terence says. 'Suddenly, from being a tiny business, we could see a future that was absolutely thrilling. We wanted to get on and do things.'

Reed took some time to reply, but when it did it was to tell Terence that it had acquired the magazine publisher IPC and would be concentrating its efforts in that direction rather than Habitat. However, an alternative partner soon appeared in the shape of the stationery retailer Ryman.

Ryman was a long-established stationery chain, dating back to 1893. The company was still family-run in the sixties – by two third-generation brothers, Desmond and Nicholas Ryman, who had expanded the business by acquiring some smaller retail chains and incorporating them into the Ryman group. Stationery retailing was something of an old-fashioned business; most retailers sold stationery loose, and there was no self-service – nothing much had changed since Victorian days. In relative terms the Ryman brothers were trail-blazers: they packaged their products, introduced self-service, and employed the services of the designer Jock Kinneir to develop a house style. In 1960 they also started selling a high-quality office-furniture range called Formation, designed by the architect Brian Henderson and made by Bath Cabinet Makers. Henderson's wife, Elizabeth, was then employed as a consultant to Ryman's to design a contract-furniture showroom in Dover Street and to choose the product range. Most of the product she selected was from Europe, but Terence had long made furniture for the office market, and Elizabeth included several of his designs. By the mid-sixties Ryman was one of Conran Furniture's biggest customers, accounting for some 15 per cent of its output.

Terence had met Desmond Ryman at a party the Hendersons gave at their home, and they found they admired each other's attempts to change the businesses they were operating in. In the wake of the Reed failure a merger with Ryman became a possibility. Morgan Grenfell, who had lent Terence £150,000 to expand the business after the success of the first Habitat, were also bankers to the publicly quoted Ryman. In the terminology of the time, there seemed to be 'industrial logic' in putting the two companies together, and Morgan Grenfell brokered the deal. There were areas of joint interest on the contract side, and Terence's companies could also provide Ryman with expertise in manufacturing. Desmond Ryman says the attraction for Ryman was that 'It was the future. We thought it would be marvellous to get design into our world.' For his part, Terence thought the Rymans were great enthusiasts and got the impression that Desmond Ryman was very keen to have him lead the business.

Terence's motivation in merging was to develop Habitat. Although he was always happiest when involved with small projects and companies where he could get intimately involved with determining the design and selecting product, he had an inner restlessness to undertake new projects and build a big business. Partly this was connected with his long-held desire to provide more people with the opportunity to buy a better way of life and partly it was to do with his own personality. Excitement for Terence was in risk-taking rather than in managing a business. He needed to prove to himself that he could take an idea and make it work – especially if either research or other people were telling him it wouldn't. There was an added *frisson* if he could prove people wrong. His view was that you needed imagination to see what was possible, and that the people who pooh-poohed his ideas simply saw what existed and failed to see what could be. That his judgement was so often proved right was because of his intuitive ability to draw on a variety of sources for his ideas and then combine them in a unique way that appealed both to him and to his customers. This was as true of his designs as of his business ventures.

In December 1968, Ryman Conran was formed with fifty-six retail outlets and combined profits of £600,000. Given that Ryman's was a public company negotiations had been conducted discreetly. However, several people were put out by the deal, and the new set-up was tarnished by ill-feeling rather than being launched on a wave of enthusiasm. Rodney Fitch remembers:

I came into Hanway Place early one morning and the place reeked of cigar smoke, which meant Terence was there. He told me that he was announcing on the Stock Exchange that day that the whole Conran business had been sold to Ryman. I was furious. It wasn't that I denied him the opportunity to sell the business, but no one had spoken to me about it. From that moment onwards my relationship with Terence would never be the same.

John Beevor left as there was no room for him on the joint Ryman Conran board, and John Mawer quit because he felt the merger wasn't going to work. David Phillips stayed with the company, but says of the initial honeymoon period that 'Hands were shaken and backs were slapped, but the period of bonhomie lasted about six weeks. There was a very quick falling out between Terence and Desmond.'

Several problems seemed to exist which, in the haste of the merger, simply hadn't been thought about. The Ryman brothers were the dominant partners in the relationship by virtue of their owning more shares. Terence was no longer the clear leader: he and Desmond shared the chairmanship, and Terence found it difficult to operate alongside someone else. Rodney Fitch remembers that what Desmond did one month Terence would undo the next. Another issue was the shortage of funds. Terence had envisaged that the merger would accelerate the growth of Habitat; instead, the available monies were fought over, as Desmond wanted money to fund the development of Ryman. However, the most significant problem was the difference in the company's cultures. Ryman was businesslike, well established and paternalistic. The Conran companies were entrepreneurial, aggressive and impassioned; they reflected Terence's personality and the values he held. Whereas in the pre-merger days everyone focused on the similarities of the two companies, afterwards everyone focused on the differences. This was epitomized by the style of the two sides. Desmond Ryman remembers:

Terence used to come to work in a sports shirt, and he'd wear a roll-neck sweater and cord trousers to the factory. And we [Nick and Desmond Ryman] used to be dressed in white collars and striped shirts and dark suits.

We were looked upon as a couple of real old squares and they were the
swingers. When we used to go into the Conran Design Group I just knew
what they thought.

However, the Ryman Conran marriage was positive in some
respects. It did, for example, see the launch of a proper catalogue for
the first time. Terence had of course produced catalogues of his
furniture ever since 1953, and in the early sixties the Summa
catalogue had been put together with a certain amount of style. The
first Habitat catalogue in 1965 was simpler and comprised a series of
loose sheets, featuring line drawings by David Wrenn, bound at the
corner. Terence's idea was to produce a full-colour sixty-four-page
catalogue (eventually it became eighty-eight pages) which he would
supervise with the help of designer Guy Fortescue and photo-
graphers Roger Gain and Dennis Hooker. Later Terence would
write:

There is an apocryphal story within the Conran Advertising catalogue studio
that I designed, photographed and wrote the copy for the first edition in
1969, entirely on my own. Guy Fortescue who, I have to admit, was in charge
of the studio then, is sensible enough to allow me my small fantasies.[9]

Guy Fortescue had been working at the London design studio of
the furniture designers and manufacturers Lupton Morton. Tom
Lupton and John Morton had built their business on producing
modern domestic and contract furniture at their factory in
Wallingford, Berkshire. Desmond Ryman remembers that people
would drive from all over Britain to buy LM furniture. The
other asset of Lupton Morton was a mail-order business. Not
only did it have a good list of customer addresses, it also had
experience in producing catalogues. However in spite of the
popularity of its furniture, LM was in some financial trouble.
Terence and Desmond saw an opportunity and in June 1969
decided to make an offer for the company. The acquisition was the

9. Terence Conran, 'Dreams that Money can buy', in *Creative Review*, Winter 1980.

catalyst for Terence and Guy Fortescue to create the Habitat Creative Living catalogue, which was launched in October 1969. This featured a combination of LM's Campus range, which had been sold through Ryman, and Habitat merchandise. Much of the furniture on offer was self-assembly, to ease transportation. The initial print run of 300,000 was sent to both LM and Habitat customers. It was hoped that the catalogue would bring in an additional £1.5 million turnover.

Although the demand from the catalogue was good, in the first few years the systems were never quite sufficiently well developed to cope with it. Nevertheless, Terence was very proud of this and subsequent catalogues: it gave him the opportunity to reach a much broader audience than he could hope to do with just the shops, and by featuring well art-directed room-set photography the catalogue was an effective way of conveying the Habitat ideal. However, no one was ever quite sure how successful it was. The catalogue was designed to bring customers into the store as well as to generate mail-order business. The latter could be measured, but additional store business was difficult to gauge. Jeremy Smith, who ran the fabrics side of the business says:

> The catalogue was a means of extending the product range to a wider audience. Because of the publicity Habitat generated, there were customers who knew about the products but couldn't necessarily get to one of our six shops. As soon as Habitat started to cover the country, it was questioned as to what the catalogue was achieving, but it did seem to be a valuable guide to personal shoppers.

In spite of Terence's enthusiasm for the catalogue, the relationship with Ryman had all but broken down by the end of 1969. Terence had gone into the merger with high hopes, and felt disappointed that the progress of Habitat actually seemed to have slowed down. In the first year of the merger, only one new store opened. While Terence was pushing for Habitat, the Ryman brothers were pushing for the development of the office side of Ryman. The merger seemed to be in name only, and neither side was willing to take a dispassionate view of the overall business. Things came to a head in a board meeting at Hanway Place. Terence lost his temper and walked out, and everyone heard his Porsche screech out of the car park. Desmond's only comment was 'Abuse of company property'.

Terence retired to his country house in Norfolk while he considered his next move. He was deeply disappointed by the failure of the merger, but he was determined to have Habitat back. He knew that Desmond didn't really understand what he called 'the little boutique business' or see its potential – he had written Terence a letter offering to sell him the business, which concluded with, 'You may be a wonderful designer, but you'll never make a retailer.' Terence started talking to the merchant bank Samuel Montagu about generating the money to reacquire Habitat. Its venture capital arm, Midland Montagu Industrial Finance Corporation (where, coincidentally, John Beevor was later to become managing director), was willing to provide the necessary funds. Habitat had been underperforming since the Ryman merger. Turnover was up because the full impact of new shops was coming through, but in the 1969/70 financial year there was a trading loss of £67,526. Also, morale among the staff was low: they had always been motivated by Terence's vision and energy, but after the merger a Ryman manager was put in charge of Habitat who 'knew nothing of the Habitat philosophy'. David Phillips remembers, 'We had a very tough time. Peter Hope, myself and Maurice were still there. There was an enormous sense of relief when Terence bought the company back.'

On 21 June 1970 Terence reacquired Habitat for the net asset value of the company, £753,384. Of the total sum, £640,000 was due to be paid by the end of 1971, while the remaining balance was deferred for an indefinite period. It seemed Terence had got a bargain. He owned Habitat, had kept the warehouse at Wallingford, and he still retained a 17 per cent shareholding in Ryman Conran. But he had left behind Conran Contracts, Conran Fabrics, Conran Design Group and the furniture-making factory at Thetford, which had a combined turnover in excess of £2 million. Desmond Ryman felt that Ryman had kept the bits of the group that best fitted his organization. Terence was disappointed to be losing businesses that he had been building since the mid-1950s, but he was now clearly focused on what was closest to his heart – Habitat.

In any case there were no restrictive covenants on what he could do, so Terence immediately set about creating a new design group, called Conran Associates, which he located in new offices in Neal Street, Covent Garden. He approached Rodney Fitch and asked him to join the new venture. Rodney says:

> Terence asked me whether I would like to go with him and set up again. He offered me 5 per cent of the equity of Conran Associates if I left Conran Design Group and brought the six key people with me. So I talked to them and thought about the offer, and Terence assumed it was going to happen. One morning I went along to see him and said I didn't want to go. He was furious. Terence doesn't like losing.

In the end Rodney bought the Conran Design Group out and created Fitch & Co., which would be one of Conran Associates' biggest competitors during the seventies and eighties. In Rodney's place, Oliver Gregory took over the running of Terence's design group, supported by Guy Fortescue, Stafford Cliff and a young designer called Keith Hobbs.

With the re-acquisition of Habitat, Terence set about creating what he called 'the Sainsbury of the furniture trade' – good quality, low prices and aimed at a wide target audience. Typically, he wanted to create his 'Sainsbury' with some speed. The management consultants and accountants Arthur Andersen were brought in to sort out the company's finances, a new financial director, Ian Peacock, was appointed, and Michael Tyson, who had left at the time of the Ryman merger, rejoined the company as managing director. Terence had long admired Sainsbury's style, and he was equally impressed with the systems of a fellow retailer, Mothercare. Terence believed that if Habitat was to grow it needed to be better disciplined and as efficient as Mothercare. Michael Tyson, who was very much the systems man, was charged with making sure the rate of expansion could be sustained.

What the shops were selling had also evolved. The late sixties had seen a movement towards a more informal approach to furnishing the home – especially among the young. Rather than traditional seating such as chairs and sofas, ideas such as beanbags and large cushions made their appearance. Habitat also stocked inflatable chairs and furniture, which for a short period were a popular and flexible means of using and creating space in the home. But the core of the Habitat range had changed very little – the links between the styles of merchandise in 1964 and 1970 were very evident. Terence continued to sell what he personally liked. He was interested in the more avant-garde furniture that Italian designers such as Ettore Sottsass and Jo Colombo were making at the end of the sixties, but only from a design perspective. His taste remained focused on the pure and the simple.

CHAPTER EIGHT
INTERNATIONAL MOVES

After the frustrations of the Ryman merger, the seventies brought Terence a sense of new beginning. Ever the optimist, once he had regained his independence he set about building up Habitat, both in the UK and overseas, with a sense of urgency. This time he wasn't constrained, personally or corporately, by the problem of finance: not only did he have the backing of Midland Montagu, but shortly after his departure from Ryman the brothers decided to sell the company to the clothing retailer Burton for some £8 million, making Terence, with his 17 per cent share, a millionaire. As well as developing Habitat, the money helped Terence establish a new design group and open a new restaurant – the first since The Orrery in 1954. With his love of food and cooking and his previous experience as a restaurateur, it seems surprising that it took him so long to open a restaurant, but throughout the late fifties and sixties he was preoccupied with designing and retailing. He says, 'We'd been designing restaurants for other people, and it was always my dream to open a restaurant the way I wanted to do it. I just didn't have the time or the money before.'

The new venture came about through a chance meeting. Although Terence and Philip Pollock's joint ownership of Habitat had been shortlived, they remained friends and were still involved in furniture-making. Philip's Aerofoam company was making the Chesterfield sofa for Habitat, as well as a number of other pieces. They also used to meet socially, and it was at a dinner party at Philip's house in Primrose Hill in north London that Terence met the art dealer John Kasmin. It was a memorable evening in that Kasmin knocked a glass of brandy over Terence. Kasmin remembers, 'Frightfully embarrassed and apologetic, I started wiping it off with lavatory paper and ended up covering him with it. He found it so engagingly unlikely he rang me up the next day and invited me for dinner.'

Although they liked each other immediately – 'Terence wasn't the bullying tycoon then: he was a *bon viveur* who exuded charm' – Kasmin thinks they also saw a point in knowing each other. He saw Terence as a potential client and believes that Terence saw him as a useful contact. Since 1963, with the backing of Lord Dufferin, Kasmin had been running 'the paradigm of contemporary galleries' dealing in modern abstract art. Although his name is now always linked with David Hockney, in a sense Hockney was an aberration: Kasmin's real interest was in American abstract artists such as Frank Stella, Helen Frankenthaler, Morris Louis and Ken Noland. Terence was not particularly interested in art, but he did enjoy Noland's and Hockney's work and he was a very keen collector of Richard Smith, who was another of Kasmin's artists and was married to one of Terence's former girlfriends, Betsy Scherman. Dick Smith's work appealed to Terence because his paintings worked within a context. Terence says, 'Aesthetically my ideas and Dick's matched. He seemed to understand the way paintings work in interiors. You could put one of his pictures in a room and it would complete the environment.'

Kasmin and Terence didn't see eye to eye about painting. For Kasmin art was very important, whereas Terence tended to look at it in a decorative sense; Kasmin liked the élitism of the art world, whereas Terence hated it. Kasmin says, 'When we talk about art we usually argue like crazy. He's much more interested in Mr Everyman having a treat. I can't stand it – I'm an élitist.'

Where Terence and Kasmin did agree was in their love of food and of France. The two combined in a holiday, when Kasmin invited Terence, Caroline and the children to stay with him in a French château he had rented. Terence and Kasmin spent their time cooking together in the vast kitchen and discussing the joys of owning a restaurant. Kasmin recalls, 'I think everybody who likes food is interested in having a restaurant. It's all part of proselytizing – of wanting people to like what you like. So we said, "Let's have a crack at it."' Having made the decision, Terence and Kasmin went off every day to a café in the hills and, while drinking cold Alsace wine, made lists of the sort of menus they liked. As with The Soup Kitchen and The Orrery, an idea was converted into reality with frightening rapidity. The location for the restaurant was to be in Neal Street, Covent Garden, underneath Terence's new offices, which were housed in a converted banana warehouse. This was more of a risk than it would now appear: Covent Garden then was still a working fruit and vegetable market – rough at the edges, not trendy. Neal Street, to the north of the market, was beginning to be transformed by Christina Smith, who had sited her wholesale firm Goods and Chattels there a decade earlier, but when Terence moved his offices there it was still largely neglected eighteenth-century shops and Victorian warehouses. The Neal Street Restaurant, as it would be called, was both a catalyst and symbol of the future regeneration of Covent Garden.

In later years Terence would have a direct involvement in the renewal of the area. When the fruit market closed and moved to Vauxhall, the Covent Garden Authority, led by Lord Samuel, was formed to advise on the redevelopment. Although the mainly Georgian architecture of the fruit market was impressive, the Authority was planning new office buildings. Together with the financier Charles Gordon, whom Terence had known since the early days of Habitat, a company called The Dedicated Market Limited was formed to fight the Authority and put forward an alternative plan. Rather than knocking down Covent Garden, their proposal was to renovate the site. Terence lobbied the Greater London Council (GLC) planners and persuaded them of the benefits of The Dedicated Market's approach. As Charles Gordon says, 'the Covent Garden Authority died a well-deserved death. Today the market is virtually the same as Terence and I originally planned.'

As well as Kasmin, Terence decided to invite Oliver Gregory to join the partnership. Oliver had some restaurant experience, having taken a sabbatical from the Conran Design Group in 1968 to open with his wife, Pagan, an award-winning restaurant in Dunmow, Essex. Terence, Oliver and Keith Hobbs worked on producing a

The Neal Street Restaurant, Covent Garden, 1971

distinctive interior. The walls and ceiling were all white, with bright recessed lighting, and there were quarry tiles on the floor. 'The Neal Street Restaurant' was set in lower-case lettering. The whiteness of the environment was offset by the powerful forms and colours of paintings from Kasmin's gallery stock. The menu card was designed by David Hockney. The restaurant is sometimes referred to as being archetypal seventies in style, but the design is classic rather than ephemeral, and Terence says, 'It's one of the designs I'm most proud of.' The restaurant, which is now owned by Terence's sister and her husband, Antonio Carluccio, has remained essentially unchanged and looks as relevantly modern today as it did in 1971.

The restaurant opened to much fanfare and some very positive reviews. At first the food was patchy, but it settled down under Santiago Gonzales, who had previously been the chef at the Clermont Club and produced consistently high-quality French cuisine. Although the menu had a set core of dishes, the idea was that as Kasmin and Terence were often travelling they would bring back interesting ingredients that would form the basis of special meals.

The restaurant was patronized by the art world, who used it because of Kasmin's connections, and by Conran Associates who entertained clients there. However, Terence remembers that its success was variable: 'One evening we would be absolutely packed and the next we only had three or four covers. Usually it was quite good at lunchtime. . . . But it wasn't that well managed – we bumped along making small profits and small losses.'

In the early days, the partners derived a lot of pleasure both from eating there and from the positive response of most of their customers. Nevertheless, there was an air of danger because the manager used to get 'appallingly drunk' and was quite likely to greet customers with a grand air but with his trousers round his ankles. It made for an atmosphere that some enjoyed, but which frightened others off. Kasmin remembers that the pleasure of the restaurant wore thin after a time. The idea had been to create their ideal restaurant, but in his view it was slackly managed, the service was erratic, and it became too expensive. Inevitably there were arguments and quarrels. Kasmin thought Terence bullied the staff and was annoyed by his – Kasmin's – lack of commitment. He recalls:

I would arrive at the restaurant at nine in the morning and say, 'It looks nice in here,' and Terence would say, 'Yes, Oliver and I were here at six cleaning the floor.' I used to think, Why does he have to tell me that? It's an implied criticism of one's way of life. He's a mad workaholic who thinks of me as a gifted person who doesn't use his talents.

Terence was more closely involved with the restaurant than Kasmin partly because the Conran offices were above it and partly because he owned 80 per cent of the shares. Once the restaurant was established, Terence then had the idea of developing something else in Covent Garden. He loved the excitement of taking on new projects, but this time it was a short-lived and fairly unsuccessful adventure. In spite of their differing views about the art world, he and Kasmin decided to open a gallery. Kasmin had given up his own gallery, leaving something of a void in the London art market for showing avant-garde work by young artists. When a space came up – an unconverted garage in Earlham Street, owned by Christina Smith – Terence and Kasmin agreed to open a new gallery, to be called, perhaps unsurprisingly, Garage. The idea was to involve a number of artists in the gallery, and everyone would then determine what was to be shown. The original directors were the sculptor Anthony Caro, David Hockney, Richard Smith, Martin Attwood (a friend of Kasmin's), Kasmin himself and Terence. Howard Hodgkin was also invited, but declined because he felt it would conflict with his being a trustee of the Tate. The gallery, which opened in September 1973, was designed and financed by Terence and fitted out by Oliver Gregory.

From the outset the gallery was beset by problems. Some of the directors took more of an interest than others, but the fundamental problem was that they all had different tastes and tried to pull the gallery in opposite ways. Kasmin remembers that at the beginning there was much discussion just to agree the name, and there continued to be an enormous number of meetings, which tended to decide very little. Terence, who was never very tolerant of meetings – especially ones that decided nothing – found it all intensely frustrating. The only amusement he found was in some of Hockney's quips. Although Hockney had been living in California since the early sixties, he still retained his Bradford accent and Yorkshire wit. Terence can recall a particularly lengthy meeting at which the relative merits of various avant-garde artists were discussed. Hockney, growing tired of the debate, said, 'What I think we ought to have is a nice exhibition of Michelangelo's drawings.' Nevertheless, in its short life the gallery did have one or two exhibitions of interest. Dick Smith had a show of his work, and David Hockney exhibited a collection of large drawings on paper, one or two of which were for sale. However, within a year everyone was disenchanted with Garage, and Christina Smith agreed to take the space back. Terence lost money on the venture, but he was given a sculpture by Anthony Caro as a thank you. Kasmin says, 'Most of the shows were of art I didn't like or understand. I just wanted to show good work, but I found it difficult to influence the managers we had. It was a frustrating and annoying affair for Terence. He got frightfully cross with Garage. He couldn't stand it.'

Apart from having too many strong-willed people involved, the enterprise – unusually for Terence – lacked any real commercial orientation. It was also a world with which he had little empathy and for which he lacked the intuition which stood him in such good stead with his restaurants and shops. In fact Garage and to a certain extent The Neal Street Restaurant were sideshows: the real business was Habitat.

With the demerger from Ryman Conran, Terence lost his manufacturing base. Although he would later go back to making furniture on a small scale, he never again owned a large-scale factory; from now on furniture, like everything else, would be bought in from suppliers. In spite of the change, however, there was no loss of control in the look and the function of products. Over 80 per cent of the Habitat range was exclusive, and, although Terence would talk about being the Sainsbury's of home furnishing, in this respect he was already ahead of them.

The ranges tended to be developed in one of two ways: the Habitat buyers would either develop product ideas with manufacturers or they would involve the Conran designers in creating products that could be produced externally. One of the best examples of collaboration was Airfix Plastics. David Phillips, who was still working on the non-furniture side, remembers introducing the managing director of Airfix, David Sinigaglia, to the design group, which then designed a range of twenty-one multicoloured plastic products. Initially the range – called Crayonne – could be purchased only at Habitat, but later, when it was carried by competitors, Habitat still sold large quantities. Such was the success of Crayonne in helping to change people's attitudes towards plastic products that the range was selected for display by the Museum of Modern Art in New York.

The value of this close cooperation between retailer and manufacturer was that Habitat could tailor what it sold exactly to its needs in terms of price and quality and it remained the brand, rather than being a retailer of other people's brands. Although Habitat's product range was still modern, it had become more eclectic. Partly this was a result of range expansion, but it was also a sign of the times. Following the stylistic demise of pop, there was an interest in reviving the styles of previous periods, and art deco, Victorian and Georgian styles – or rather pastiches of them – became popular. On the back of this, the seventies represented the flowering of Laura Ashley and her traditional and quintessentially English style.

People lost their faith in progress and sought reassurance in images of a romanticized past. Nostalgia as an industry was born in the late Pop years.[1]

1. Nigel Whiteley, *Pop Design: Modernism to Mod* (The Design Council, 1987), p. 216.

In Habitat there were still a lot of vibrant colours, but there was also the introduction of more browns and natural colours. Alongside modern crockery, there was now a larger range of traditional ware. But in furniture there was more use of plastics. As Habitat grew, the core of its market changed from the tightly defined Fulham Road shoppers to a broader middle-class base. This was partly a reflection of the success of Terence's crusade: he had changed attitudes towards the home and how it should be furnished among a growing segment of the population. More people now wanted the Habitat style – or at least elements of it. The Sunday supplements in the late sixties and early seventies often featured Habitat furniture – in 1971, for example, the *Observer* colour magazine ran an eight-page feature on four Wates homes all furnished by Habitat.

Habitat was still a niche business, but Terence was trying to make it a bigger niche. From a product point of view this required some compromises, which reduced the clarity of the package. Terence's view is:

> If you're reaching a mass market you have to compromise. In merchandise meetings products used to be presented and I'd say I didn't like them. But if the buyer believed they would sell they would sometimes be accepted. But if I hated anything it wouldn't go into the shops.

What surprised Terence and his team was that, until IKEA entered the UK in the mid eighties, no one followed Habitat into the market gap they had created with any conviction. In fact it might have been beneficial to Habitat to have had some good competitors to help expand the market, but the worry in the early years was that a major competitor would come in and snatch Habitat's position. To avoid this, Terence was keen to develop the chain as quickly as possible. As well as averting an external threat, new stores increased the volume of products sold, improved margins, and enabled the company to produce more exclusive products to Habitat's own designs. Expansion was a signal to everyone that Habitat was moving in the right direction after the Ryman Conran hiatus. In September 1971 Habitat opened in Bristol, and in 1972, guided by the geographic profile of shoppers garnered from the mail-order catalogue, in Cheltenham, Guildford, Birmingham, Nottingham, Watford and Croydon.

To help ensure the infrastructure was in place to sustain the expansion, Terence began the development of the Wallingford site where the warehouse was situated, asking the architectural practice, Ahrends, Burton and Koralek (ABK) to develop a new complex which would centralize store administration and ware-housing and provide a retail showroom. It was Habitat's first experiment with out-of-town retailing. The building that ABK produced was functional and, within the context of a large warehouse space, interesting. Terence was excited by it, and the architectural press enthused over its design: 'The new building is designed as a day out for the family and as such is fresh, welcoming and works extremely well.' The spatial relationship between the buildings – the 'jolly green giant' warehouse and the white showroom – was described as 'superb'. There were also a restaurant, an outdoor terrace and some play sculpture that Terence had had designed by Eduardo Paolozzi. The warehouse won three architectural honours: the *Financial Times* award, the Structural Steel Design Award and the Architectural Heritage Year Award.

The next year, 1973, saw the opening of a further five shops, including one in the King's Road which was massive by comparison with previous outlets. Most of the Habitat shops had been in the range of 12,000 to 15,000 square feet; the Kings Road shop – on the site of an old Odeon cinema – was 34,000 square feet. The space was large enough to display the whole Habitat range and also to provide good in-store room sets, which Maurice Libby designed. The interior was in classic Habitat style, but there was a notable addition in the form of a French-brasserie-style self-service café on the first floor.

The King's Road shop was number eighteen, and Terence was predicting another thirty shops at the rate of four to six a year. In spite of the industrial problems in Britain – 23 million working days were lost to strikes in 1972, the highest in any

ABK's shed at Wallingford

Habitat, King's Road, 1973

industrial country – Habitat had benefited from a decade-long spending boom. Between 1964 and 1973 consumer expenditure more than doubled, from £21 billion per annum to £44 billion. With more and more people buying their own homes – owner-occupiers accounted for more than 50 per cent of housing for the first time in 1971, and 62 per cent of new mortgages went to people under thirty-five – there was a boom in home furnishings. It was against this background that Terence decided on two fresh initiatives: a new shop to be located in the original Fulham Road site and a move into the French market.

The Conran Shop, as it became, was born out of the frustration at merchandise meetings of having to reject products which, although to Terence's liking, were seen to be too expensive or esoteric for Habitat. While Habitat was setting off in pursuit of the expanding middle class, The Conran Shop was almost a reversion to the principles of the very first Habitat. It enabled Terence to escape the growing bureaucracy of Habitat and to make quick decisions. Nevertheless, not all the board thought the new shop was a good idea – some saw it as a diversion from Habitat and an indulgence. However, Terence prevailed, and Maggie Heancy, who had joined Habitat in the mid-sixties to work in the Tottenham Court Road shop, was asked to be the buyer – something she was nervous about: 'It showed great perception on Terence's part that he dropped this project into my lap, as my buying experience was limited to shopping at Sainsbury's. He seemed to have great faith in my ability, so I just got on with it and had a great time putting it all together.'

Maggie spent much time researching the product range, visiting manufacturers and going to trade fairs, and the eventual selection was full of modern classics. It was very much to Terence's taste. The opening leaflet described the range:

> Furniture produced from the drawings of Mies van der Rohe, Le Corbusier, Marcel Breur. The brilliant work of Tobia Scarpa, Vico Magistretti, Jo Colombo. Ancient hand-loomed rugs from Afghanistan. The jewel-like precision of Finnish stainless steel pots by Opa Oy . . . The Conran portoflio of designs, so painstakingly collected, is spare and pure. There is no ostentation, no vulgarity. There is shape and line, texture and clear colour. Close attention to detail.

But The Conran Shop also took work from young designers and craftsmen as well as from famous designers. Without the pressure to feed the needs of a chain, it was easier to experiment with new ideas and commission small quantities. If the products worked and were not too expensive, they were then introduced into Habitat.

In spite of Terence's considerable retail experience, when the shop opened – in November 1973 – it wasn't a runaway success. This was as much bad timing as anything else. The bank rate was 13 per cent, emergency regulations caused by public-sector strikes prevented the heating of stores, and there was an IRA bombing campaign going on – Waltons Restaurant, just round the corner from the shop, was bombed. Habitat's own sales were 11 per cent below budget. The failure of The Conran Shop to perform adequately proved to some that Terence had been wrong to divert scarce resources from Habitat, but Terence, as always, persevered, and within two years the shop was a success.

Terence's move into France had in many ways been a long time coming. It also contained an element of irony: for twenty years Terence had been trying to bring French style and culture to Britain; now he was re-exporting it. 'I suppose that if there's one thing I'm proud of it's that through design and through the shops I've been able to bring something of those experiences I had in postwar France back to Britain.'[2]

Terence first sold furniture in France in 1968. He had been approached by the young buyer of the home-furnishings department of Prisunic, Francis Bruguière, to provide some designs for a furniture catalogue. Prisunic, which was owned by the Au Printemps group, had some three hundred and fifty shops throughout France, selling clothes, food, household goods, records and furniture. However, the nature of the shops – *The Times* described them as Woolworth, Marks & Spencer and British Home Stores rolled into one – didn't really allow modern furniture to be displayed properly. Francis Bruguière's solution was to produce a catalogue which could be mailed to customers. To help create some excitement, he had the idea of featuring an important designer in each catalogue. Francis says, 'At that moment I was advised by the style director, Denise Fayole, to approach Terence Conran. So I went to London, and I was extremely seduced by the products and the person.'

Although Terence created one very sixties room set in bright colours, featuring a graphic leaf design, most of the range was modern-classic designs with a predominantly light-wood feel. Francis Bruguière had the furniture produced by LaFargue, a French firm of school-furniture specialists, and the catalogue was launched just before the 1968 riots with this description of the furniture: '*Le style Conran est actuellement le plus représentatif du mobilier moderne, rationnel, séduisant, à prix modique.*'

The prices were indeed *modique* – being about 25 per cent cheaper than modern furniture in other shops – and, perhaps not surprisingly, Terence's designs sold very well.

2. Terence Conran, *Terence Conran's New House Book* (Conran Octopus, 1991).

Francis Bruguière launched subsequent catalogues featuring other designers, but he was keen to do more than just sell from a catalogue: he wanted to launch a retail chain of modern furniture stores. For this he knew he would need a large injection of funds, and he produced what he believed to be a well-argued proposal which he delivered to the directors of Au Printemps. Although there was undoubted merit in the idea, they were hesitant and deferred making a decision. Francis, however, was impatient, and worried that someone else might come into the market and seize the opportunity. He therefore wrote to Terence with the idea of setting up Habitat in France. Francis remembers:

> Terence wrote back straight away and said, 'We'll do it when the UK joins the Common Market.' I wondered whether it was a nice excuse, but as soon as it was clear that the UK would join he wrote and said, 'Are you still interested in doing something, because I have someone who is keen to work on this project and put some money in?'

That someone was Michael Likierman, who had recently met Terence. Michael Likierman had been running a family business which had been taken over by ICI. He was in his early thirties, ambitious and entrepreneurial, and he hated working at ICI. He had read in a newspaper that Habitat, which Terence was buying back from Ryman Conran at the time, was in trouble, so with typical chutzpah he called Terence and offered to save the company. Terence, who always made himself accessible to people, was taken by such audacity and invited Michael to come and talk. Terence wasn't sure what the meeting would lead to, but, when Michael told him that he had been to business school in Geneva and spoke French, he saw an opportunity to develop the expansion of Habitat into Europe. Michael recalls: 'Terence said, "Habitat isn't in trouble – it's all false propaganda – but we are interested in moving abroad. Why don't you come and join us, and we'll see if we can do it together?" Terence is a man who knows how to use other people's talents.'

Michael didn't need much persuading, and Terence was very excited by the idea of moving into Europe. Although France was high on the list of target countries, the two agreed they wouldn't prejudge the issue and that Michael would conduct a feasibility study on the project. It started with Paris. Terence drove Michael there at high speed in his Porsche to meet Francis Bruguière. Michael remembers, 'It was a great pleasure driving to Paris with him – in the early stages of any relationship Terence is extremely charming; he's very good at building up relationships. We arrived in Paris at about ten o'clock and went straight to the Café de Flore in Boulevard Saint-Germain for dinner.'

Michael spent three months touring Europe before providing the Habitat board with a report which recommended that Habitat should go ahead with its overseas expansion and that the initial target should be France – the Prisunic catalogue had shown that the Habitat style would be popular; there seemed to be a demand for good-value modern furniture in France, which was not being met; and the French market was accessible to new stores. With Terence's wholehearted support, the plan was agreed, and on 1 January 1973 – the day the UK joined the Common Market – the project got under way. Michael Likierman moved to France and was joined by Zimmie Sasson, who at the time was buying for the UK stores. Francis Bruguière arrived with his buyers, Michel Cultru and Yves Cambier, and stylist Janine Roszé. An empty flat was found in the Boulevard Saint-Germain and converted into an office. The aim was to open by September, but the sights were always set beyond just one shop: this time the plan from the outset was to create a chain, and everything was developed on this basis.

Terence felt liberated by the developments in France – it was like starting all over again, except with more money and a proven concept. In the early days he gave a lot of time to the product range and to the development of the French stores, but he had great faith in the abilities of his team in France. There was no need to create a Habitat ethos – everyone involved was already deeply committed to the ideals of the company.

Habitat was also launching into France with seemingly perfect timing, as there were many similarities between Britain in 1964 and France in 1973. Furniture retailing in France was dominated by reproduction furniture. Apart from the Prisunic catalogue, there was really no modern furniture on offer, unless you were willing to pay designer prices. In cookware there were two small shops selling white porcelain and cooking utensils. However, there was a new, questioning, young urban audience – the very people who had rebelled in 1968 – who wanted to express their distance from the cultural values of their parents, not least in the way they furnished their homes. The young were demanding a more modern society. This modernism was reflected in the government's commitment to new architecture, the apotheosis of which was Richard Rogers and Renzo Piano's winning in 1971 of the competition to build the Centre National d'Art et de Culture Georges Pompidou. Completed in 1976, the building had an inherent freedom and flexibility appropriate to the recognition of people's ever-changing needs. Similarly, whereas the older generation had tended to live in one house in one way all their lives, there was an emergent mobility and restlessness which meant young people wanted flexibility within their home and the freedom to change where they lived with increasing frequency. The furniture on offer didn't allow them to do this: it was inflexible, and too expensive to be discarded when they changed house. What Habitat offered, as it had in Britain ten years earlier, was an appropriate lifestyle.

Although Habitat was providing French cookware and Scandinavian-influenced furniture, to begin with it was seen as an English shop, and this added to its cachet and appeal. The sixties style might have long gone in London, but French ideas of trendiness at this time were still connected with England – from Mary Quant's 'mini-jupe' to the Beatles to British Leyland's Mini. Though François Truffaut was damning about the British film industry, a lot of the imagery of a happening Britain had also been sustained by films set in England, such as Nic Roeg's *Performance* and Antonioni's *Blow Up*. British retailers were doing well on the back of all this. By 1973 Burton was already the second largest menswear retailer in France, and Richard Shops was also opening in Paris, alongside Habitat. The only seeming limitation in France was the lack of media interest in the home – the national newspapers weren't interested in design, and neither was there much in the way of home-oriented magazines. However, one magazine, *Maison Marie Claire*, was concerned with the sort of products that Habitat would be selling, and later it was joined by others, such as *Maison Française* and *Elle Décoration*.

The location chosen for the first French Habitat was in the controversial Tour Montparnasse building. This was the only tower block in Paris, and architecturally it was rather uninspiring – especially compared with something like the contemporaneous Kings Road Habitat. The location was perfect, however: it was at the junction of four Métro lines and ten bus lines, and was alongside Montparnasse railway station. Some 3.5 million people lived or worked within fifteen minutes' travelling time. On the lower floors of the building was space for some eighty shops, including a 20,000-square-foot site that Habitat chose. Whereas previous Habitats had been opened on a shoestring, the fitting-out cost of Montparnasse was over £200,000. Except for some dominant yellow service piping, the interior was typical Habitat – white brick and plaster walls, slatted ceilings and brown quarry tiles. Although the majority of the product was the same as in British Habitats, some 25 per cent was new. For example, in spite of a large number of French people having second homes in the country, Habitat found there was less of a market for countrified furniture than in Britain, so Conran Associates helped develop new product ideas. Francis Bruguière recalls:

The English market was much more interested in cosy, comfortable products. The French at that time were attracted to an urban, modern style and less towards traditional country things. It was a reaction against the endless traditional furniture. Then people were also mostly living in flats and wanted smaller, less bulky furniture.

There were also some innovations from Britain. Although the idea of bringing British culinary experience to France may have seemed incongruous, such items as pie funnels were sold in the French Habitats – Yves Cambier remembers Terence drawing a

The first French Habitat, Tour Montparnasse, 1973

pie funnel on a paper napkin in a restaurant in the Boulevard Saint-Germain, to show him what it was. It had to be sold with an explanation for French customers, in much the same way as chicken bricks had to be explained in Britain. There were other points of difference. The French wanted square pillows, saucepans without lids, breakfast bowls, and individual pieces of china rather than sets. Overall the lifestyle was less formal and traditional, so, without losing the idea of what Habitat stood for, the range was adapted. However, there were also occasions when, rather than adapting to the French market, Terence pushed his team to change attitudes – it was the truism that people can't buy what they aren't offered that had encouraged Terence in the first Fulham Road store. The French had never used duvets, and Michel Cultru was deeply sceptical of the idea of introducing them. However, with Terence's encouragement, he decided to try. He remembers:

I thought duvets were so bulky and difficult to transport that we would have to make them in France. But all the French manufacturers thought we were mad. They said, 'The French like sheets and blankets. It's not a French habit to have duvets, so it won't work.' After six months we persuaded them to try.

The duvet – which was promoted on the basis of '*20 seconds pour faire un lit!*' – was a huge success and symbolic of Habitat and its liberated customers.

Terence refused to spend any money advertising the store, but the Tour Montparnasse was such a talking-point that Habitat rode on the back of its press coverage, and the moment the shop opened, in September 1973, it was packed. As with the first Fulham Road Habitat, it wasn't the uniqueness of individual products that created the attention but the combination of products and their presentation. When Terence had tried briefly to sell his products in a concession in Au Printemps it had been a total failure, because they were in an environment that was totally irrelevant. In Montparnasse the package was coherent – from the products to the store design to the displays and the labelling. Michel Cultru remembers, 'People were so amazed by what we had done. There were revolutionary things in the shop, and the layout was revolutionary. There was a big space so that people could walk around the products, and piles of merchandise that people could touch.'

Terence was delighted with his new success, but almost as soon as the store was open there were problems. In October 1973 war broke out in Sinai. Although the conflict was relatively short-lived, the war resulted in the Arab oil producers restricting oil exports. Both France and Britain were heavily dependent on Arab oil, and the reduction in supply accompanied by a rapid rise in prices that in Britain raised the oil import bill to something like four times its former level made an already tough economic problem even worse. This was further exacerbated in November, when the National Union of Mineworkers implemented a ban on overtime and weekend working, which was followed by a similar ban by the electricity power engineers and the locomotive engineers. The result was that from 1 January 1974 British business had electricity for only three days a week. Not only did this cause problems by reducing the level of custom in Habitat's shops, it also meant that Habitat couldn't get products through from its suppliers. In the short term this created problems because Habitat France, which had three shops planned for opening in 1974, was heavily dependent on UK suppliers. In the longer term the business of both countries was affected by the recession that resulted from the end of cheap energy and the consequent ills of inflation and unemployment.

To overcome shortages, the French team had to find French manufacturers who were willing to make the Habitat range in small quantities. This wasn't always easy, because, as with duvets, the manufacturers were not easily convinced that the products the buyers were trying to develop would work – for example, Michel Cultru remembers having to battle against manufacturers' scepticism to get brightly coloured sheets made. Although Terence was keen that the French product range reflect to some degree the different attitudes and buying patterns in France, the process of having to find a separate manufacturing base started a process of sending the British and French shops in radically different directions. This was evident by the time the first French catalogue came out, in 1974. Styled by Terence's sister, Priscilla, who had been living in Paris, and Zimmie Sasson, photographed by Michael Nicholson and designed by Conran Associates, the new catalogue was smaller than its British counterpart and different both in terms of style and product.

In its first year Montparnasse was budgeted to achieve sales of 8 million francs; in spite of the economic climate, sales were 12 million francs. However, the second French shop was disastrous. Terence and Michael Likierman had found a site in the Paris suburbs called Les Ulis. It was the first shopping centre in France to use a hypermarket – Carrefour – as its anchor. Terence and Michael reasoned that Carrefour would be a major draw and that a young mobile population would shop there. By siting Habitat next door, they believed they would get Carrefour's customers coming in to buy home furnishings. With the strong performance of Tour Montparnasse, the budgets for the new store were set high, but Michel Cultru says that he knew that the store wasn't going to work and he refused to order the merchandise until he was made to do so. For the opening, everyone went down to the shop to help, but the customers were so few that there was nothing to do.

Terence felt that the French team hadn't been behind the new store and said to Francis Bruguière that it wasn't working because 'You don't love this shop enough.' The reality was that Michael and Terence had misinterpreted people's shopping habits: customers came to shop for food and petrol, but they weren't in the mood for browsing round and looking at things for the home. Francis Bruguière also thinks that, although there was a strong movement towards the suburbs, the market for Habitat at that time was 'people who were trendy and snobbish' – *branché*. Shopping for furniture in the suburbs was not a good way of demonstrating trendiness. The shop was soon costing a fortune to keep open, and Habitat France was proving a drain on resources. Another shop opened in the spring at Orgeval, just west of Paris, where the company had its warehousing, but its performance too was uninspiring.

Terence was now coming under pressures from his bankers – he remembers that they told him 'You've got to stop the bleeding in France.' However, he thought they were just being short-termist and that France in time would prove to be profitable. In fact Terence had an emotional attachment to his French operation, and wasn't willing to countenance closing it down. He was also loath to get rid of Les Ulis because he had never closed a shop before, but the French team felt it was a waste of resources. In 1975 it was shut. By then Terence and Michael had found another site in Paris, near the Arc de Triomphe, and one in the South of France at Montpellier, both of which were successful, but plans for opening a shop in Lyons had to be postponed because of the crisis caused by Les Ulis. In retrospect Michel Cultru thinks, 'We were overambitious and overdimensioned – we had too many people, and the warehouse was too big. We wanted to be too big too quickly.'

The problems in France and underperformance in the UK led to internal battles. Michael Tyson, who was running the British Habitat, thought the situation could be improved if there was more consistency in product and also in the catalogues for France and the UK. This would achieve economies of scale and reduce duplication of effort. Although intuitively Terence felt it was important that the independence of the French operation should be maintained, he was open to persuasion. When it came to product, Terence possessed a clarity and confidence about what was right, but in operating a business he could be swayed by people who seemed to have intellect. Not having had an academic background or business training, he could be impressed by the rationality of people who had. Looking back, he believes a lot of his mistakes in business stemmed from 'admiring people's brains', whereas his best decisions have been made by trusting his feel for products and places. In this case Tyson, whom Terence regarded as a good businessman, converted him to the logic of more harmonization between France and the UK. Michael Likierman, who was in a weak position because of the poor performance in France, refused to cooperate and in the end resigned. He says, 'I fell out with Terence, although at the time it appeared I was falling out with Michael Tyson. There was quite a lot of emotion about it, but I think it became apparent that Tyson could run the company better without me, and Terence went along with it.'

With the departure of Michael Likierman, Tyson took over the running of the Habitat group and tried to implement his plan for integrating the product ranges by unifying the buying teams of France and the UK. He offered the job of director of buying to Francis Bruguière, but Francis turned it down, believing that it was important to retain the individuality of the two countries' operations. Tyson then offered the job to Michel Cultru, but he too was convinced that, although there should be better communication between the two operations, full integration was a bad thing. Michel recalls:

There was quite strong pressure from Terence for me to accept the job, but I said no. He said I was pigheaded. Fortunately Habitat was starting up in the US and Michael Tyson went off to run it. Terence then agreed that the two buying teams would work together, but would retain their independence.

With the growth in the number of shops in the UK and the launch in France, Terence found less and less time for home life. His fifth child, Ned, had been born in 1971 and St Andrew's Place had become too small for the family. Terence and Caroline scoured the newspapers for a country house and discovered a thirty-two-room eighteenth-century redbrick house called Barton Court near Newbury in Berkshire, just a few miles from the former Sloper family seat at West Woodhay. It had a walled garden, a stable-block and a river running through the grounds. It had been a school, but, like all Conran purchases, it was derelict and needed a large amount of time and money spent on it. Caroline was captivated by the house, and for the bargain price of £100,000 they bought it. Terence immediately set about redesigning it. He turned the house round by moving the driveway and putting the entrance to the back of the house. The

In the kitchen at Barton Court

ground-floor billiard-room was converted into a large kitchen and dining-room, and the hall was transformed into a long living-room.

The cost of making the property good and incorporating his changes to the layout was considerable, and, to Terence's horror, within sight of completion his quantity surveyors told him that there was an overspend on the work and that a further £80,000 would be required to finish it. Terence didn't have the additional funds, so a halt had to be called, and the Conrans had to move into the annexe which was called The Bell House until Terence raised the cash. Sophie remembers that her mother would organize picnics to the main part of the house. For the children it was an adventure, but for Terence it was a nightmare.

Although the house was grand, it was furnished quite simply, with a combination of antiques and simple modern furniture. Not surprisingly the dominant colour throughout was white. The

furniture designer Rodney Kinsman believes that Barton Court is a good indicator of Terence's character:

> Terence is not interested in money personally and is in fact quite frugal. His big house in the country – he treats it as if it were a small house. He and Caroline always lived very simply. It's a house that demands to be lived in on a grand scale, but he's quite happy living there unpretentiously.

As Barton Court was close to Wallingford, where Terence had his warehouses, offices and showroom, the move seemed practical. However, the reality was that Terence was now travelling a lot of the time. In the early days of Habitat France, he was spending much of his time in Paris, looking at sites for shops and helping to choose the merchandise. He was going on buying trips all over the world and also working with the design group in Neal Street. To give himself some sort of London base he had the basement in Neal Street converted into a windowless office-cum-*pied-à-terre*. Of that period, Caroline says, 'From the time we moved to Barton Court, Terence became a complete workaholic. The business had got quite big by then, which is how we managed to afford the house. He always felt that everything was on the brink of collapsing all around him, so he had to really push himself.'

Terence thrived on the excitement of all his projects, but by moving to Barton Court he was in danger of losing control. So, to ensure he knew what was going on, he started having meetings at Barton Court once a week. He liked mixing his home with his work life, and the people who worked with him enjoyed the lifestyle. Yves Cambier remembers:

> Barton Court was very lively – we spent so much time working and relaxing there. During lunchtimes Terence or Caroline would cook simple but sophisticated food. Sometimes I would stay and Terence would go and get the vegetables from the garden and cook dinner. It was a great pleasure for him, but he never stopped thinking about Habitat.

While the arrangement suited Terence, Caroline felt that the family home was being taken over by work: she would have preferred the

Terence and Caroline outside Barton Court

two to be separate. The situation was further exacerbated in 1976, when Terence started up a design studio in the stable-block. Conran Associates, which had a turnover of some three-quarters of a million pounds, more than half of which was generated out of Europe, was left in Neal Street to develop designs for Habitat shops and other clients; the new studio was set up to work on new product development. Oliver Gregory moved down to run the studio, and in the late seventies Michael Wickham was persuaded to join them to make prototypes. Michael remembers, 'Terence had some bright young men working at Barton Court, but he said, "They're all totally illiterate – they only know about cars and design." He asked me to come and educate them a bit.'

One of the things that Michael introduced to Terence and the studio was Shaker furniture – simply designed wooden chairs and boxes made in the style of the Shakers, an American religious sect founded in the late eighteenth century. Although the style has since become famous, it was unknown in Britain at the time. Terence liked it because the Shakers had not consciously designed anything – they were craftsmen who were inspired by their deeply held beliefs. It was exactly the kind of 'undesigned' design that appealed most to him.

Although having the studio at Barton Court meant that Caroline and the children saw more of Terence than before, on any deeper level he was as remote as ever. In the early days, the cycle of work had been broken by family holidays to Positano, St Tropez or to the house they owned (a conversion of a derelict café) in the small Dordogne village of Le Bastit, but as time went on Terence's appearances became more infrequent. In the summer Caroline would take off to Le Bastit for a month with the children, and Terence would come down for the odd weekend. Although most of their friends were related to Terence's work in one way or another, Caroline, because she was warm and open, often became the focus of friendship. People such as Michael and Cynthia Wickham and Kasmin regarded her with affection. The children remember one summer holiday in a château with Kasmin and a coterie of artists such as David

Hockney, who spent many hours drawing with Sophie, Dick and Betsy Smith and Howard and Julia Hodgkin. Terence, however, came only for a few days. He found family holidays too noisy. He was a very robust and energetic person, but he had problems with his back, which made him grouchy, and his working life sometimes simply got too much. To recuperate, he preferred to go off on his own. Caroline and the children had an enormous amount of freedom in their lives, but what they lacked was support from Terence.

The real interaction between Terence and Caroline was in their love of cooking. In their billiard-room kitchen they would experiment with new ideas, and Caroline would write about them. Every Christmas she would produce a cook's calendar for Habitat, and she was a regular contributor of cookery articles to the *Sunday Times* and *Nova*. Caroline had also co-written two cookery books and produced translations of classic chef's books, and in the late seventies she embarked on a translation of Michel Guérard's *Cuisine Minceur*. Terence also produced two books in the seventies. The first, *The House Book*, published in 1974 by Mitchell Beazley, grew out of the Habitat catalogue and from Terence's experience in converting houses. The book not only provided inspiration about how houses could be furnished, it also gave very practical advice about how to do things in the home. In the first two years of publication 75,000 copies were sold (total lifetime sales were over 2 million). Terence followed up *The House Book* with *The Kitchen Book* (1977), *The Bedroom and Bathroom Book* (1978) and with Caroline, *The Cook Book* (1980).

Terence tended not to interfere much with the lives of any of his children, and Caroline was the dominant influence on her three: Tom, Sophie and Ned. Sophie remembers that her father wanted her and the others to do well at school and would berate them over their reports, but her mother's influence was more constant. Caroline encouraged the children to enjoy themselves and nurtured their interests. When his eldest children, Sebastian and Jasper, reached school-leaving age, Terence started to take an interest in their possible careers – it gave him the basis for a relationship. Having previously had a remote father, however, neither of the children was willing to do what Terence wanted them to.

Terence was very keen that Jasper become a restaurateur, but Jasper's passion was clothes and he wanted to be a fashion designer. He achieved his ambition by running away. After he had finished his 'O' levels, Shirley took him to New York on a trip. Once there he decided to fulfil his long-held desire and talked himself into a place at the Parsons School of Design, refusing to return to Britain with his mother. Jasper says his father was furious: 'I presented him with a *fait accompli*. The reaction was one of cold fury because he hadn't been asked. He hadn't been asked because I was too frightened of him. He was a very powerful figure.' Terence's recollection is that part of the reason for his fury was that Jasper was only sixteen and shouldn't have been in New York by himself.

Sebastian also initially reacted against the expectations for him. The two eldest children had taken over the lease of St Andrew's Place from their father. Sebastian had become involved with punk music and managed the group The Clash, who collectively moved into the house with him. Large stereo systems, musical instruments, graffiti on the Corinthian columns and pinball machines took over, where Eames chairs and Marimekko fabrics had once reigned supreme. After this flirtation with rebellion, however, Sebastian changed tack and trained as an industrial designer. An interesting aspect of both Jasper and Sebastian's careers is that, although Terence's involvement with them as they grew up was minimal, they both came to believe in Terence's views about function and simplicity in design.

People at work could also be intimidated by Terence. He once said, 'I use my temper to stir the blood of my designers. I like the idea of people thinking I am idiosyncratic so they can gossip about me behind my back. I hate the dull pattern of sanity.' Terence never wanted to be a conformist: he always looked at the world with new eyes, and wanted to change what he saw. He also wanted the people who worked with him to see things in the same way, and he would in turn cajole them or bully them into sharing his point of view. He was very good at hiding any weakness of his own, and sometimes this would lead him beyond bullying and he would seem to take pleasure in picking on people's failings. Maurice Libby says, 'Children do that – they find your weak spot and play on it. It's to keep a hold over you; to maintain an advantage. He likes to control everything.'

At home Caroline would tend to walk away when Terence pushed her too far, and at work people would mostly do the same or buckle under. But occasionally people would stand up to him – and in some ways Terence rather liked this. The merchandise meeting, where stock was selected for Habitat, was the forum for the fiercest confrontations, especially during Michael Tyson's time. Tyson was an intelligent man who was very good at generating ideas, but he also deliberately created a regime of uncertainty – it was his way of keeping people on their toes. In contrast to Terence's vision, Tyson provided hard-nosed reality. Geoff Davy, who had graduated from store management to running Habitat's second warehouse, at Wellingborough in Northamptonshire, remembers his first merchandise meeting:

> There were a number of varied interests at the meeting. The buyers were there, who Michael saw as Terence's creatures: effete, not numerate, not businesslike – people who ranted about colour and form. To counter the buyers, Michael packed the meeting with his own people.
>
> The first product put forward was a table from a supplier who was of medium to low reliability. The idea was that the meeting would pass comment on it, but being Habitat it was never enough to say 'Yes' or 'No' – 'Yes' or 'No' had to be articulated. That's when it got violent. Michael made some derogatory comment about the table and Terence said, 'That's typical of you,' and turned to some young store manager and shouted at him, 'That'll sell, won't it?' And Michael screamed, 'No, it fucking won't!' The meeting degenerated. They would throw things around and at each other. I can remember Terence storming out of a meeting and Michael saying 'I'm glad that fat bastard's gone', at the top of his voice.
>
> It was like a soap opera, but the negative energy between the two of them appeared to work.

David Queensberry, who through his design consultancy, Queensberry Hunt, was a regular supplier of products to Habitat, recalls hearing about a merchandise meeting in Paris, where one of the Habitat buyers was going to show an Italian glass which was square-shaped. Before Terence's arrival the buyer showed the product to everyone else and they all agreed it was an interesting shape, even though they knew that Terence would hate it because he would say, 'What's wrong with a bloody cylindrical glass?' The reaction was inevitable: 'Terence arrived and he was in a foul mood and he picked up the glass and said, "Whoever selected that should be sacked." And the buyer looked round at everyone else and she suddenly realized that she didn't have any supporters.'

On another equally combative occasion, Priscilla was the recipient of one of Terence's outbursts. At the first merchandise meeting she attended, she was presenting some bathroom fittings when Terence interrupted. Priscilla recalls, 'He said, "How dare you present something that doesn't work," and he laid into me for a quarter of an hour. At first I was horrified and thought I was going to burst into tears. Then I thought, No, it's not me that's wrong – it's him.'

Terence's concern was to instil in others the same kind of fierce belief in the principles of Habitat that he held. He enjoyed a row and the rush of adrenalin. Sometimes compromises were reached; on other occasions Terence stood his ground. Whatever the outcome, he never bore grudges. If he wanted to, he could also make his points by teasing. When Priscilla was responsible for display in The Conran Shop one Christmas, she produced a table layout which was all white. Terence came and saw the display and asked the shop manager to put teddy bears at the front of it. The manager in turn asked Priscilla, who refused. When Terence next came into the shop he said, 'Where are my teddy bears?' As Priscilla was telling him that it would look ridiculous, she realized that he was mocking her – that he knew as well as she did that the teddy bears were wrong.

When it came to what he saw as unwarranted criticism from people outside the company, Terence could be quite pointed in his put-downs. After Roy Strong, the then director of the Victoria & Albert Museum, criticized the 1976 Habitat catalogue in *Design*, Terence delivered a full-blooded riposte. The cover was indeed very un-Habitat-like, showing a girl in a Liberty dress – Strong said she looked like a 'forties tart' – photographed in soft focus in a sitting-room, but Terence wrote:

> While I am deeply flattered that *Design* should have consulted such an eminent authority to analyse the sociological content of our products, perhaps we should add that while not wishing to detract from the glamour of this learned dissertation, we are simply trying to fulfil the desire of many of our customers for comfortable furniture which supports their tired old heads and shoulders – you may not like the appearance but undoubtedly this furniture fulfils the function. You comment that it seems only suitable for a 'Hendon semi'; so it might be, but it is also suitable, as I have seen, for a modern flat, a converted Victorian town house, or for the Georgian country house where I live – comfortably![3]

When Terence later became a trustee of the V & A, he memorably suggested that Roy Strong be stuffed and placed with the other exhibits in the museum.

By the mid-seventies the company was growing rapidly, but Terence remained intimately involved with the detail of product and with the catalogue – seeing every layout and photograph and insisting that those that he felt were wrong would have to be reshot. Stafford Cliff, who had taken over the design of the catalogue, remembers that he had a chopping-board photographed with some sliced mushrooms. Terence looked at the transparency with his eyeglass and said, 'We can't have that – the mushrooms are all wrinkly at the edges. You have to put lemon juice on the mushrooms after you've cut them.'

As the years went by the catalogue became more sophisticated. Rather than using studios for room sets, Terence and Stafford decided to use houses. This had already been done occasionally by

---

3. Terence Conran, 'Whither Habitat', in *Design*, March 1976, p. 61.

shooting in Terence's homes, but by using different houses –
mostly in France – a higher degree of reality was obtained.
Although the catalogue was very dense, to communicate the
idea of Habitat, Stafford also included old things among the
new. The idea was to put across a look and to indicate how
an effect was achieved. However, people would often take the
ideas very literally and want to know where the props could
be bought. Stafford says, 'In a gentle way Terence was
educating people with the catalogue. It was a book of ideas –
it gave people a sense of security to lay out money knowing
what something would look like. Now magazines do that for
people.'

The catalogue, along with the books that grew out of it,
became a full-time project with specialist staff and systems. With
the growth in the number of stores – by 1976 sales had reached
£21 million and pre-tax profits exceeded £1 million – the
operation had become so big that it needed to be overhauled.
Terence had long cast envious eyes at the computerized stock-
control systems of the baby- and mother-goods retailer Mothercare. He believed that stock control was the key to Habitat's
success, and was keen to have something similar. Some people,
such as David Phillips, believed that Habitat had already become
too obsessed with systems. He says:

In many cases the systems people were allowed to predominate. Michael
Tyson saw Habitat as a selling-machine. I don't think Habitat should have been
run like that – we were much too driven by accounts and controls. It's why I
became disenchanted with it – the systems overtook the inspiration. That's
probably a buyer's view, but to me it was the inspiration that mattered.

Geoff Davy sees the systems problem from a different perspective. He thinks that the systems in the company were not as
effective as they could have been, because the company culture
said they didn't really matter – 'style, presentation, form
mattered'. Certainly systems weren't a personal interest of
Terence's – he just wanted other people in the company to get
them right.

Advised by the consultants Arthur Andersen, Michael Tyson chose a till and stock-control system driven by a Burroughs computer. The tills came from another US company, Data Terminal Systems. The cost was £1.5 million, and the system was beset with problems from the outset. Habitat was pioneering the electronic point-of-sale (EPOS) system in the UK. This worked by the now familiar method of giving each product a code number. When the number was punched into the till, the price would be shown automatically, and the till would store the sales information. At night, the data was transmitted via a Post Office land-line to the central computer. This should have meant almost instantaneous sales information, thereby ensuring that the status of items on the shelves and in the warehouse was always known. As Terence says, 'It should have meant that we always knew what our bestsellers were. In retailing you find that 20 per cent of products make up 80 per cent of sales – you always need to make sure the 20 per cent are in stock.' However, having installed the system, there was a continual problem with lost data and incorrect sales information. The memory of the system was insufficient, and it had not been tested on European telecommunication links. Even more irritating was that, after the investment had been made, IBM announced a better package.

In time the system was made to work – but only after months of not knowing what the stock situation was at all. In spite of the tribulations involved, which continued to hound the company for some time, Terence was immensely proud of Habitat's EPOS system: for him it symbolized Habitat's arrival as a serious business. Some sections of the media and some banks might still look at Habitat as a 'boutique' business, but Habitat was now leading other, better-known, retailers.

Terence was also galvanized into another innovation of which he remains proud. Habitat had been very much his creation, but it had also been built on the loyalty of others. Terence wanted to reward that loyalty and keep people fully involved in the business by letting them share in its success. This was not old-fashioned paternalism; rather, it was born out of Terence's belief that industry needed to involve people in the work they did. There were some employee incentive schemes in Britain – for example, the John Lewis Partnership, which Terence consulted, had long given dividends to employees – but no one seemed to be offering employees shares. Habitat's scheme, for which the Inland Revenue had to be persuaded to change its rules, worked by diverting a proportion of profits each year to pay for an allocation of shares to new and existing shareholders. As a result of the scheme Terence's shareholding fell from 100 per cent to 73 per cent. Launched in 1976, the scheme set the standard for a number of companies, and in the late seventies the *Financial Times* and the business sections of other papers were awash with stories of employee share schemes.

Terence revelled in challenging conventions – he had been doing it ever since everyone told him not to open the first Habitat in the Fulham Road. The bigger the barrier, the more exciting the challenge, and after building Habitat in Britain and France, Terence wanted to take on the graveyard of British retailers, the USA. Stretched as he was by the shop-opening programme – Habitat now had thirty-four shops in Europe – Terence needed more money. As had been done for the Continent, a feasibility study of the United States was undertaken – this time by Michael Tyson. His recommendation was to concentrate the development of a chain of between twenty and twenty-five shops in the North East, starting with New York. The recommendation was put to Habitat's bankers, who turned it down flat. Terence says, 'When we wanted to raise money to go into America we couldn't find anyone to back us. The banks thought that Habitat was a fashion business – to them it was no different from a jeans shop – here today and gone tomorrow. That's why we went off and worked with a Dutch bank.'

Terence contacted Bank Mees & Hope, a subsidiary of the largest Dutch bank, ABN. There were no Habitats in The Netherlands, but Conran Associates was doing a lot of work there, most notably for the retailer De Bijenkorf. Bank Mees & Hope saw Habitat as a mainstream business, rather than a fashion retailer, and advanced the funds required – about £4 million.

Subsequently Terence invited one of the bank's directors, Hugo Haarbosch, to join Habitat as a non-executive director.

The location for the first Habitat in New York was the new Citicorp Center. Terence already had a small but positive reputation in the United States. *The House Book* had been published there by Crown in 1976, selling some 60,000 copies, and he had designed some furniture for Macy's. To boost awareness, Terence launched himself into a PR campaign, playing on his Englishness and choosing to be controversial. It generated a lot of press coverage.

He started by being critical of American interior decorators:

Are American consumers – especially the younger ones – fed up with interior designers, high-priced furniture and the mystique of decorating? And do they have more taste than American manufacturers give them credit for? Terence Conran, an energetic English interior designer, thinks so, and he is ready to do something about it.'[4]

He followed up by lambasting American furniture manufacturers. At the Southern Furniture Market in North Carolina, the *New York Times* reported Terence as being critical of almost everything he saw:

'That chair will give way in no time,' said Mr Conran, the ombudsman. 'There's a bloody wooden bar across this sofa bed. Who could sleep on that? It's abominably uncomfortable,' he said, lying on it, 'upholstered tables are a way of adding cost and taking money off the customers. To pay money for stuff so badly made, forget it.'[5]

Although there were American designers and manufacturers that Terence did admire – such as Charles Eames, Knoll and Herman

4. Norma Skurka, 'A Slap at the Decorating Mystique', in *New York Times*, 17 January 1977.

5. Joan Kron, 'British Merchant Invades American Furniture Market', in *New York Times*, 21 April 1977.

Miller – none of them was producing furniture that was priced to be accessible to a typical Habitat customer. There was also a plethora of reproduction, imitation and ornate furniture that was anathema to Terence and the antithesis of the Habitat style. The main competition in America was likely to come from the Chicago-based Crate and Barrel, from a shop called Workbench and, in china and glass, from Pottery Barn. There would also be some competition from the big department stores, but in his favour Terence had the cohesiveness of the Habitat look and a range that covered not only furniture, but also textiles, crockery and kitchen goods.

Having started looking for a site at the end of 1976, the aim was to find and open a shop by the following autumn. Michael Tyson was to be the president of the new operation. David Pasmore moved from London, where he had been stores director, to run the new store, and Tina Ellis, who had been designing Habitats for the last four years, was given the task of developing the store design. However, Terence knew that he also had to have an American to guide the product range. Fortuitously he had met someone called Pauline Dora, who seemed perfect. Previously she had been working for a modern furniture retailer based in Massachusetts, called Design Research. Pauline had seen Habitat in the UK, and through a restaurateur friend, George Lang, who had been advising the Citicorp Center on its restaurants, she met Terence. Terence knew the architect, Ben Thompson, who ran Design Research, and had seen his shop in Boston. Although Terence was appalled by Thompson's lack of commercial awareness, he was much taken by the shop and its product range – which was the closest thing to Habitat in the USA. Terence believed that if Pauline Dora could produce such a good range for Design Research she could do it for Habitat, and he offered her the job of head of buying.

However, Pauline was appalled when Terence told her the location – 'I thought they were fools.' The Citicorp Center a distinctive skyscraper with a wedge-shaped top that was originally designed to obtain energy from the sun – is in what is now a prime space on Third Avenue and East 54th Street. However, in

1977 the area was an unlikely one. There was very little retailing of note in the immediate vicinity, and customers would have to be drawn away from the department stores on Fifth Avenue. The area was seedy – right next door was a topless/bottomless bar – but in spite of this Terence felt the location was right. Just as with the Fulham Road, it was an area that was beginning to change. Also, the location and the fact that it was a new development meant Terence could get good terms from the landlords – a twenty-year lease at $10 per square foot for 40,000 square feet on two floors with a good frontage along both streets.

To stock the store, Pauline Dora started by buying from the British and French operations. Where there were gaps – such as in lighting, where the wattages were incompatible – or where cheaper alternatives were obtainable locally – such as in uphol-stered furniture – products were sourced from US manufacturers. Everything seemed to be running smoothly until rumours of a dock strike in New York created concern. This was nothing, however, compared to the next bombshell – which was the discovery that the Habitat name had already been registered in the USA by a number of companies, one of which went to court to prevent Terence using it. The decision was taken that the operation in the USA would be known as Conran's – presented with a lower case 'c' to echo the presentation of Habitat – but the new name meant that 'Habitat' had to be erased from all the products that had been brought over from Europe. Even the base of the chicken bricks where the Habitat name had been stamped had to be ground off.

On Terence's birthday, 4 October 1977, the new shop opened. The opening party was exuberant, but the sales were anything but. For the first four months Habitat was the only retailer in the Center; others had been more cautious about the location and whether it would open on time. Customers were unsure about Conran's quick-assembly furniture, and there had been insufficient adaptation to the American market. Partly this was because of the timing problem, but it was also due to Terence being insufficiently attuned to the thoughts of

American consumers – he didn't really believe that Americans would only buy glasses the 'size of ice buckets' and over-dimensioned beds. Whereas he had had a lifetime love affair with France, his understanding of the United States was much more limited.

To break even in the first year required sales of $3.5 million. Conran's didn't make it. In fact it would be six years before it did make a profit. Although the Citicorp site began to work well in time, the company's subsequent location decisions were not successful. New Rochelle, where Conran's sited a shop and its first warehouse, had, as Pauline Dora says, 'died years ago', and Washington was a logistical nightmare because it was too far away from the other shops. But once Pauline Dora took over the running of the company, some three years after its start-up, she tried to fill in the locational gaps and to build up mail-order business, as mail order was much more sophisticated in the USA than in Europe. During her presidency of the American operation, which lasted until the late eighties, Conran's made a profit.

The seventies marked a period of rapid growth in the development of Terence's businesses. By 1980 sales had reached £58.2 million, with profits of nearly £4 million. France was performing very successfully under the guidance of Francis Bruguière, with sales of £21 million and approximately a quarter of the trading profits. In fact sales in France between 1975 and 1980 had grown by 47 per cent compared with 21 per cent for the UK. The Habitat catalogue, which had started with a 25,000 print run in 1965, had expanded to an 800,000 print run with a cover price of 75 pence. Conran Associates had grown rapidly and had undertaken interior-design work for the Centre Commerciale de la Defense in Paris, for Renault cars and for hotels in the West Indies among others. Although Terence remained the guiding light of Habitat and his other businesses, he had in Ian Peacock, Michael Tyson and John Stephenson a capable management team to support him. When Habitat's fellow sixties pioneer Biba closed its doors in 1980, speculation was rife in the press about the timing of Habitat going public. Terence had proven to everyone that Habitat was more than just a fashion business – it had real substance.

CHAPTER NINE

HABITAT MOTHERCARE

The end of the seventies marked a turning-point in British society. As Peter Jenkins pointed out in the *Guardian* in September 1978:

No country has yet made the journey from developed to underdeveloped. Britain could be the first to embark upon that route. That is what it would mean to move away from a century of relative economic decline into a state of absolute decline.

The 'absolute decline' seemed to be happening in the 'winter of discontent' that followed. In January there was a nationwide strike of lorry drivers. This was followed by industrial disputes in public services, including ambulance drivers and dustmen. The Labour government's pay policy collapsed, and inflation was rampant. The spring election that year was comprehensively won by the Conservatives under Margaret Thatcher, who came to office determined to reverse the decline. By the end of her first term in office in 1983 they had resolutely failed. Gross domestic product and industrial production had fallen, unemployment had increased from 1,253,000 to 3,021,000, and taxation and public spending had gone up.

For Terence, whose political hero was the staunchly socialist Aneurin Bevan, the advent of Thatcherism was in most ways a disaster. Terence's father, who had come to live at Barton Court, was equally critical of her, although Terence thinks his comments were probably more sexist than political. However, Terence could find some things to admire:

I hated her policies, arrogance and total conviction that she was right, but I admired her determination. I think she changed Britain out of all recognition.

By making sure that the trade unions weren't so powerful, she created more opportunities. However, her vision never equated to mine – it was very uncaring, and she was dismissive about the arts – that seems to be endemic in the Conservative Party.

Famously, Terence refused an invitation to lunch with her, because of his strong disapproval about her attitude to the Falklands war – he felt that, like Suez, it was a backward step, driven by jingoism. But on a more prosaic issue – over Sunday trading – they did see eye to eye. Since the 1970s Terence had been behind a campaign for letting retailers trade on Sunday, called Open Shop. He saw that many couples' work commitments meant that their opportunities to shop during the week were limited. His solution was to open on Sundays. As he was breaking the law, Habitat was regularly fined. He mobilized other retailers and argued that there was no logic to a system which allowed someone to buy a pornographic magazine on Sunday but not a Bible. He also claimed that the staff liked it, both because they were paid double time and because customers were in a relaxed mood. Caroline disagreed with Terence over Sunday trading – she felt it was bad for family life – but Margaret Thatcher was more supportive. He went to see her and remembers that she told him that her father had been a religious man but that he had opened his shop on Sunday during the war. In spite of her backing, however, getting a bill through Parliament turned out to be a long and tortuous process.

Even though there was a fall in personal disposable income in the 1980–2 recession, as well as street riots and violent industrial disputes, consumers did not stop spending and retailers were not so badly affected as in the recession a decade later. Indeed in this period retailers began to exert their authority. Although Habitat had long presented itself as a brand in its own right, the shift of power from manufacturer to retailer, which has continued unabated ever since, really got under way. In supermarket retailing, for example, the price wars that had preoccupied the multiples came to an end as the emphasis was switched to creating strong retail identities with a much greater proportion of own-brand products. Perhaps not surprisingly, Terence's favourite, Sainsbury's, led the way with a high-quality own-label range. Retailers were moving to the centre stage both in the minds of consumers and in the City. It seemed the time was right to take Habitat public.

This had first been mooted in the press in 1978, and seemed to be imminent at the end of 1979 when the *Financial Times* ran a feature on Habitat's impending flotation. However it was some time before Habitat came to the market, as Terence wanted the American operation to break even first. In 1979 that was predicted for the summer of 1981. The flotation itself was to be sponsored by Habitat's Dutch bank, Mees & Hope, and by Morgan Grenfell, who had been Terence's advisers, through Philip Chappell, since the early sixties. However, Chappell was too busy with other commitments at the time and recommended that Terence use one of the young stars of the bank – Roger Seelig. Terence recalls, 'Philip said, "Roger Seelig is young, bright and energetic – he's the man for you." I was doubtful about Roger at first. I'd been used to the wise, gentlemanly Philip Chappell, and here was this brash, slightly flashy man. But the more I got to know Roger the more I liked him.'

Roger Seelig, who was in his mid-thirties when he met Terence, was to become one of the best known of the eighties deal-makers – partly because of his involvement with the controversial Guinness bid for Distillers. Roger had a strong academic background and had worked briefly for Esso before he joined Morgan Grenfell, where he discovered his talent for finance and deal-making. Although in the context of flotations Habitat was very small, Roger thought it was an exciting prospect because Habitat was so fundamentally different from other retailers.

However, as soon as the detailed planning for the flotation was under way, a £28 million offer was made for Habitat by Selim Zilkha of Mothercare. It was a tempting offer because it was a quick, clean and risk-free way of liberating the value of the company. Negotiations took place on Terence's role in the new venture but when he asked Roger Seelig's advice about whether he should go ahead, Roger advised him against accepting. He recalls, 'I persuaded Terence – and there was a certain amount of vested interest in it – that the price was too cheap and that by floating we could do better. I incurred Selim Zilkha's irritation in stopping Terence from going ahead with the Mothercare offer.'

The float itself turned out to be traumatic. It involved an enormous amount of work in the preparation of documents, and America was still losing money. Even though Habitat overall had increased its sales and profits from the previous year, inflation of nearly 20 per cent meant that in real terms the performance was static. Also the stock market was becoming nervous, and the *FT* index fell from 550 on 14 September to 460 two weeks later. The economic situation in Britain was parlous, there were developing problems in Poland as the Solidarity free trade union flexed its muscles, and an American economist was predicting that the end of the world was nigh. However, when Terence was interviewed by Deyan Sudjic in an article entitled 'Optimists', a month before the flotation, he said that, while recognizing the impact of the 'present economic blizzard', he believed that 'Habitat must go on presenting a confident and attractive face.' Also, Roger Seelig's view was that the combination of the small scale of the offer and the long-term reputation of Habitat would carry the day.

As there was no comparable company, it was difficult to determine Habitat's value. Roger recommended they should go for a tender offer, where investors would be asked to state what price they were prepared to pay above a specified minimum, which was to be set at 110 pence. If the demand for the shares was high – as Roger believed it would be – Terence and the employees would benefit. The novelty of the tender was that although just over 25 per cent of the shares were available, the number actually sold was to be set by the sum of money being sought – £12 million. This meant that if the average price was higher than 110 pence, a lower percentage of the total shares would be sold. In spite of the problems in the market, when the offer closed, Habitat had achieved an average price of 118 pence.

Terence had cause for celebration, which he combined with his fiftieth birthday on 4 October in a grand party at Barton Court. There were champagne and fireworks – one of Terence's great loves – fine food and drink, and music by George Melly. Even though he lavished money on the event, there was an interesting example of his inconsistent attitude to money. Rodney Kinsman recalls that, after most people had gone home, Terence said to him, 'You're interested in machinery – come and see the boiler.' He took him downstairs to a room like a ship's hold in which sat a massive, panting boiler with coloured pipes. Rodney agreed with Terence that it was a beautiful piece of engineering; 'Terence said, "Yes, but it costs a fortune to run. I'll have to turn it off." It was a cold night with a house full of people. I was incredulous. I said, "You can't – everyone will freeze!"'

In a sense, the party was also a prelude. Buoyed up by the success of the flotation and the rapid rise in the company's market capitalization, which reached some £57 million by the end of the first day's trading – Terence and Roger were receptive to a new opportunity. Having failed to buy Habitat, Selim Zilkha was now looking to be bought, and Terence was invited to make a bid. Terence, who didn't like the confrontation of putting a deal together, remembers that Roger negotiated very hard to get the best price and infuriated Selim Zilkha. Roger says, 'Mothercare was capitalized at about £139 million. It would have been unthinkable in the summer that this midget company, which Selim was prepared to pay £28 million for, was now bidding for him. Selim wouldn't have me on the board of the merged company because he was so cross about it all.'

Mothercare proved to be an extremely good deal. It had good systems, and a chain of 423 shops in Britain, Europe and the USA. However, sales had started to fall off, the American operation was struggling, the product range was starting to look dreary, and, in an attempt to compete with other retailers, Mothercare had started reducing its prices and paying less attention to quality. Market analysts had started to be very critical of the Mothercare management. What the company needed was vision – something Terence had in abundance. His view was that:

> Mothercare was the perfect niche business – and a very major niche. Originally there was a vision, but as it grew Selim didn't know what to do with it; he didn't know what the product should be and he didn't understand that young mothers were interested in style. Money was the only thing that seemed to matter. It was a business driven by percentages.

Terence liked Selim Zilkha, who had originally come from a banking environment, but he couldn't comprehend his lifestyle, which, unlike Terence's, was divided into two very distinct parts. Terence remembers that Selim's home was a very large apartment in Langham Place, full of grand paintings and with footmen in white gloves. However, although he would go to work in a chauffeur-driven Rolls-Royce, the Mothercare headquarters was an old run-down sweet factory with 'rotten furniture and holes in the carpets – a real shit-heap of an office'.

Selim had absolute control over every aspect of the business, but he wanted to move to America. Terence asked to remain a director in the transition period of putting the two companies together, but it was his long-standing partner, Barney Goodman, who was more actively involved in the integration of the two companies and stayed on as chairman of Mothercare. Terence felt the need to have a chief executive in addition to Goodman to control Mothercare and, although Habitat had been the acquirer, he felt the role should go to a Mothercare person. Selim's advice was that Kevyn Jones, who was the stores director, should be given the role. To drive the design development of the store, Terence asked John Stephenson to spearhead a dedicated in-house design group which, along with the buyers, would redesign the stores and the products. This operation – the Habitat Mothercare Design Group – was run separately from Conran Associates, which was focused on work for non-group clients.

Terence knew that, as a public company, Habitat Mothercare would not be given much time by the City to prove itself. He believed the company needed to change its position in the market-place and, with some irony, said at the time that it should aim for Marks & Spencer's customers, not British Home Stores'. Terence felt the best way to achieve the transformation was to focus on those elements of the Mothercare package that could be changed quickly and economically. In store design, this meant concentrating on lighting, colours and graphics. In the space of one year, a team led by Oliver Gregory, who had returned to Neal Street following the break-up of the Barton Court group, transformed some two hundred stores with new carpets, sweet-pea-coloured decor and easy-to-read signs. The clean feel of the original shops was retained, but was softened by the new environments. The products were also dealt with in a similar way. In the short term, products were enlivened by new bright colours; in the longer term, a complete review of all products was undertaken. Sebastian Conran came to work with the in-house design group and was responsible for redesigning new 'hardware', such as pushchairs. Two of his more interesting products were a stroller in which the baby faces the person pushing and a stylish, top-of-the-range pushchair. Inevitably these took longer to develop because of the considerable time required to tool the products and to meet safety standards. Clothing was also changed: out went the dowdy and synthetic and in came colourful clothes made from natural fibres. When a new catalogue was launched to the press some eighteen months after the acquisition, everyone was impressed by the speed and the substance of the turnaround. Sales had increased by 15 per cent and profits by 32 per cent.

However, Terence was not content to let the development of the group rest there. At Habitat he relaunched a range called Basics. The catalyst was that Terence always felt that his vision of providing simple but affordable design was in danger of being lost. Although Habitat's products were never expensive, he believed there was an opportunity to provide a no-nonsense, well-designed, minimal-decoration range. He had originally launched Basics in the recession of the early 1970s as a specific response to the squeeze on consumer spending, but it was an idea that Terence often revisited. This time 178 products were developed and launched in March 1982. The range caught the imagination of the press and the public, but in merchandising terms it was less successful because the products sold out quickly and couldn't be replaced fast enough. In fact, although Basics was popular, over the years it lost its 'basicness' – rather than just being repromoted each year, it tended to get more fashionable – and it was finally dropped. Nevertheless Terence remained a keen advocate of it. Geoff Davy says:

> Terence never ever let go of Basics – it's part of his evangelical thing. He would say, 'If I can bring my version of good taste to the masses, then I'll rest a happy man.' He always had this hankering to be the man who made the Model T of sofas.

There were also more Mothercare and Habitat stores, both in the UK and in Europe, and Habitat France acquired some large outlets from Maison de la Redoute – a subsidiary of Au Printemps which had three large stores in the suburbs of Paris and Lyons and the largest mail-order company in France. The deal was agreed between Terence, Roger and the Redoute directors at a meeting near a new home Terence and Caroline had acquired in Provence, called Brunellys. Even though Terence was now a man of considerable wealth, he still liked getting a bargain. Roger remembers this was well illustrated by an outing to a local restaurant with one of the finest wine lists in France. Terence asked Roger to choose the wine for dinner. He narrowed the choice down to a Château Lafite, a Latour or a Mouton-Rothschild. The price difference between good and bad years was huge: there was a Latour at 9,000 francs and one of 900 francs. Roger asked Terence whether he thought a Latour could be good even in a bad year. Terence said he was sure it would be good in any year, so Roger chose the 900 franc bottle. The sommelier presented a bottle without a label which, when decanted, was perfect. Roger recalls:

> I said to Terence, 'We have plucked a jewel.' Two minutes later the sommelier said, 'There's been an awful mistake' – we'd got the 9,000 franc bottle. Terence

was just deliriously happy at the bargain he'd got. On the Monday we had lunch with the Redoute people and we had the bad year. It wasn't undrinkable, but it was what it was.

> Whereas the early experiment with a suburban store in France had been a failure, the trading environment had changed: there had been a migration towards the suburbs, and the concept of edge-of-town shopping had been developed. The Redoute out of town stores, which were rebranded Habitat Grand H, cut out the problems of having to find sites and get planning permissions. The product range in the shops was extended and clearly aimed at a broader segment of the market than the city-centre Habitats, which remained focused on their *branché* customers. What worried Terence and Francis Bruguière most was the arrival of the Swedish home-furnishing retailer IKEA, with its large warehouse-like shops in the suburbs selling low-priced modern furniture. IKEA proved to be very successful in France. Having started with some small suburban stores, it acquired ever bigger sites and closed the original stores as the new ones were opened. Also, unlike Habitat, IKEA advertised extensively. Terence was never keen on spending large sums on advertising if he could avoid it – something Pauline Dora felt was a problem in building the reputation of Conran's in the USA. Yves Cambier says:

When we had meetings about advertising, Terence would always ask about the shops. His view was that if the shops weren't right then there wasn't any point in advertising. When we presented results from market-research studies, he would say, 'Are you sure about these findings?' Generally, for him it was enough that we all worked together to agree what we had to do. Good products and good displays were what mattered most. He believed that taking care of the customer was the key to success.

> The timing of the Redoute acquisition was poor. The French government moved to reduce retail margins, and the franc was weak. In the year to March 1983, although turnover went up by 43 per cent in local currency, profits fell.

The other new venture for Habitat was the development of the Japanese market. Japan was notoriously difficult to penetrate without a local partner, so Terence decided that Habitat in Japan would have to be a joint venture. There were about six different possible partners, but Terence was particularly taken with the chairman of the Japanese department-store and leisure group Seibu, Seiji Tsutsumi – not only did he write poetry, he also had a passion for architecture and design. The process began with Terence visiting Japan to see Seibu's operations and to discuss a possible tie-up. This was followed by a visit to Britain by Seibu executives to look at Habitat. As with America, there had to be some product adaptation, both in the scale of the furniture and in kitchenware. The difference in the latter was minimized, however, because, just as Habitat was busy introducing the wok to Britain, so the Japanese were becoming more interested in European cooking and utensils.

The first Habitat within Seibu stores and one stand-alone shop opened in October 1982 with considerable advertising support. By the end of 1983 there were eleven Habitat outlets in Japan. The main income from the operation was derived from the royalty payments on goods sold, but from Terence's perspective the most important aspect of the venture was the sense of taking British design and making it work in a country which he had long admired for the beauty and simplicity of its designs. The Japanese were particularly taken with the Basics concept and developed shops under that name, which became the inspiration for Muji – a high-quality no-brand-name retailer.

Although he was proud of the popularity of Habitat in Japan, in retrospect Terence recognizes that he didn't tie up the franchise agreements tightly enough. Seibu maintained the essence of Habitat, but Terence says, 'We kept going there and finding they'd put their own quite unsuitable merchandise in.'

The growth of Habitat overseas, the company's Stock Exchange listing, and the merger with Mothercare were all indications of Terence's enhanced status in British business. Although he had always been highly adept at generating press interest, more and more that interest was moving from the style

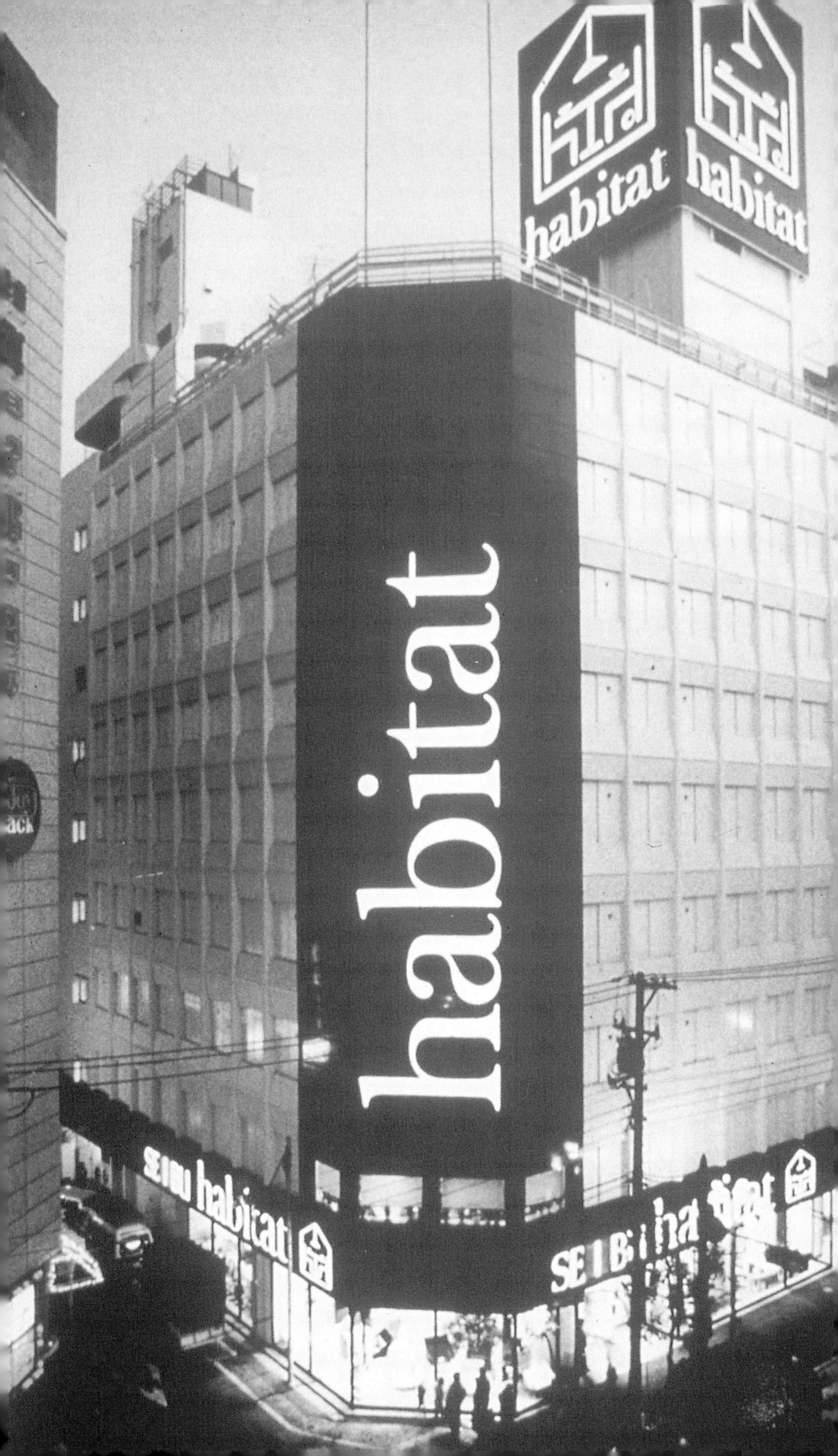
habitat
habitat
habitat
SEIBU habitat

pages to the business ones. In a 1981 interview, Terence said, 'The most cheering thing I've seen this year is a stockbroker's report which, in an analysis of retailing throughout the world, identified design factors as being crucial to success. To get the financial community talking about design – that's a real success.'[1]

The belief that design could differentiate retailers and enhance performance drove a near-decade-long obsession with retail design. As the social commentator Peter York noted, 'Good design sells, they said in the sixties, and now, in the eighties, industrialists believe it.' Although by the end of the eighties 'design' would become a pejorative term – Peter York was deriding it in the early eighties – for the most part the status of designers was raised. At the forefront of the movement was Terence. He was always a maverick in the pantheon of business leaders, but he had moved a long way from the youthful rebel who had rowed with the Society of Industrial Artists. In fact the Society – now the Society of Industrial Artists and Designers (SIAD) – had made him a Fellow and awarded him a design medal in 1980, and in 1982 this was followed by the Royal Society of Arts Bicentenary Medal.

In 1979 Terence acquired his first external directorship, at the long-established Yorkshire-based menswear retailer J. Hepworth & Son. He had been invited to join the board by Eric Crabtree, a former solicitor who had owned a successful chain of womenswear shops called Cresta, which he had sold to Debenhams before joining the Hepworth board. When asked by the avuncular chairman of Hepworth, Robert Chadwick, to find someone who could bring some more style to the board, Crabtree, who had met Terence, thought his blend of retail and design knowledge would be perfect. Terence was very flattered to be asked and was intrigued by the prospect of being in the clothing business and of getting the opportunity to work for a large public company. Hepworth had a major presence on the high street, with some 365 menswear shops, but the style of clothes was uninspiring –

1. Deyan Sudjic, 'Optimists', in *Design*, August 1981.

even though the designer Hardy Amies had previously been a consultant.

At first Terence's influence was marginal, but at the end of 1980 the retirement of the incumbent chairman was announced and Terence was asked to replace him. The company began to accelerate the process of change. Conran Associates began a refurbishment programme of the Hepworth stores, and a shoe chain of some 120 stores, called Turner's, was acquired. This was important in its own right, but it also brought into the company a very good retailer called Trevor Morgan who was bright and ambitious and active in seeking out opportunities. Trevor Morgan uncovered an old Leicester-based family business called Kendalls, which specialized in rainwear. It had no real image, unexciting product and run-down stores, but from a property point of view it was a bargain. The board had long discussed the idea of going into womenswear; Kendalls seemed to provide the opportunity to do it. To help move the idea forward, Terence got the design group to conduct a study on the opportunity for womenswear and to devise some mood boards to show what might be done with the stores in terms of layout, clothes and accessories.

Terence was very excited by the ideas, and the board was further motivated when a merchandise director called George Davies was found to develop it. Davies presented a series of merchandise concepts, developed by his designer, Liz Devereaux-Batchelor, which were aimed as he describes it at 'somewhere between Jaeger and Marks'. Starting early in 1981, the aim was to get the new chain launched by February 1982.

The strategy for the new idea was to offer good-value coordinated fashion and accessories to professional women aged over twenty-five. The clothes themselves would be simple, but elegant. However, the idea needed a name and a design concept that could be quickly implemented across seventy-eight shops. John Stephenson, who was in charge of design on the project, came up with a name which he had thought up when he had worked at Burtons: Next. All the designers liked it, as did Terence and George Davies, but the rest of the board were nonplussed. Trevor Morgan, who was unwilling to spend much money on the stores, wanted Terence to see if the design group could use an anagram of Kendalls, so that the existing fascia lettering could be used. The others felt the name was too odd, and it was agreed that the name would be researched. The findings were negative, but Terence and George Davies were so sure of the idea that they undertook some further research using carrier bags with mocked-up Next lettering. This time the result was more positive. Although the exercise only confirmed Terence's cynicism about market research, the name was finally agreed.

In true Habitat style, the shop designs concentrated on simplicity – 'the merchandise itself was the message rather than the store design'. Whereas mid-market womenswear retailing normally involved very high stock density, the Next concept was focused on providing comfortable shopping environments with plenty of space to walk around and look at the clothes. The fittings for the shops were modern, with natural wood finishes. Terence recalls:

> We wanted the shops to be flexible, because we wanted to show how to put things together in different ways to make a wardrobe. The look was to be clean and fresh and bright. The clever thing was that the clothes looked upmarket, but were very reasonably priced. That was down to George.

Once the store design was agreed, it was rolled out across the whole chain in a two-month period with only one week's loss of trading in each location. Supported by an advertising campaign devised by Conran based on the theme of accessible collectables, Next was an immediate success and spawned an empire that would in time encompass interiors, jewellery and menswear shops. In design terms it also determined the look of the high street for the coming decade. Terence enjoyed the whole experience from both perspectives. However, he didn't stay to nurture the idea. The commitments associated with running a public company combined with the launch of his own range of fashion outlets (NOW and Richards) made it inappropriate for him to continue as chairman, and he resigned in 1983.

In the early 1980s Terence was energetically pursuing a variety of projects. There was a new architectural practice, called Conran Roche, which Terence had set up with Fred Roche, the ex-chief executive of the Milton Keynes Development Corporation, that had immediate work in Nigeria, Docklands and Milton Keynes itself; a new publishing venture with Paul Hamlyn, called Conran Octopus; and the development of Terence's long-cherished idea of a museum of modern design. While Habitat was his commercial attempt to change people's attitude to the look of things, Terence also felt there ought to be a process of educating people about modern design in a museum context. There would be some criticism of Terence for this. Some felt that the line between museums and retailing was becoming too blurred – something which Roy Strong exacerbated by suggesting that the V & A 'could be the Laura Ashley of the 1990s'. Terence saw the parallels, but felt that the imparting of knowledge was the key thing – cultural commentators could whinge all they liked. As a student at the Central School he had spent endless days at the V & A copying old textiles. His main recollection of the experience was there was never anything modern to look at. Except for the influence of Eduardo Paolozzi, much of the Central course tended to be backward-looking and parochial. Terence says:

When I was a student the only source of information on what was going on in the modern world was magazines such as *Domus* and *Art and Architecture*. Later on I was inspired by my visits to the Milan Triennale. But in England there was nothing to do with modernity: it was all to do with history. I thought, Wouldn't it be wonderful to have an international museum of contemporary design?

The opportunity to turn the idea into reality came when Terence decided to float Habitat. This would generate sufficient income to set up the Conran Foundation, which would support the museum. In any case Terence was keen to ensure that not all of his money would be left either to his children, who he thought should be able to stand on their own two feet, or to the taxman. Terence discussed his idea with Paul Reilly, who had opened Terence's Thetford factory in the early 1960s and who had since become a director of Conran Associates. Reilly, a key part of the design establishment and director of the Design Council (the former Council of Industrial Design) for many years, had also had a similar conversation some years earlier with a young academic called Stephen Bayley who was looking for a rich backer. Reilly put the two men together, and Terence had soon commissioned Bayley to produce a report on the project.

Bayley was a lecturer in art history at the University of Kent, but was ambitious and keen to extend his career beyond academia. Terence seemed to offer a lifestyle far removed from that at Canterbury. Bayley says, 'When I worked with Terence I had the genuine impression that I was at the centre of the world.' With £1,500 of Conran funds, he visited museums in Europe and the Museum of Modern Art in New York. Although there were some collections of design, and also occasional exhibitions on design-related topics, there was no museum wholly devoted to the subject of industrial design. The result of his research was published in a 1979 report, which was then submitted to the Charity Commissioners. However, the project now had to wait on the flotation of Habitat which took two years to come to fruition. In the interim a space had to be found.

The director of the V & A, Roy Strong, who had previously been on the receiving end of Terence's anger over comments about the Habitat catalogue, had also cherished the idea of a collection of industrial design, and offered Terence space at the V & A – 5,000 square feet in the old boilerhouse yard on the western side of the museum. Terence says, 'It was a hole in the ground – completely derelict.' Initially provided for five years, the space was transformed by Conran Associates into a brilliantly lit white space with tiled floor – The Boilerhouse. When it opened at the end of 1981, following the Habitat flotation, the first exhibition – Art and Industry: A Century of Design in the Products You Use – set the tone for the future aims of The Design Museum.

The Boilerhouse immediately generated a lot of publicity, not all of it positive. Peter York enjoyed himself by making fun of the whole idea:

Emergency Ward 10. And the trolley goes down the New Brutalist concrete ramp into the basement, round the corner and into . . . a laboratory? a main service area? a gym? a men's room? Anyway, past reception it's all white tiled, every living inch of it's white tiled . . . it takes a while to suss out where the *exhibits*, so to speak, actually are in the Victoria and Albert Museum's Boilerhouse annexe exhibition of hand tools. There is, however, one irresistible tableau in the Hyper-Realist style, the best thing there. On the far right hand there *seems* to be a kind of window with venetians against it, and if you peer in there seems to be *a young man with everything* on display in an office interior in the style popularly known as Hi-Tech. And this young man *seems* to wear a bow-tie, a perky but tasteful day-time bow-tie of the kind worn on special occasions by those who have been to art school, and everything else a modern person should have . . . When it moves, however, one realizes it's little Stephen Bayley, who runs the show here, living the Design Life.[2]

Peter York was not averse to making of fun of Terence directly. In another article, 'NW1's First Family', he lampooned the lifestyle of the Conrans – 'the sixties Visuals who took over the world.' After this appeared in *Harpers & Queen*, Terence made his views known to the then editor, Willie Landels, forcibly:

Willie was bicycling past the great glass ship-shaped Conran Shop nosing Fulham Road between Draycott and Sloane Avenues, probably wearing his green shawl and definitely his flower buttonhole, when his old acquaintance Conran rushed out, grabbed him angrily and pulled him off his bike so roughly the buttonhole fell out.[3]

2. Peter York, *Modern Times* (Futura 1985) p. 26.

3. Ann Barr, '£150 million down and still smiling', in *Harpers & Queen*, July 1991, p. 84.

In spite of such cynicism, The Boilerhouse was very successful. With its constantly changing exhibitions – everything from Memphis (the Milanese avant-garde design group) to hand tools to robots – it generated a steady flow of visitors. Terence believes that Roy Strong soon got fed up with its success, which irritated the keepers of the V & A's own collections, who were having to struggle along on limited funds. In particular there was an exhibition on 'Coca-Cola – The Making of a Brand' which attracted more visitors than the rest of the museum. Terence described The Boilerhouse as 'an energetic carbuncle, which very quickly a number of people wanted to get rid of'. To cater for the number of people who wanted to visit the Boilerhouse shows, Terence offered to fund a proper twentieth-century gallery in the V & A. The idea was rejected, so Terence and Stephen Bayley decided to find a new location. The initial idea was to move to Milton Keynes – it was the only wholly modern city in Britain, and seemed an apposite choice for a museum devoted to the twentieth century. However, Terence was also interested in developing a site he had found in London's Docklands.

Butlers Wharf was an eleven-acre site on the south side of the Thames by Tower Bridge. Terence had first noticed it when he had been on a riverboat party with the design group, and he had asked Fred Roche to investigate. He found out that the land was owned by P & O, which had never managed to develop the site because all its planning applications had been turned down. In 1983 Terence bought the property, subject to planning permission being obtained, for £3 million. Conran Roche designed a plan for the area, which was presented to the London Docklands Development Corporation. The strength of the plan combined with Fred Roche's excellent connections meant that the application was approved at the first attempt. A company was formed, called Butlers Wharf Ltd, to develop the site. The directors were Terence, Fred Roche, Roger Seelig, the builder Lord McAlpine and the financier Jacob Rothschild. The funds for the project came from the directors and also from bank borrowings. The site contained a complex of seventeen mostly nineteenth-century warehouse buildings that had lain empty since the early seventies, when the move to containerized transport meant that London's docks ceased to be used. Terence regarded Thameside with particular affection from his boyhood visits to his father's warehouse, but he was also a passionate believer in London and the importance of its regeneration, and, as with Habitat, to be an agent of change was his main motivation. He says, 'It never looked as if Butlers Wharf was going to make a lot of money, but I wasn't doing it for that. It was an opportunity to create a new bit of London out of rubble.'

The plan for the site aimed to realize 1 million square feet of homes, shops, offices, workshops and a design museum, with all the elements of the site feeding off one another. Architecturally the plan was to combine restoration with new buildings. The main Butlers Wharf building, which fronted on to the Thames and was linked by a high-level bridge network across the street to the building behind it, was to be renovated, while Spice Quay alongside it was to be an uncompromisingly modernist, all-new, glass-box construction. The Design Museum itself was to be housed in a brutish three-storey 1950s brick-and-concrete warehouse which the Conran Roche design planned to transform into an all-white Bauhaus-like building complete with a glass-brick-fronted staircase.

The Design Museum concept was shown in model form to the Prince of Wales, who was beginning to take an active interest in architecture at this time. The Prince took an immediate dislike to the design and started talking about the scale of architecture and the desirability of pitched roofs and arched windows. Roger, who heard the story of the encounter, relates:

Terence was sitting there with clenched fists, and in the end he said, 'I live in an eighteenth century house' – he omitted to mention that he'd gutted the interior – 'and I love and respect the qualities of eighteenth-century architecture, but we have to progress.' He made this little speech, 'And in any case,' he said, 'you wouldn't want to be remembered as the repro monarch.'

The Design Museum design went ahead as Conran Roche conceived it. Although Terence was an active participant in the

The Design Museum, before and after

239

Butlers Wharf project, on a day-to-day basis it was managed by Fred Roche – Terence was simply too busy elsewhere to devote too much time to it.

As his involvement with building Habitat Mothercare grew, so Terence had less time for other projects and for family life. To reduce the strain, he and Caroline bought a house in Eaton Terrace, near Sloane Square. Terence never felt any great affection for the house – probably because there wasn't the usual opportunity to restore it – but it did provide them with a family base in London. A house he felt much more excited by was the farmhouse they had bought near Les Baux, in Provence. The property comprised 200 acres of hay fields and olive trees and – typically – a derelict house (built to the design of a Tuscan count as a prototype of the ideal farmhouse at the beginning of the last century) and an overgrown garden. Renovated and simply furnished, it provided a haven for Terence when he wanted peace and quiet and an opportunity for him and Caroline to entertain guests – albeit mostly business-related ones. As always, Terence was quite happy for his life to revolve around business. On a very rare occasion when Terence was drunk, Rodney Kinsman, thinking he might catch him off guard, asked him what his goals were outside of business. 'Terence looked at me as if I were mad,' Rodney recalls. Not surprisingly, with so many projects circulating in his mind, Terence would find it difficult to focus on the minutiae of family life, and his children found it was sometimes difficult to hold his attention. Sophie can recall that often when talking to him she could see his mind wandering. It wasn't that he didn't care about his wife and children – once, when Terence was away, Sophie and one of her friends borrowed his Porsche and crashed it; she was terrified at having to tell him about it, but his only reaction was 'Thank God, you're all right.' His failing was that he wouldn't communicate his caring, except in adversity. For Caroline, who was an emotionally needy person, it left a gap in their relationship.

Once Terence had digested Mothercare he was keen to expand again. Although many observers have accused Roger Seelig of manipulating Terence to keep on acquiring, Terence

Ned, Caroline, Sophie, Terence, Jasper, Sebastian and Tom on the balcony of the house in Eaton Terrace

denies this. His view is that if anything Roger held him back and tried to make sure he exercised caution. Roger agrees: 'I often used to lecture him how easy it was to buy companies, but how much more difficult it was to get a management team of sufficient depth to absorb the acquisitions.' The reality is probably that Terence and Roger egged each other on. Terence was much more excited by new challenges and projects than by the ongoing management of a company, and likewise Roger loved the thrill of deal-making. Whenever either refers to a particular acquisition, it is always in terms of 'We . . .' They were both very driven people and optimistic – they believed that effort and intellect would overcome most problems – and their abilities were largely complementary: Terence as designer and marketer, Roger as financier. They also enjoyed each other's company, and shared a keen sense of humour. Roger was an entertaining story-teller and appreciated Terence's wicked but penetrating wit. He remembers introducing Terence to a fellow Morgan Grenfell high-flyer, George Magan. Magan, who came from an old Irish family, was in his mid thirties, had slicked-back hair, and wore very smart three-piece suits complete with watch-chain.

Terence has great perception. Once, when Terence and I were in New York, I invited George Magan to come and meet us for a drink at the Carlisle Hotel. George, as always, was impeccably dressed. Terence asked him what he'd like to drink, and George said, 'A split of champagne.' Terence called the waiter over and said, 'Mr Wooster here will be having a split of champagne.'

The next target for Terence and Roger was Heal's. Terence had had a long relationship with Heal's. It was a shop he had grown up with – it had supplied his childhood Christmas presents – and he felt some reverence for the simple, functional furniture that Ambrose Heal had produced in the early part of the twentieth century. However, Heal's had lost direction and was languishing in the past. Oliver Heal had become managing director in 1980 and had tried to claw back the shop's image with exhibitions featuring classics of modern design and stylish advertising. However, this was largely superficial: behind the scenes the systems were antiquated. Secretaries were still using manual typewriters and calling the managing director 'young Mr Oliver'. Heal's was losing large amounts of money, and decided to look for a buyer. Terence knew the Heal family and was approached to see whether he would be interested in acquiring the company. He needed little persuading. 'It was a fantastic building with huge potential. My thought was that Heal's could become to Habitat, what The Conran Shop is now – the mature person's Habitat.'

Terence acquired the Heal family shares for some £4.8 million and immediately set about transforming the huge retail space – 250,000 square feet on Tottenham Court Road. Geoff Davy, by then Habitat's buying director, was appointed managing director of Heal's, and Priscilla was brought in to review the products and identity of the store. The aim was to get the store in shape for Habitat's twentieth birthday in May 1984.

Although Heal's had a second, smaller, store in Guildford, the attention was initially focused on reworking Tottenham Court Road. This huge, rambling building had been built at various stages in the company's development and was full of interesting architectural features which the architect who oversaw the work, Les Meldrum, and the Conran Design Group were keen to retain and restore. The layout was replanned. By focusing Heal's product range and moving the company's bed factory, the ground floor of the building was split between Heal's, Habitat, Mothercare and NOW – a development of the Mothercare concept aimed at ten- to sixteen-year-olds. Heal's itself was concentrated into three floors at the southern end of the site. With Habitat and Heal's sitting side by side, Terence knew that both the product and the interior style of each had to be clearly defined, so that it was clear to people what each shop offered. Heal's graphic style was redesigned and a new logo was developed. The quality of finishes used in the interiors was high, and plenty of space was allowed to browse the shop. The dominant wood used for the fittings was Ambrose's favourite – oak. Two restaurants were developed. The first was a sophisticated restaurant with detailing inspired by the Vienna Secessionist architect Josef Hoffmann – one of Terence's favourite designers. The second, the Café des Artistes, looked like a public restaurant but was in fact the staff canteen. There was aluminium furniture combined with natural wood tables and finishes. In spite of the attention to detail, however, when Heal's was relaunched the performance was poor. Geoff Davy and his team tried to rework the space and remerchandise it, but sales were consistently under budget. Not surprisingly, Terence was very disappointed. In the last trading day before Christmas 1984, Geoff Davy had a meeting with the Habitat Mothercare board and recommended that 'they rough up the interior and make it more commercial and less precious'. The board agreed, but Geoff knew it was his last chance to get it right. About eight weeks after implementing the new approach sales began to lift, and by the summer Heal's was the star of the group.

The upper floors of the Heal's building were transformed into working space for the administrative side and for the in-house design group, which was now physically split off from Conran Associates. However, the arrangement was to be short-lived, as the fortunes of the design side of the business were mixed. The emphasis placed on design by all the Conran businesses meant there was a steady flow of product, interiors and graphic-design projects from Habitat, Mothercare and Heal's. There were also some major external projects, such as interiors for Europe's largest shopping centre, at La Défense in Paris, and the North Terminal at Gatwick, which involved planning for 50,000 square metres of space. None the less there was a feeling among some of the designers that, as Terence became more and more involved with developing the scale of the business, the design group began to lose direction. Terence's long-standing allies, such as John Stephenson and Stafford Cliff, tried to continue Terence's ethos, but there was too much change at the top. In 1984 nearly a quarter of Conran Associates designers left the company, and while other consultancies were growing at 30 per cent or more per annum on the back of the boom in retail design, turnover was falling at Conran's. To try to restore credibility a new managing director was appointed, and the in-house and out-house design teams were remerged under the chairmanship of John Stephenson.

Design work from within the group continued to grow, both from further organic growth and from acquisitions. In addition to the creation of NOW, Terence bought a minority stake in Richard Shops from Hanson Trust, which had recently acquired the chain. The rest of Richard Shops' shares were held on behalf of Habitat by Morgan Grenfell, and in time Habitat would acquire these. Richards, as it became known, was in the same market sector as Next and Terence's and the design group's experience in launching that concept was invaluable in redesigning and remerchandising a chain of 130 shops in just over a year.

The early eighties had been a great success, and Terence was rewarded in 1983 by the offer of a knighthood in the New

Year's Honours list. Terence was very surprised by the idea, and says that initially he thought about turning it down – he felt awkward about being known as 'Sir Terence', and thought that his designers would think it was 'some terrible Pseuds Corner joke'. However, his business colleagues thought it was an honour not only for him but also for the company. Caroline told him he should take it – joking that it would get her to the front of the queue at the local village shop. He decided to accept, although he would rarely use the 'Sir' prefix: it didn't fit easily with his unassuming and unpretentious self-image.

Even though others could be awed by his knighthood, Terence was always accessible to people; he would never throw his weight around because of who he was. Maggie Heaney recalls being invited to lunch after he had opened Bibendum. Unfortunately there were no tables available, so, rather than pushing to have a table set up for him, he and Maggie ate in the corridor. Similarly, his aversion to parties and his social shyness when he didn't know people meant he disliked being the centre of attention. On social occasions, most often he could be found in the kitchen doing the washing-up.

However, after his knighthood Terence did acquire a houseman called Rogers, who had once worked for Lord Halifax. The notion of Terence having a houseman amused his work colleagues. Geoff Davy remembers:

> Rogers was a big burly man with a Brylcreem quiff and a Yorkshire accent. He was used to working for people who were comfortable with servants, but Terence was so ill at ease with this bloke – he couldn't cope with it. Rogers used to bring coffee into meetings and would say, 'Sir Terence, would you like the coffee now?' Terence would look uncomfortable, and we'd giggle.

Later Terence would acquire a driver and helper in the country-and-western-playing Reg Dixson, but Reg was much more down-to-earth and was regarded by Terence as part of his extended working family, which was growing rapidly to meet the needs of the business.

In five years the turnover of the Conran businesses had increased from £67 million to nearly £447 million. With the next merger it would pass the £1 billion mark.

CHAPTER TEN
STOREHOUSE

The £1.2 billion merger between Habitat Mothercare and British Home Stores in January 1986 created a huge retailing empire. It was an uncontested arrangement, but in other respects it epitomized the frenetic merger and acquisitions era of the mid-1980s. Whereas in the early eighties take-over activity in the UK accounted for about £1 billion a year, by 1986 it had exceeded £20 billion, with Morgan Grenfell accounting for £14 billion of the bids. That was also the year when the attempted purchase of Westland Helicopters cost Mrs Thatcher two of her cabinet colleagues and Guinness launched its controversial bid for Distillers.

The move to acquire British Home Stores had in fact started with Burton's aggressive take-over of the department-store group Debenhams.

The managing director of the Burton Group was Ralph Halpern, whom Terence had known since the early sixties, when the Conran Design Group had designed interiors for the Peter Robinson chain that Halpern was then working for. Halpern, who was in his mid forties, had spent almost his whole career with Burton and was a passionate and assertive retailer. Both he and Terence were ambitious to develop their respective organizations and had several conversations about possible take-over targets. Halpern, who was very keen on clearly focused retailing, had also tried to persuade Terence to sell Habitat Mothercare to him on more than one occasion. Terence discovered in one of these exploratory talks that Halpern was interested in buying British Home Stores and had already made an approach.

Terence and Roger had also been eyeing British Home Stores, and were now worried that they might lose out. British Home

Stores was a big, underperforming stores group, with its main business in the sort of clothing and housewares areas in which Habitat Mothercare had experience – although BHS's range was much more mass-market than Habitat's. Terence was worried about losing his opportunity with BHS, but his Hepworth contact, Eric Crabtree, recommended he look at Debenhams instead. Terence and Roger did study Debenhams, but decided it was not for them.

Terence then suggested to Ralph Halpern that Debenhams might be a better acquisition than British Home Stores for Burton. Halpern agreed it would be perfect for the Burton Group, and asked Terence if he would like to be a partner in the bid. Terence wasn't interested in making a financial commitment, but he told Halpern he would be prepared to support the bid and would consider taking space in the acquisition if successful. The idea behind the bid was to retain the Debenhams brand as an umbrella, but to have other specialist retailers operating under their own names in the same building. This galleria concept, as it became known, replicated what Terence had achieved with his collection of retailers in the Heal's building. Terence's agreement with Burton in May 1985 provided him with the design contract for the refurbishment of the Debenham stores, the opportunity to occupy 20 per cent of the floor space in Debenhams, and an option on 20 per cent of the shares. If exercised, the contract would have increased Habitat Mothercare's trading space in the UK by 50 per cent.

Debenhams, however, did not want to sell to Burton, and the bid was acrimoniously contested. Terence and Ralph Halpern appeared together in an advertising campaign to promote the Burton offer, and eventually the combination of Halpern's retailing nous and Terence's design and merchandising skills swung the shareholders behind the acquisitors.

With Burton preoccupied with digesting Debenhams, Terence was now free to pursue his own quarry. However, having seen the mud-slinging in the Burton bid, Terence was willing to proceed only if British Home Stores agreed to a merger. He knew he could count on the support of the head of Sainsbury's,

John Sainsbury, who had an edge-of-town food and clothing joint venture with BHS called Savacentre. John Sainsbury had made it clear to Terence that he was disappointed with BHS's management – not least because the BHS board had tried to poach Peter Davies, who was Sainsbury's managing director. Buoyed up by Sainsbury's support, Terence and Roger made their approach. British Home Stores believed Terence would give it the flair needed to lift the company and, because it was a merger rather than an acquisition, it also believed continuity could be maintained, with none of the blood-letting that was so prevalent in aggressive take-overs. The merger was agreed, and a new holding company, Storehouse, was created which offered Habitat shareholders 158 shares for every 100 held, while BHS shareholders had a one-for-one swap. The merger went through without being contested on 7 January 1986.

Generally the merger was positively received – the *Daily Telegraph* commented:

> BHS and Habitat have different needs, but this merger looks set to satisfy both. BHS is a cash rich company with slow sales growth and image problems . . . For Habitat 'image' has never been a problem. It has demonstrated its ability to sell fashion goods, whether they are clothes or furniture, in attractive surroundings. The problem is that its aggressive takeover policy of the last few years has left its liquidity stretched.

Ralph Halpern, however, was furious. Terence had certainly been disingenuous, and in many areas Debenhams and British Home Stores were direct competitors. The 20 per cent share option in Debenhams was withdrawn, and the 20 per cent floor space and use of Conran design services were questioned. Terence then managed to exacerbate the problem by writing an article for *Draper's Record* which called on Halpern to 'pull his finger out' and allocate Habitat space. Both sides were arguing that they could not spell out their intentions until they knew what the other was planning. The squabble drifted on for most of the year, and was settled only after Roger Seelig met with Derek Higgs of Warburg's (Burton's advisers). The Conran

Design Group would get the contract to redesign the Burton stores, a modest cash settlement and the possibility of some trading space in Debenhams for Habitat Mothercare, but the big design contract for the Debenhams galleria concept went to Fitch & Co.

The focus for the immediate future was on improving British Home Stores' performance. What Terence had taken on and believed he could change was BHS's product. His argument was exactly the same as when he had started Habitat: people can't buy well-designed goods if they aren't offered them. However, whereas Terence had essentially always operated in clearly targeted businesses with which he had personal empathy, with BHS he was taking on a mass-market store which was not directly related to his own lifestyle. Some were sceptical about his ability to make the transition, and with the benefit of hindsight some argued that the failure to transform BHS was attributable to this. His long-standing friend David Queensberry felt that 'Terence was like Augustus Caesar, who confused the Roman Empire with the world,' but the reality of the failing of BHS was complex, and Terence believes that people problems were the root of the failure, not the idea itself.

British Home Stores had been started in 1928 in East Ham by two American brothers who originally intended to compete with Woolworths at the lower end of the housewares market. With the depression of the early thirties this market positioning was fortunate, and by 1935 there were fifty-nine stores. After the war the company acquired more sites and changed its emphasis to compete more directly with the middle market, dominated then as now by Marks & Spencer. The company strategy was to provide core product lines plus ranges which M & S did not offer, such as lighting. However, British Home Stores was an underachiever, and couldn't match M & S for quality in those areas where they did compete; its sales per square foot were less than half those of Marks & Spencer. The requirement for change was obvious to everyone, but the first problem Terence faced was that change was difficult to implement.

The merger meant there was no dominant partner in the

relationship. Terence, as chairman, was the senior director, but underneath him was a large board composed of the erstwhile Habitat Mothercare directors and BHS directors, with both groups seeming to be pursuing their own agendas. As with Ryman Conran, there were two distinct cultures pulling in opposite directions. The Habitat Mothercare culture was largely a reflection of Terence's personality and values: it was informal – everyone called each other by their Christian names – entrepreneurial and open. People were encouraged to express their own points of view – to the extent of being rude. In contrast, British Home Stores was formal – everyone was 'Mr' – bureaucratic and factional. People didn't express their own views: they toed the line. Geoff Davy says:

> Within BHS there were tribes. As an employee, your first loyalty was to your boss, the second to your tribe and the third to the company. Instant death was embarrassing your boss in front of a competing tribe. Career over. There was a whole heritage of not saying what you thought. Terence was a bit naïve about this and would say, 'Why can't people tell me what they think? I'm just an ordinary bloke.'

Breaking down the factionalism which put 'tribes' in direct competition with each other and forging a new culture were prerequisites for success, but the nature of the balanced board stimulated rather than limited the warring between rivals. Roger Seelig says:

> You often get a problem of cultural differences in mergers. It's capable of being addressed if you try to establish a new culture that draws on the strength of both partners, but you can only do that if it's clear that there is group authority. So long as you allow there to be two camps under one holding company it's a nonsense – you haven't got a merger; the benefits don't come through. I came off the board when the merger happened, because I didn't believe in the concept.

The City was expecting quick results from the merger, so Terence was under some time pressure to pull things round. But even as the merger went through, the situation was exacerbated by reports of a poor Christmas and New Year at both Habitat Mothercare and BHS. One analyst commented that 'Trading turned sour the day after the merger was announced.' Increasingly Terence was being pulled away from where his real talents lay and into endless meetings which resolved very little.

In spite of the problems within the boardroom, Terence's view was that the same approach that had been used with Mothercare was the way to improve performance. This meant focusing on those areas where things could be changed quickly. The Conran Design Group had already been working on a store-modernization programme for BHS before the acquisition, and now the name was changed from the laborious and dated 'British Home Stores' to 'BHS'. The logo was reworked to be more colourful and exciting, and new graphics were developed to brighten up the stores. However, all this would have been purely cosmetic without some change to the product itself. Clothing was given priority, and a specialist studio was set up to work with the buyers to produce better-quality ranges. Terence's view was that the buyers needed to have some conviction about what they were doing – generally they hadn't because the BHS culture encouraged them to play safe. The standard approach to product development within BHS was for buyers to trawl the world for ideas, which they then had copied. Terence wanted to see 'simple, well-made clothes that are well cut and shaped in good-quality cloth in good colours'; mostly what he got was frills and cheap decoration. Terence, who was always a prodigious memo-writer, started firing off notes to the Storehouse board about the lack of creative thinking and the need for change in the product and its merchandising. He kept citing the American retailer, The Gap, as a perfect example of what could be achieved with simple but good quality wares.

Within a few months he was getting very frustrated with the lack of action. The retail consultancy Management Horizons had been analysing the company for some time, but Terence's view was that there was too much research and not enough leadership.

He wanted to see a focus on those areas where BHS could be the best in terms of value and design.

For a while he hoped that a more precise food offering could be an area of excellence – food occupied a large amount of footage in terms of both selling space and storage – but BHS simply wasn't big enough to compete with the likes of Sainsbury's and Tesco, and by the summer it was agreed to close down the company's food operations. This was dangerous in that it would reduce customer traffic in the stores, but Terence felt this could be compensated for by better ranges in such areas as clothing, accessories, books and stationery. He says, 'Food was losing money and we couldn't see how we could make it profitable, and there was some evidence that other parts of the store were underspaced. Being involved with food was emotionally appealing to me, but there seemed to be no future in it.'

The exit from food freed up space so things like clothing could be better presented, and it also provided the opportunity to carry out the galleria idea by introducing Richards, Habitat and Mothercare shops in the BHS space. The original intention had been to include NOW as well, but in the summer of 1986 the decision was made to close it. Terence had launched NOW in 1983 with some hubris – 'Does anyone think we can fail?' – however, the chain had lost its way. The original intention had been to focus on ten-to-sixteen-year-olds, but the range had been extended to include older age groups. This put NOW into a highly competitive sector where image was all-important, and the teenage market was put off by the connotations of a store so closely associated with Mothercare. High-street rents had been growing rapidly and NOW was not large enough to buy big quantities of product, both of which put margins under pressure, and, looking back, Terence also believes that the merchandise itself became less adventurous. If Terence had been operating NOW as a private company he would have tried to ride out the problems, as he had done with some frequency in the early days of Habitat, but the City was not prepared to wait. The short-termism of the City was one of Terence's ongoing irritations – 'If things didn't work immediately, you came under pressure to make changes.' The City reacted positively to the decisions on NOW and food, but there was some obvious scepticism about the value of retaining the previous BHS management, who had been guilty of long-term underperformance.

The new-look BHS was unveiled in September 1986. Although there was an on-going refurbishment programme, the graphic facelift was applied to all stores in one weekend and was then presented in the Kingston store to City analysts and investors. It was intended not only to make the shopping experience at BHS more pleasurable, but also to attract a younger customer, as well as the twenty-five-to-forty-five-year-olds who were BHS's core market. The project, called Exclamations, was meant to be a signal of change and was supported by a £2 million advertising campaign. It seemed to have a positive effect on performance – at the year end in March 1987, BHS profits had increased from £60 million to £70 million. However, there were fundamental problems developing elsewhere.

As high-street rents went up in the mid-1980s, Terence and the Board decided that the stocking policies of Mothercare had to be changed. In the mid-1970s Mothercare's systems had been held up as a paragon of efficiency. By the early eighties they were creaking, and by the mid-eighties they were coming apart. Part of the problem was that each store carried its own stock and made orders direct to its suppliers. This was anathema to Terence, who right from the first Habitat had believed in using as much shop space as possible for selling. Mothercare had basements full of stock, and because each outlet was buying individually there was no central control. A study was undertaken and it was decided to centralize stock in one warehouse from which each store could order stock when it needed it. A new warehouse was designed by Conran Roche and IBM EPOS units were installed in all the shops. Terence had already gone through a similar exercise with Habitat, with disastrous results; he encouraged the Mothercare management to use the best consultants available to advise on the change as he knew that it was fraught with danger. History repeated itself. Neither the warehousing nor the EPOS systems worked properly. Suddenly store managers, who before had always had the buffer of their below-stairs stocks, found themselves out of key product lines. Terence says:

> We had a huge problem with distribution – the stock was in the wrong places at the wrong time, and morale was very low. There were a lot of management recriminations. We'd done it before, so I was telling my executives to exercise caution, but the advice was ignored. Mothercare once had a completely dominant position in the market, but we let other people in.

The problem in a sense went deeper. The driving force behind all Terence's businesses had always been his own personal vision. In the early days, when there were managers who shared his beliefs, that vision was endemic throughout his companies. As the businesses grew, however, Terence was not able to exert such a direct influence, and often new managers came in with their own ideas. As Terence became focused on developing the group, he had to delegate to new people. Largely he held to the view that the managers leading the individual businesses should have responsibility for them, but this resulted in a succession of wrong turns that could have been averted if Terence had chosen to intervene. Although Terence was a perceptive man, he was also very trusting, and as a result he misjudged some people. Maurice Libby says:

> For years he was bad at delegating, and then when he did start to he overdelegated and the business got into the hands of all kinds of opportunists. He'd pick up new people and believe what they offered. And he did find a number of outstanding people. But equally he employed a number of damaging people. Some of us desperately tried to carry on his ethos, but the more newcomers there were the more we got swamped.

Habitat itself had a succession of chief executives who tried to steer the company in different directions. It seemed to be crying out for Terence to put his personal stamp back on it, but, as he now says,

'I think I listened to others too much.' The company moved away from its growing niche and increasingly into the mainstream market. Terence didn't want Habitat to be marginalized, but, rather than having a clear positioning as it grew, it started to see itself as competing with the large out-of-town home-furnishings retailers such as MFI, IKEA and Queensway. Product quality started to be compromised to compete in this sector – earning the company the soubriquet 'Shabitat' – and Habitat went out-of-town into MFI-like sheds. Not only did this confuse the image of Habitat, it also created horrendous logistical problems in servicing the rapidly increased scale of operations. Locations now started to be chosen on the basis of a broader market profile that was wholly inappropriate to the old concept. Habitat had become an organization driven by research and without a philosophy.

In contrast, France remained a successful part of the Habitat operation precisely because it retained its direction. The French team – Francis Bruguière, Yves Cambier and Michel Cultru – had been there since the beginning and believed in the original ideals of Habitat. They knew that it was a niche business, and the growth there was strictly controlled. Francis's view was that about twenty-six shops was the optimum number for the French market:

We were much more focused on a style-conscious market. In about 1987 I said, 'We must stop opening stores or we'll run into the UK's problem – we'll end up going to locations which are too small and conservative.' It was a vicious circle in the UK: the company had to create products that would appeal to the mass market – largely unsuccessfully – which then disappointed the core market. They were saying, 'What's happened to Habitat? It's lost its imagination.'

The shared beliefs also meant that delegating authority was not problematical in France. Francis Bruguière found that it was very clear what he was authorized to do and not to do. He says, 'Terence delegated well. I always had a clear direction – probably because I shared 99 per cent of his views.'

Terence knew he had to address the failings of the Storehouse group, and he finally decided to appoint a chief executive to help him steer it. This had been discussed for some time. Roger Seelig had been of the view before the merger with BHS that the management team wasn't strong enough. In fact Terence had once discussed the job with Roger, but Roger wanted to know what Terence meant by a chief executive: 'Did it mean making his coffee and doing the dirty jobs? We never quite got to what the role was.' Nevertheless he was tempted to accept the offer, and had discussed it with his boss at Morgan Grenfell. He knew he didn't want to do the job for more than a few years, so he wanted to see whether he could remain a non-executive director at Morgan Grenfell while he was with Habitat Mothercare. Morgan's turned him down. Additionally, Terence would only pay him £100,000, whereas Roger was already earning over £300,000. Terence was never keen to pay people too much – he was far too much the puritan, and had spent most of his life scraping through. Not only did he take a relatively small salary himself – £80,000 in 1985 – he also believed that people should be rewarded by performance. Compared to the million-pound salary that his fellow retailer Ralph Halpern took that year, the offer to Roger looked paltry. In the end Roger declined – but not before the idea had been discussed with the man who would later become the chief executive. Roger recalls:

> I thought it would be great fun to be chief executive. I liked Terence – loved him in a way. During the two months we talked about the job, I said I would only do it if I had the authority to recruit the best financial director. That was Michael Julien.

Terence and Roger had already met Michael Julien, before the BHS merger, when they were sniffing round the Littlewoods group of department stores, where he was a non-executive director. After Roger pulled out of the running for the chief-executive role, Terence decided to see whether Julien was interested. He needed someone who could deal with the administrative and financial side of the business – who could improve the systems and the controls. Julien seemed perfect. Originally trained as a chartered accountant, he had been a group financial director at BICC and was performing a similar role at Midland Bank, which was trying to extricate itself from its disastrous acquisition of Crocker in America. Terence invited Julien to meet the Habitat Mothercare board, but after the meeting the board decided it didn't want to proceed, and for a time the chief-executiveship was shelved, with Terence maintaining the responsibility.

The need for a chief executive became more accentuated after the creation of Storehouse. The job had been promised to Dennis Cassidy, who had been running British Home Stores, but Terence found it difficult to work with Cassidy, who seemed to be resistant to change and very conscious of his position. Terence knew that to be effective BHS had to be seen as more than a second choice to Marks & Spencer, yet in too many product areas BHS failed to compete. To Terence's mind, Cassidy was insufficiently focused on the core issues. Large sums of money – £10 million on the Oxford Street store – were being spent on refurbishment programmes and restaurants, but the products seemed to be receiving scant attention. With the rising costs, static sales and bureaucratic management, Terence decided to break the deadlock on the board – a new chief executive had to be appointed from outside the company, which meant the promise to Cassidy would be rescinded. Terence felt guilty about going back on an agreement, and it caused a huge furore and split the board even further into two camps. Cassidy decided his position was untenable, and in September 1987 he resigned.

His resignation coincided with an interest in Storehouse by potential acquisitors, who could see hidden value in the company. The first of these was Tony Clegg of Mountleigh, a fast-growing and acquisitive property company. Clegg's interest in the company was twofold – the values in the properties that Storehouse owned and a belief that the break-up value of the parts of the group was greater than the sum he was intending to pay. Roger had worked with Clegg and suggested he meet Terence. Clegg came down to Terence's house in Provence with Roger, and a possible offer was discussed. He was willing to pay 445 pence a share, which valued the company at £1.8 billion. Terence stood to make £132 million personally from the deal. Roger believed it was a very good offer, and thought Terence should force it through the Storehouse board. Terence was more ambivalent. The two years of 'warring barons' and the slow progress of the group had been frustrating, but on the other hand he still believed in the Storehouse concept. He decided the bid should be put to the company's advisers – Kleinwort Benson, Rowe & Pitman, and Scrimgeour Vickers – for their views. Their conclusion was that the company was worth more than was being offered and that the minimum offer would have to be 520 pence per share. The original offer was discussed by the Storehouse board and rejected; Clegg was told that he would have to go higher for any chance of acceptance. He was unwilling to do so, and with the intervention of Black Monday in October 1987, when share prices plummeted, he would in any case have had difficulty in carrying the deal through with his own shareholders.

The Mountleigh bid, however, encouraged others to try. In November 1987 a take-over vehicle called Benlox marshalled a bid for Storehouse. Led by the take-over specialist Peter Earl, Benlox was only a £45 million company, but, in spite of the fact that it was a share-exchange offer rather than for cash, Benlox's £2 billion bid had to be taken seriously. Benlox was suggesting that the amalgamation of the various companies under the Storehouse banner was not adding any value to the component parts, so the company should be broken down into six separate operations. Whereas the offer from Tony Clegg had had some merit, to Terence the Benlox bid was an irritation, and he spent much time touring round Storehouse's institutional investors, explaining the company strategy and convincing them to remain loyal to the existing team. Terence found that the institutions were nervous about the departure of Dennis Cassidy and also the slow rate of change at Storehouse. In the end, however, they backed him, and the Benlox bid collapsed in December — but they made it clear that they expected Cassidy to be replaced quickly.

The two candidates for the chief executive's role now put forward to the board by Terence were Michael Julien and Alan Smith, who was Marks & Spencer's senior man in America. Smith in many ways seemed ideal: he was an articulate man with wide interests who had top-level experience with Britain's foremost retailer. In contrast, Michael Julien's background was primarily financial, but he had built a good reputation with the City, who saw him as a 'sorter-outer'. He had spent most of 1987 resolving Guinness's problems in the wake of the Distillers affair. Alan Smith withdrew, which effectively left Michael Julien as the only candidate. Nevertheless, his interview with the board seemed anything but a courtesy: 'I was interviewed by the whole board for two hours. They were asking awkward questions not so much of me but of Terence, who sat in, because I was Terence's candidate.'

In spite of some reservations about his lack of retail experience, both the media and the City were positive about the appointment of Julien in February 1988. Like Roger Seelig, he had tried to make it clear that he was going to be his own man but would work in partnership with Terence. Terence himself had made it clear that his own tenure as chairman would end on his sixtieth birthday in October 1991, and that the forty-nine-year-old Julien was the heir apparent. He was hopeful about the new relationship:

'Where it would be perfectly just to criticise me was my failure to bring these two cultures (Habitat Mothercare and BHS) together and get them to work together,' he admits. 'I was not able to get BHS people to give up their fiefdoms. If I'd had Michael there it would have been no problem at all . . . I knew that Michael was exactly the person who would be complementary to me in the future direction of the company.'[1]

1. Anne Ferguson, *Management Today*, July 1988, p. 34.

Terence and Michael Julien, 1988

Terence, as he saw it, could get back to sorting out the product and its presentation, from which he had long been diverted – though even at the height of his involvement with corporate affairs he would still regularly attend the furniture fair in Milan. Rodney Kinsman recalls one year when he met Terence on the plane to Italy and they decided to tour the stands together. Terence ignored the famous designers and headed off down one of the side halls, which featured 'miles and miles of mediocrity'. At one of the stands, showing a range of garishly painted chairs, he stopped. Rodney couldn't understand why, but the display had one wooden chair unpainted to show customers its construction. The salesman tried to tell Terence it wasn't for sale, but Terence insisted it was the one he wanted. As Rodney says, 'It was a gem, and I suddenly realized what an eye he had.'

Although Terence got a certain buzz out of dealing with the City, it meant being tied up in company presentations to institutions, board meetings, shareholder meetings, and fending off bids – none of which he liked. As far back as 1979 he had said, 'I don't look forward with much enthusiasm to the problems of being chairman of a public company.' While the company was riding high and he had Roger Seelig by his side, however, he had got some fulfilment out of it – partly because Roger dealt with finance and the City. But now he was looking forward to Michael Julien taking over that side of the business.

Quite consciously, Terence had chosen Michael because he was the seeming opposite to himself in almost every way. This was starkly illustrated when Michael Julien arrived at Storehouse and had the opportunity to furnish his own office. Maurice Libby remembers that he chose rosewood units. However, dark rain-forest woods were taboo in Terence's eyes – morally and aesthetically – and when he found out he had the order changed to ash without telling Michael. No one knew whether they should inform the chief executive that his office had been changed, but eventually he was told and the order was changed back again. When the units arrived, Terence was annoyed. Michael's perception was that Terence kept interfering throughout their working relationship. Michael was determined to do what he wanted, but many of his ideas would be totally at odds with Terence's deepest beliefs. It was to be a relationship of conflict rather than harmony – starting with the choice of the wood of Michael's desk.

Within the rest of the group there had also been change. Francis Bruguière had become chief executive of Habitat, and Geoff Davy moved over to run BHS. Ray Nethercott, who was originally a BHS man, was put in charge of Habitat UK. With Michael's arrival Storehouse was restructured into four divisions, each of which reported to him. There was an urgent need to stem the problems. Group pre-tax profits in 1987/8 were £121 million, but Mothercare's profitability had plummeted with the distribution difficulties – from £35 million to £22 million – Habitat was stagnating, and BHS's turnover and profitability were showing only marginal increases. Although Habitat and Mothercare were causes for concern, it was BHS that needed the most radical surgery.

Terence's office in the Heal's building

Terence and Geoff Davy had already decided to implement a new version of the BHS in-store upgrade programme, called Exclamations II. As the merchandise itself had been improved, so it was seen to be important to have stores which created the right sort of ambience and showed off the product to best effect. Exclamations II had been exhaustively researched and tested in six stores, and sales had lifted by 42 per cent. Thirty million pounds had been allocated by the Storehouse board to implement Exclamations II in half the estate. There seemed to be cautious cause for optimism. However the space-management programme, involving the reallocation of space that had been freed by the exit from food retailing, was not proceeding as smoothly as planned.

The idea had seemed sound. More space had been allocated to clothing and to other Storehouse companies, such as Mothercare, Habitat and Richards. This should have created a clear positioning for BHS, based around the theme of 'the family store', which would distinguish it from Marks & Spencer and give customers a good reason for visiting. There were also two further potential benefits: the percentage of selling space in-store should have been improved, and the high-street space occupied by the stores that moved into the BHS sites could be sold. However, the reworking of the space had caused enormous disruption and had also resulted in some degree of cannibalization – the new shops within shops had taken business away from BHS. Terence had had the vision to create the new concept, but the implementation and management of it had been delegated. Terence says, 'The idea of putting Richards and Mothercare into under-utilized space seemed like a good idea, but it wasn't too competently done and it was too expensively done.'

The space problem was further exacerbated by the high levels of stock that BHS was carrying. Terence had been berating the board about this since the early days of the merger: his view was that stock should either be on the shop floor, in a separate warehouse, or at the supplier's factory. In reality very little had actually been done. Even after relinquishing food, the overall percentage of selling space was low, because of the huge area with stock sitting on it. Although it would dent the profits, Michael Julien's view was that old stock would have to be written off, and when the interim results were announced in November 1988 pre-tax profits had dropped by 29 per cent.

Everything that was going wrong within the store was compounded by the decline in high-street sales that started in the middle of 1988 and which heralded the onset of recession. Terence felt that the only way out of the impasse was to try to improve margins by cutting back on all unnecessary expenditure and adding more value to the product range by good use of design. He had been having a running battle to get the Storehouse board to think more carefully about the highly expensive refurbishing of stores. He found that a lot of money was being spent on research to make decisions, and then when something was agreed the BHS bureaucracy was causing budget overruns. When he visited the new stores, he was aghast to find such things as heavy teak doors being used in the staff areas. For someone who had spent a lifetime designing simple and economical shop interiors, the waste at BHS made him furious. Before Geoff Davy's arrival at BHS, he had also found every effort to involve the Conran Design Group thwarted by concerted foot-dragging. Even with Geoff at the helm, change was still difficult, because the other BHS directors tried to counter his initiatives. Irritated memos winged their way to him from Terence with regularity.

Even with Terence's whole-hearted attempts, something fundamental needed to be done to ensure the survival of the group, and, to give the company more focus, Michael Julien felt that some of the more peripheral activities would have to be sold. Terence was reluctant, but it was agreed that the profitable Savacentre joint venture would be sold to Sainsbury's and a 20 per cent shareholding in the French book and music retailer FNAC, which had been acquired in 1985, would also be sold. Michael says, 'At an early stage I realized Terence was like a magpie – he's a great collector of all sorts of jewels, such as the Heal's building and FNAC.'

At the end of 1988 the third potential acquisitor in just over a year came after Storehouse. The American arbitrageur Asher Edelman believed he could do better for the Storehouse shareholders than the present management. He started to acquire shares in Storehouse, and on 9 December he notified the company that he held nearly 21 million shares – 5 per cent of the company's equity. He was followed by the British arbitrageur David Rowland, who acquired 4.2 per cent. It was a worrying time, because it was clear that the institutional shareholders were disappointed by the performance of Storehouse and might well look for salvation elsewhere. Michael Julien brought in the

American investment bank Goldman Sachs to defend the company.

Edelman first wrote to Storehouse suggesting a meeting. He was rebuffed. He wrote again in January with more specific proposals, suggesting the breaking-up and sale of Storehouse assets. Again he was rejected. From the outset it was clear that the campaign was to be a public one – the initial exchange of correspondence between the two parties was published in the press by Edelman on both sides of the Atlantic – and for seven months Edelman harassed Storehouse. He appeared on television and radio, and gave press interviews. He talked about the terrible state of Storehouse and its poor management. The attention was very much focused on Michael Julien, who was convinced the American was using underhand tactics to get information on the company; Terence stayed out of the way. Edelman may have thought that he could get Terence on his side; however, in spite of all the problems of Storehouse, Terence was determined to ride out the problems if he could. By July 1989 Edelman had neither made a bid nor managed to stimulate anyone else into doing so, and the regulatory authorities ruled that the phoney war could not go on. Edelman was forbidden from making a full bid for Storehouse for a year. He decided to increase his shareholding to 8.9 per cent, but by the autumn he was carrying a $20 million loss on the investment. The bid had been fought off, but it had been a costly and time-consuming exercise for a company that needed to have all its attention focused on the job in hand.

Exclamations II had been implemented in the autumn, but it wasn't achieving the results expected of it. The merchandise wasn't as good as it had been in the spring, when the pilot store test had been undertaken, and the logistics of implementation caused some disruption. Terence also felt that the style in which it was installed was dour and underlit. The previous failings of BHS's management to effect positive change had encouraged Michael Julien to seek outside advice, and the problems with Exclamations II confirmed his view.

Almost as soon as he had been appointed as chief executive,

Michael brought in Bain & Co. – the American-owned management consultancy that had been working at Guinness. Terence maintained a healthy disregard for consultants – especially expensive ones – as his previous experience of employing expert advice had been almost wholly negative. He believed that the experience of management was the key to directing a business, not the views of consultants, who were likely to obfuscate the real issues. One of his favourite cartoons is of a well-dressed tramp on Wall Street selling matches with a sign round his neck saying, 'I lost it all on expert advice.' Geoff Davy says, 'Michael didn't know a lot about retailing, so he was reliant on the advice of others. He discriminated against advice from the managers within the organization – we were tarred with the brush of diminishing profits.'

Michael also sought advice from his investment bankers, Goldman Sachs. They advised him to stop thinking about BHS as a problem and to see it as an opportunity. They suggested that Storehouse employ someone who knew how to turn round a large-space retailer. Michael says, 'It was that meeting in March 1989 which decided me to remove Terence's appointee, Geoff Davy, and then to start a search for a new chief executive for BHS. It was a terrible disappointment to Terence – Terence had a great affection for him – but, to be fair, he didn't make a big fuss over it.'

Geoff Davy was followed by Francis Bruguière, who resigned because he felt Terence had become too removed from the business. Francis missed Terence's involvement, and had become convinced that Terence would soon leave the company.

A gap was opening up between Terence and Michael Julien. Terence had begun to lose the team that had grown up with Habitat, and he was increasingly isolated. This was emphasized physically in the summer of 1989 when Michael Julien took over Terence's atrium-lit office in Tottenham Court Road and Terence removed himself to an office in Butlers Wharf. Partly this was because he was worried about the Butlers Wharf development, but it was also a way of reducing the discomfort he was feeling. Michael was a serious man, who had a disciplined and analytical approach to business and believed in taking the advice of the consultants he employed – although most of Bain's advice was never acted upon. This was in direct contrast to Terence's intuitive approach, which treated the interpretation of research with caution and trusted to gut feeling. Rather than complementing each other, they had begun to conflict. Looking back, Terence's view is that he didn't appreciate how much Michael Julien wanted to put his own personal seal on the business. Roger Seelig endorses this view: 'I believe to this day that Terence's and Michael's skills were entirely complementary, and if they could have worked together they would have been the most magnificent partnership. I think Michael was naughty in that he was overambitious and sought too much power.'

Michael now began to build his own team around him. He believed that the big-space retailer he was looking for would have to come from America. The man that he found was David Dworkin. Dworkin, who was in his mid-forties, had been buying director at Saks Fifth Avenue, and had also worked for the big department stores Neiman Marcus and Bonwit Teller. Terence had reservations about someone who had always worked in up-market stores. Although he was trying to inject style into it, BHS was much more prosaic than Saks Fifth Avenue. The fluffy slippers and frilly underwear were still staples of the BHS range, in spite of his best efforts:

Once I held up a pair of particularly awful knickers and asked who on earth would wear them, except a tart. One was treading on people's toes with that – especially the knicker buyer, who no doubt thought they were jolly nice knickers and had fantasies about wearing them.

Michael Julien believed that Dworkin would bring with him a degree of objectivity and ruthlessness that couldn't be found in a Briton; Terence remained sceptical.

In the summer of 1989 there was a dinner for Maurice Hodgson and Ian Peacock, who were retiring as non-executive directors on the board. The appointment was discussed, and it was agreed that Dworkin should be taken on as chief executive of BHS. Michael Julien negotiated a package which enabled Dworkin 'to make a lot of money' over the space of a four-year contract – the last year of which yielded a salary of over £400,000 and a bonus of $4 million. Terence was absolutely disgusted at the huge disparity between what shop staff were paid – about £6,000 – and Dworkin's package. He says, 'I was horrified by the appointment of Dworkin, and I was even more horrified by the terms of his contract. I think it was one of the most disgraceful things that happened at Storehouse.'

Dworkin arrived in the autumn of 1989. He was a hard-nosed retailer with a big ego who wanted to run BHS his way. His first actions suggested Terence was absolutely right to be sceptical about his appointment – the initial range that Dworkin presided over was very clearly American-influenced and a complete disaster. He also sacked 900 people in head office and the stores, many of whom were Terence's appointees. Michael Julien fully supported Dworkin's radical action.

There were also other new appointments which diminished Terence's influence. Ann Iverson, who had worked at Blooming-dales and Bonwit Teller, was brought in as stores director for BHS, Barbara Deichmann, who had also worked at Bloomingdales, joined as styling director of Habitat, and Michael Harvey, who had worked in management consultancy and at Viyella, had come in as the new chief executive of Habitat. All of Terence's people, including his merchandise director, Jan Kern, and his sister, Priscilla, were overlooked for key positions. Gradually they either left or were pushed – including Priscilla – and Terence was pretty much powerless to stop them going. He tried to reassert his authority, but he knew he couldn't put the clock back and that he couldn't raise the stakes. Although the institutions had been amused by his speech at the 1989 Storehouse annual meeting, when he said, 'I stand here clothed in humility and a BHS suit,' he knew they would not look kindly on a war between him and Michael Julien.

Terence realized his position was getting more difficult, and it also began to get uncomfortable when Michael Harvey started a process of what he called deConranization – of abandoning what were left of the original Habitat principles. Michael Harvey believed that the key to developing the business was America. The company had only sixteen stores in the USA, and it was his view that this market needed money pumping into it to fund expansion. Pauline Dora had developed the merchandise in America so that it was more clearly tailored to the market: half the product range duplicated what was sold in Europe but half was exclusive. She had also pushed prices higher, as the more affluent Americans were willing to pay more than Europeans for the Conran style. Pauline too was keen to expand the American operation faster, but, like other managers in the group, she felt there had been a lack of direction, and she wanted Terence's support and involvement. Instead, as he got drawn more and more into trying to sort out BHS, she got a succession of different bosses with different agendas.

Like Habitat in France, with its *branché* customers, Conran's in America under Pauline tried to keep a focus on its largely 'yuppie' market. However, Habitat in the UK was still trying to broaden its customer base, and it was felt that the American operation ought to be following suit. Fiercely loyal to Terence as she was, Michael Harvey decided that Pauline Dora was an obstacle to progress in the USA and had her fired.

A similar scenario occurred in France, and Harvey was soon in conflict with the French chief executive. Harvey had brought in another Bloomingdales émigré, Glen Senk, to run a coordinating operation, Habitat International. Senk tried to push the organization into focusing more on china and glass, but the French resented the intrusion into their affairs and simply refused to cooperate with his plans.

By the Christmas of 1989, virtually all of Terence's allies had gone. Michael Julien went to see Terence at Barton Court between Christmas and New Year. The meeting wasn't stormy: unlike Terence's relationship with Michael Tyson, which had been aggressively confrontational, Michael Julien and Terence disagreed in a rather gentlemanly way. However, their positions had become directly opposed. Terence needed to be in control of what he was doing, but he found himself without real influence. He was proud and energetic, but his energies were being marginalized. The position Michael Julien was offering was that of figurehead – something that was impossible for Terence to accept. He decided he wanted to get out of Storehouse. An agreement was reached with Michael Julien, which was then confirmed with the board: Terence would buy back The Conran Shop and move to a non-executive position.

For Terence, who had always been such an optimist, his inability to run Storehouse in the way he believed necessary was very depressing. Caroline Conran says, 'Terence's leaving Storehouse devastated him. He bounced back from it in a way, but I think it changed his outlook on life and made him pessimistic.'

A few months before his meeting with Michael Julien, the American magazine *Forbes* had written an article which dated Terence's slide into the 'discreet humility of a powerless chairmanship' from the time he had agreed to appoint a new chief executive. *Forbes* wrote Terence off – 'it is all a rather tarnished ending to an otherwise brilliant career' – Storehouse had been a failure, and Michael Julien was in control. But Terence didn't regret what he had tried to achieve with Storehouse. He had seen it as a golden opportunity to bring well-designed goods to the mass market. The successes of Next and Mothercare and other retailers such as The Gap had convinced him of the viability of the strategy, but the reality was that BHS was imbued with a culture that was resistant to change. Terence lacked the right lieutenants to overcome that, and he was too stretched to impose his vision. The *Forbes* obituary was also premature: his departure from Storehouse was merely the end of one career and the start of another.

CHAPTER ELEVEN

BOUNCING BACK

Nineteen ninety represented a low point in Terence's life. Having spent forty years building up an empire, he suddenly found himself with much less to do. He had planned his retirement for several years, but Terence's concept of retirement was not connected with having more leisure time, merely with leaving Storehouse and pursuing other ventures. Terence's attitude to such things as 'golf' or 'sailing' was always sneering: what he needed was projects. As Jasper says, 'The worst thing for my father is not to have enough projects.' He had bought The Conran Shop for £3.5 million and had become joint president of the design part of the French advertising group RSCG, which had bought the Conran Design Group. He also had a furniture workshop, restaurants and The Design Museum to oversee – a not inconsiderable workload for a retiree. However, it was not enough, and in the space of the three years following his 'retirement' Terence created a new empire – smaller, but more cohesive and, from his point of view, more enjoyable.

Many of these ventures had their origin in the eighties, when he had been creating Storehouse. The Conran Shop, which had been launched on the original site of Habitat in the Fulham Road, had moved in 1987 across Sloane Avenue to the Michelin Building – the former British headquarters of the French tyre company. Terence had bought the building some two years earlier with Paul Hamlyn, with whom he had set up a publishing venture, Conran Octopus, to produce high-quality illustrated books – including his own – in areas such as cookery, homes and gardens. Terence had always loved the wit of Michelin's corporate symbol, Mr Bibendum – the inflatable tyre man so often seen perched on the cabs of French trucks smoking Monte Cristo cigars – and he had long coveted the Michelin Building.

The renovated Michelin building, 1987

Built in 1911, it was a strange mixture of styles. There were elements of art nouveau, Edwardian design and also art deco – even though the building predates the style. Glazed tiles in various colours clad the front of the structure, the columns carried tyre-shaped cylinders at the top, and originally there were three big stained-glass windows featuring Mr Bibendum. The Fulham Road frontage featured a large drive-in tyre bay. Although the styling was eclectic, it possessed a unity and charm that was wholly appropriate to Michelin. When Terence and Paul Hamlyn set about renovating the building, they were keen to preserve as much of the original structure as possible. The tyre bay and its tiling were restored and the stained-glass windows and tyre cylinder turrets, which had been removed, were re-created. However, there were entirely new

The Conran Shop in the Michelin Building, 1987

elements. Two new floors were added and to replace the loading-bay at the back of the building, a glass-fronted building facing Sloane Avenue was designed by Conran Roche. This was to be the main frontage of The Conran Shop, which was to occupy some 32,000 square feet. The glass wall provided a highly visible fascia and the interior featured wooden floors, subtle lighting, and stainless steel handrails. The external structure and shape of the building were reminiscent of a grand passenger ship, and the interior with its light space and central staircase continued the theme.

Almost from the moment that work began on the structure of the new building, Priscilla began work on the product. The shop would be more than three times the size of the previous one, so the ranges had to be rethought. Priscilla started from the beginning and reviewed everything. If she thought something could be bettered, it was replaced. With managing director Geoff Marshall and buying director Polly Dickens she built the products up into departments tailored to the specific needs of customers, each section of the store having its own identity within the umbrella of a consistent style. There was an extensive cookware department, featuring original ethnic cooking utensils – everything from pasta-makers to yakitori skillets – a home-office section offering stylish desks and accessories, and of course extensive ranges of furniture and fabrics. The furniture was a mixture of modern classics, Shaker styles, and products designed and produced by Terence's workshop. The shop seemed to have chosen the best and most interesting products from the four corners of the world – which was indeed the case. It was expensive, sophisticated, modern and exciting – 'the most exciting new store since Biba.'

In many ways, Terence's 'dream store' had taken him back to where the first Habitat started: it had the same consistency of style that had created such a stir some twenty-three years before. The product took two years to select and was largely chosen by Priscilla, but of course Terence's eagle eye was also passed over the range. In fact there was very little they disagreed about – they have an amazing similarity in taste. Terence likes to tell how he and Priscilla once independently looked at thousands of Indian rugs and ended up making an identical choice of the best two dozen styles.

The Conran Shop was only part of the new enterprise. The front of the building featured a stained-glass window of Mr Bibendum quaffing a glass of wine to the words 'Nunc est Bibendum' – 'Now is the time to drink' – and the motif was repeated in mosaic on the entrance floor. Originally the phrase had been part of the company slogan 'Nunc est Bibendum, Le Pneu Michelin Boit l'Obstacle', but it acquired a new connotation with the company's involvement in creating the *Michelin Guide* to the best restaurants in France. Terence had been hankering to create a new restaurant: now he had the space and the opportunity – and also it seemed the exhortation – to do so.

And there seemed to be a real appropriateness in creating a restaurant in the building that had housed the company that had created an awareness of good French cooking.

Terence's desire to open another restaurant had been fermenting in his mind for some time. In 1984 he and Caroline had gone out to dinner at a restaurant in South Kensington called Hilaire, where the chef was Simon Hopkinson. They had all met briefly once before, when Terence had been thinking of buying a house in Cheyne Walk, Chelsea, where Simon had been the in-house chef. Terence was very taken with Simon's strong-flavoured but simple food and said that if he ever wanted backing to open his own restaurant he should call. Simon telephoned the next day, and a five-minute meeting followed some weeks later. Terence tended to think that all chefs were prima donnas, but Simon seemed down-to-earth and unassuming. He came from Bolton, in Lancashire, and had learned his trade from a rotund French chef called Yves Champeau at the Normandie in Birtle. He had run his own restaurant in Wales and had worked for the *Egon Ronay Guide*. When he met Terence he had just turned thirty and looked rather cherubic. Terence knew what a success Simon had made of Hilaire and was confident of his abilities. If Simon could provide the quality of food, Terence could provide the design and the direction. Simon was charged with finding a site. Initially he looked around Fulham and Chelsea and found some interesting possibilities, but Terence had already begun thinking about the Michelin Building and in June 1985 he acquired the site. Terence then suggested that Simon stay at Hilaire until they were ready to start the detailed planning. A year later Simon and the manager of the restaurant, a young New Zealander called Joel Kissin, left Hilaire and joined Terence.

Simon found the next few months miserable:

Terence is very good at planning, but I'm not. I hated all the meetings deciding what we were going to do. And I missed cooking. I used to go to Barton Court at weekends to cook. For me those few months were the worst period of my life.

However, there was an enjoyable part — deciding the menu. Just as Terence had done with Kasmin for The Neal Street Restaurant, Terence and Simon went and sampled other people's foods and drew up menus of the things they liked. The idea was to have a big à la carte menu – predominantly French, but also including Italian and Thai influences, using the best ingredients. There would be both classic dishes – *steak au poivre*; lemon sole with tartare sauce – and new ideas, such as ox tongue with beetroot and horseradish. What there wouldn't be was *nouvelle cuisine* or fussy food. Terence's attitude to cooking was not unlike his attitude to design – he liked authenticity, robustness, simplicity, substance; he hated unnecessary decoration and preciousness. He trusted in Elizabeth David's dictum '*faites simple.*' Simon remembers going to a well-known restaurant in Valence in south central France and having a huge slab of beef surrounded by a dainty array of vegetables, 'Terence thought it a very dull meal – he called it "hunca munca food".'

The restaurant space was on the first floor of the building, on the corner of Sloane Avenue and the Fulham Road. It was the part with the most character, but it was also the part with most listed features, which created problems with ducting. Terence, as he had so often done in the past, fused the old with the new – 'It had to link through to the heritage of Mr Bibendum.' The stained-glass windows were re-created and combined with elements of modernity. Like the food, the interior was designed to be simple and stylish. Terence was intimately involved with the design of every detail, and he took great care to create the right ambience – somewhere between the hushed grandeur of old-established restaurants and a brasserie. He says, 'Bibendum is the least compromised restaurant as regards my personal taste. I'm very proud of it.' There were elements of Hoffmann in the geometric patterns, chairs made by Thonet for the Vienna Post Office in the waiting-area, and tub chairs covered in fabrics by Jasper. All the other furniture was designed by Terence and made by Benchmark.

Much of the budget of £650,000 was spent on the look of the restaurant, whereas, at the time, Simon Hopkinson thought more of it should have been spent on the kitchen.

Terence and I argued about what to spend money on. I wanted a special oven – which in retrospect was wrong – while he wanted to spend money on buying a dozen Post Office chairs. Now I see the reason for it, but in those days, all I could think of was the food.

What Terence recognized was that restaurants – like shops – need to start with the customer. Traffic flows have to be considered; the food has to be presented and merchandised; there has to be an appeal to all the senses and a high quality of service. Terence's restaurants always look and smell beautiful. At Bibendum, there would be fresh flowers and a lot of attention paid to the quality of light both during the day and at night. The menu itself would be developed, and even Jasper's seat covers would be changed according to the season. Waiter stations were positioned throughout the restaurant, both to break up the space and to help with speed of service. Everything, from the plates to the building, was branded consistently with Mr Bibendum's organic shape, and downstairs in the entrance hall was a display of crustacea which in its plenty and sumptuousness was reminiscent of the sculptural stacked displays of the early Habitats. What Terence was able to do was to create a unity between the food and the interior.

Bibendum opened to very good reviews and full houses. Joel Kissin thinks that, although Simon's food was good at Hilaire, under Terence's guidance it got even better at Bibendum – 'more muscular, simpler and better tasting'. There was a general feeling that the restaurant was expensive, but this was hardly surprising given the staffing levels: the emphasis on quality and service meant that there was a staff of seventy-five to serve seventy-four covers. In spite of this ratio, the first eighteen months were problematic, for the large à la carte menu at both lunch and dinner-time meant that food was often very slow coming out of the kitchen. But after this initial period, with a simplified menu and the experience of running the restaurant, Bibendum started to deliver consistently good food and service. By keeping the back-of-house operation spartan, Joel and Terence also managed to make it profitable. Although somewhat ironically the *Michelin Guide* has failed to decorate Mr Bibendum with its stars, it was later chosen as Restaurant of the Year (1992) by *The Restaurant Show*.

Once Bibendum was under way, restaurants began to absorb more of Terence's attention. He'd always seen being a restaurateur as a hobby, not a career; however, in 1989 he opened a new restaurant in The Design Museum, called The Blueprint Café. Whereas Bibendum was aimed at a specific gap in the market, The Blueprint Café was partly a result of having an available site on the mezzanine floor of the museum. Terence believed that it would be used by visitors to the Design Museum and also by local and City businessmen.

Almost three years after The Boilerhouse had closed at the V & A, The Design Museum itself had been opened in July 1989 by Margaret Thatcher, who had become a convert to the value of design in industry. Although the museum would come in for some criticism, mainly for placing the banal on a pedestal and thereby celebrating consumption – 'design become a commodity, ready to be marketed as style' – it was immediately popular, with 40,000 visitors in the first three months. It contained a permanent collection of twentieth-century artefacts such as chairs, cars, washing-machines and telephones; one-off shows on subjects such as corporate identity; and a review section which presented an international survey of new products and prototypes. The review section was Terence's response to the things he had missed as a student. Whereas he could only read about Eames's chairs in *Art and Architecture*, students were now able to see products that had never appeared on the British market.

> Practising designers and design students can therefore scrutinize products which they may have read about or seen pictured in the design press, but which they have never examined 'in the flesh'.

The Blueprint Café itself was radically different from Bibendum, as befitted a more relaxed eating occasion. With its river views and large balconies, it had a Mediterranean feel. The interior was mostly white, with wooden floors. There were more Thonet chairs, and

The Blueprint Café in the Design Museum

furniture designed by Terence. The waiter stations were placed around the structural pillars and decorated with jars of pickled vegetables. The food was simpler and cheaper than at Bibendum, but also more eclectic and fun. The chefs, Lucy Crabb and Rod Eggleston, who had come from Bibendum, produced dishes that owed much of their heritage to Californian and Italian cuisine, but there were also English and French dishes – grilled goat's cheese with rocket and roast peppers featured alongside plaice and chips. The Blueprint Café was Terence in a light mood.

Although in the late eighties Terence was still in the heat of the Storehouse kitchen, he was pursuing his other interests avidly. Some would argue that he was too widely spread and not in real control. However, it was always in Terence's nature to need the stimulus of new adventures, and the more his chairmanship of a public company removed him from the designing and making of products that he loved, the more he felt the need to find outlets for his ideas. The restaurants in part met this need, as did the workshop which he created at his home in Barton Court. The workshop took over the offices in the stable-block that had been vacated when the design group returned to London. There was a romance for Terence in re-creating his earliest days as a designer/craftsman, but he couldn't commit much time to his idyll, so he decided to advertise for a furniture-maker. Sean Sutcliffe, who was just completing his studies in furniture design and making at John Makepeace's school at Parnham, applied and came for an interview with Terence one Sunday. Sean recalls:

> When I came for the interview, Rogers the butler let me in and showed me into a room. Then this chap came shuffling in with the coffee, in a pair of shabby trousers and wearing an old shirt. I thought he was another butler. He started chatting away, and I then realized it was Terence.

Terence offered him a job straight away. Sean joined another furniture-maker, Ed Nicholson, and they set about working on ad-hoc projects.

Initially most of the work was in making prototypes for Habitat, but after a few years the relationship was formalized in a company, called Benchmark, with Terence and Sean as partners. (Ed Nicholson decided to remain working in the stables but didn't want to become involved in the partnership.) Terence was following a familiar pattern. He always liked to have the people he worked with share in his ventures, partly because he regarded most of the people he worked with as his friends. Once people dropped out of his working environment, however, he would still regard them as his friends but the initiative to maintain the relationship would have to come from them. Terence was never a person to call anyone for a casual chat – there had to be a relevance to his life for him to make the first move. Many people have found it difficult to get to know him, but those who have have found it worthwhile. Sean says:

Underneath the bullying exterior, Terence is very kind. He wants things to happen for other people; he certainly wanted Benchmark to happen for me. I've seen him support a lot of people in a lot of enterprises.

Benchmark would be as much Sean's as Terence's. Similarly Simon Hopkinson is a partner at Bibendum, and Joel Kissin is a shareholder in all the restaurants.

To fund the start-up of Benchmark, Terence provided Sean with a tiny budget of some £7,000 to buy equipment and machinery. Although Terence could have afforded more, he was again trying to make it clear that Benchmark was to be a business like any other – that it would have to make money to justify investment. Terence liked the romantic elements of arts and crafts, but he also believed wholeheartedly in things being commercial. He was also acutely aware that a small business like Benchmark couldn't afford to be wasteful. He had always had a strange mixture of generosity and parsimony. John Mawer remembers that back in the early sixties Terence used to pull pieces of paper out of his wastebasket and leave a note asking why they hadn't been used. With Benchmark, it was the offcuts of wood that attracted his attention. On Fridays, the offcuts for the week would be sent over to the main house for use as firewood. Sometimes they would come back with the value of the wood written on them with suggestions that they could be used for book-ends or photo-frames – both of which Benchmark now sells. However, Terence could be remarkably inconsistent in his attitude to spending money. Sean says:

Terence hates to spend money on something he thinks we don't need. He'll say, 'What's this bill for servicing the fire extinguishers? Absolutely outrageous – £25.' Give him a bill for £100 for eating out and he'll just say, 'Good meal?'

Benchmark really began to develop as a business with the commission to make the furniture for Bibendum and products for The Conran Shop. Mostly Sean would meet the buyers to determine their requirements and would then discuss the products with Terence. Terence would come down to Barton

Court on Friday evening, often in a bad mood from having sat in traffic jams on the motorway – he could rarely be philosophical about such things – and Saturdays would then be devoted to work. Sean would brief Terence on what was required and Terence would then loosely sketch out ideas. The day would be broken up by lunch, which Terence would sometimes cook, and perhaps a walk round the garden or a read

Chair design by Terence and made by Benchmark

of the papers. Occasionally Sean would convert Terence's sketches into detailed drawings, but mostly he would go straight to a prototype.

Terence's designs always had a typical robustness and simplicity – simple lines and forms, but executed with attention to detailing. This was Terence at his most confident. Drawing on a lifetime's knowledge of making and selling, he knew the right look and materials. Sometimes his sources of inspiration would be very personal – he designed a cabinet full of little drawers reminiscent of a lepidoptery case, and also tables with spindly legs, bearing a resemblance to his fifties furniture – but other designs showed him at his derivative best. He still liked to take shapes and ideas and adapt them to his own needs, and his designs for a piece of furniture would sometimes include a cutting from a magazine with an element that he wanted to use. Sean says:

People accuse Terence of plagiarism, but what he does is find an element or an essence of something that he thinks is worth while and he'll want to use it. What he won't do is a direct knock-off – he's adamantly against that. Sometimes the buyers will say they want something that they've seen elsewhere, but Terence would always say, 'You can't just copy it.'

As Benchmark grew on the back of the work for The Conran Shop, so there was a need for more staff. Steve Stonebridge, who had been manager of the Heal's cabinet-making factory, joined and an apprentice scheme was started.

Terence got a lot of joy from Benchmark and its steady growth (turnover reached £800,000 in 1994), and he enjoyed Sean's company – partly because Sean was prepared to stand up to him. Sean recalls that at first he was intimidated by Terence and his ranting and raving, but because the business was in Terence's home he soon got to know him on a deeper level. That vulnerability that Priscilla recognized was also obvious to Sean, who says, 'I got through the suit of armour quite quickly.' Sean realized that Terence had tantrums largely because he couldn't compartmentalize his life. He had always merged home and business together – although business tended to dominate –

and so was unable to separate problems in one area from the other. If things were going badly in his personal life it would affect business, and vice versa.

In spite of the tension that Terence could create, Sean was always aware of his honesty and generosity and humour. Generally the latter is not very sophisticated. Caroline says of him that, like his mother, his preferred jokes are about nuns or bottoms – or preferably nuns' bottoms. Terence also rather enjoys embarrassing people. On one occasion Terence, Sean and Simon Hopkinson were driving down through France and stopped overnight at a hotel in Burgundy. Two rooms had been booked in advance. Terence was to have one room and Simon and Sean were to share the other. When the door to the first was opened there was one big double bed. Simon and Sean looked at each other. Behind them they could hear Terence chortling. Sean says, 'I was sure Terence had set us up, although he swore he hadn't.'

Even though Terence was enjoying considerable success with his restaurants, The Conran Shop and Benchmark, he also suffered at the end of the eighties, from the onset of recession. This impacted not only on the performance of Storehouse but also on his long-cherished development at Butlers Wharf. This had suffered from problems since the beginning. The main Butlers Wharf building which fronted on to the Thames was to be restored rather than redeveloped. When the building was originally surveyed, the foundations were checked at one end only, and were found to be in good order. When work began, it was discovered that the other end of the structure had no foundations. A massive and costly project had to be undertaken to underpin the structure.

The next-door building, called Wheat Wharf, again had no foundations, and was Grade-II listed. Rather than try to renovate it, Conran Roche designed an all-new large glass box. The intention was to have the street, Shad Thames, that ran along the back of the Butlers Wharf building continue through what was called Spice Quay. The street would thus become a glass-covered walkway. There was to be a large brasserie opening on to the quayside and a glazed riverside façade that would be lit at night. Spice Quay was to be the focal point of the Butlers Wharf development, and Terence had interested the computer company Logica in the building, but English Heritage put a block on the development by objecting to the removal of the existing building to another site, despite the fact that they recognized that it had to be rebuilt because of the foundations problem. Conran Roche appealed against the decision, but this was an inevitably lengthy process, and by the time the appeal had gone through and permission had been granted the recession was in full swing and the commercial property market had collapsed.

The development was having difficulties. Fred Roche had become terminally ill with cancer, Terence was fighting his corner at Storehouse, and no one was interested in acquiring property. The project needed a tough full-time manager, but there was no one available. The cutlery designer and manufacturer David Mellor built a high-tech building designed by the architect Michael Hopkins, and the Association for Business Sponsorship of the Arts had taken space in Nutmeg House, where Conran Roche had its offices; otherwise, nothing much on the eleven-acre site was moving. Butlers Wharf Ltd had borrowed heavily to fund the £90 million development and now couldn't service the interest. Terence was desperate to save the project if he could. He put in more of his own money and tried to restructure the borrowings with the bank. However, the constructors of the project, McAlpine, decided to put in a large bill for extra work. Terence and his professional advisers felt the bill was unjustified – if anything, they felt there should be a claim against McAlpine – but it made the bank nervous, and in December 1990 Butlers Wharf Ltd went into receivership.

Coming after the problems at Storehouse, this made it seem that Terence had lost his touch. He had long enjoyed a very good press, but there was now some carping and Terence's natural ebullience was dampened. To the outside world he erected his façade of quiet confidence, but those close to him could see the effect of the problems. Terence's way out of this situation was to find yet more projects. He needed to prove something both to himself and to other people.

The Riverfront at Butlers Wharf

With the completion of the main Butlers Wharf building, Terence had taken a suite with views over the river. Now that the opportunity to develop Spice Quay had disappeared, Terence decided to switch his attentions to opening a restaurant on the quayside of Butlers Wharf to be called Le Pont de la Tour. This time the vision was on a grander scale than before. Although his funds had been seriously depleted by the collapse in share values, he was still wealthy enough to conceive of a complex of food-related activities. And there were again to be analogies with the original conception of Habitat.

Along with the decline of commercial property values, residential sales had all but dried up – especially in London's Docklands, where the opportunity to generate local custom for a restaurant was consequently diminished. Terence knew that to pull custom from across the river, and from the City in particular, his new restaurant would have to be special. As with the Fulham Road in 1964, most people were sceptical about Terence's choice

of location – 'Everyone said, "Who's going to go there?"'
Nevertheless Terence had an emotional commitment to Butlers
Wharf and believed in its long-term viability. The question was,
would it work in the short term? Terence was extremely anxious
about it. Keith Hobbs, who worked on the design of it with
him, says:

In restaurants, Terence's biggest self-doubt was Le Pont de la Tour. He was
very twitchy and kept asking, 'What do you think people will say?' and 'Do you
think they'll come?' It was very risky, but Terence has got balls.

Rather than just drawing people to a restaurant, Terence decided
to generate custom by also offering a wine merchant, a food store
and a bakery – what someone suggested he call the Gastrodrome:
'a collection of food-related activities which appeal to those who
are particularly interested in the variety and quality of food and
drink.' The idea was that each component would generate
custom for the other and would create a total identity. Des
Gunewandena, Conran Holdings financial director, says, 'The
shops provide a service and give the area a sense of quality of
experience which benefits the businesses as a whole.' The
restaurant itself which opened in 1991 was conceived at various
levels. For people who wanted a quick meal there was a bar and
grill; for those with more time and wanting to indulge themselves
there was the main restaurant, and for those who were interested
in a private occasion there was the *salon privé*. Terence had
already tried a similar concept at Bibendum by offering a
downstairs bar, originally run by his son Tom, which offered
lighter and cheaper meals.

The total space was some 10,000 square feet, offering 250
seats. To design the restaurant Terence was reunited with Keith
Hobbs. Keith had originally been at the Conran Design Group in
the sixties and had worked on the design of The Neal Street
Restaurant, before leaving to work for himself. He says, 'Terence
and I are like one of those George Burns jokes. We worked so
well together on our first restaurant that it took us twenty years
to get another one organized.'

The Oyster Bar at Bibendum

The Oil and Spices shop at Butlers Wharf

Le Pont de la Tour was a long narrow space. Terence had already conceived of the idea and designed it, but he needed someone like Keith to make it work – a role that Oliver Gregory had fulfilled before he left the group in the mid-1980s. The interior space was elegant and cool with much use of white, which was offset by Terence-designed bur-oak chairs inspired by the dining-rooms of the *Normandie* liner. Caricatures by Sem of early-twentieth-century Parisian café society lined the wall. A huge wire chandelier of shellfish by the designer Tom Dixon was to adorn the entrance to the informal bar and grill, and there was a marble crustacea bar covered in seaweed and ice for langoustines, oysters and lobsters. Terence also decided to make the kitchens visible both to the customers and to people walking down Shad Thames. He believed it was wrong to cut off the kitchen from the dining-area – it was part of the spectacle, and he personally always enjoyed watching people cook. David Burke, who had been a sous chef at Bibendum, came over to be chef director and partner in the venture along with Joel Kissin and Terence. The menu was predominantly regional French, but there were also touches of British and Irish cuisine. Everything was to be cooked with the best ingredients – quality was to be the guiding light.

As with the restaurant, so with the other parts of the Gastrodrome. The bakery used only unbleached flours and sour dough in its creations, such as bacon and onion panchetta and spinach and nutmeg bread. The food store offered a range of largely Mediterranean produce – charcuterie and cheeses, spices and oils – and the wine merchant stocked 12,000 bottles in its cellars. Terence would also add his own personal touch to the restaurants and shops by bringing up herbs from his garden at Barton Court to be sold in the oils and spices shop, or a bootful of vegetables to be used at Le Pont de la Tour.

Terence's Gastrodrome has since been taken further by the addition of two more restaurants. Whereas Le Pont de la Tour took a year to develop, the next restaurant, Cantina del Ponte, intended to provide high-quality but less expensive Mediterranean food, was conceived and opened within four months.

Terence had thought up the idea for the Cantina while on holiday in Morocco. He and Keith Hobbs then took the sketches he had made to Provence, and worked out the details in the course of a long weekend. In contrast to Le Pont de la Tour, the interior was more colourful and relaxed. With the addition of the Chop-House, a restaurant offering the best in British cuisine and inspired by the recipes in Caroline's book *Delicious Home Cooking*, and particularly by Peter Williams' photography, the Gastrodrome was completed for the time being. Collectively the restaurants at Butlers Wharf can seat over seven hundred people. In spite of the initial scepticism over the location, all are successful. However, even the Gastrodrome has been overshadowed by Terence's most high-profile venture – Quaglino's.

Quaglino's had been started in 1929 by Giovanni Quaglino on the site of the St James's Palace Hotel in Bury Street, SW1. It offered high-quality food and service and late-night entertainment with music and dancing. It competed with the great restaurants of the day, such as the Savoy, Claridge's and the Kit Kat, but was distinguished from the others by the charm of its owner. Barbara Cartland wrote of it:

After the super snobbishness of the great Luigi at the Embassy Club; the condescension of Charles at Claridges; the lack of individuality at the Kit Kat, Quaglino was always smiling, always welcoming, made each of his clients feel a very special guest. Apart from the attractiveness and the soft music in Bury Street, the food was superlative and original.

In its heyday it was patronized by the future Edward VIII, the tango-dancing Charlie Chaplin, the Mountbattens, Winston Churchill, Evelyn Waugh and Lady Cunard – Nancy's mother. However, when Giovanni Quaglino returned to Italy during the war, to avoid internment, it changed hands and lost some of its status. In the mid-1970s it was gutted by a fire and then acquired by Trusthouse Forte for redevelopment. However, nothing was done with the site, and when Joel Kissin first saw it, it was just a subterranean black hole.

This time there was no doubting the location – just off Jermyn Street, in London's West End – but there was every doubt about the process of transforming the space into a restaurant, and also the timing. Work had just started on designing Le Pont de la Tour, and Joel wasn't sure whether Terence would risk everything on trying to develop both restaurants simultaneously, especially in the depths of the worst recession since the early 1970s. However Terence loved the location and the associations of Quaglino's, and once Forte agreed to sell the name he was absolutely committed to the idea. As always Terence was taking a long-term view, and he also saw that those restaurants that offered very good food and service, such as the The Ivy and Le Caprice nearby, were continually full. In any case, Giovanni had made a success of Quaglino's in the depression years of the thirties. Confidently, Terence acquired a ninety-nine-year lease and then he and Joel Kissin spent two years and £2.5 million creating their version of the perfect brasserie.

The design of the restaurant was inspired by the big French brasseries. Terence and Keith Hobbs spent time in France looking at restaurants, and in particular at the large and much admired La Coupole in Paris. However, whereas La Coupole had been faithfully renovated in its *fin de siècle* style, Terence decided to create something entirely new for Quaglino's – something with a sense of theatre and excitement. As Keith says, 'It's a good-time West End restaurant.' As with their other conceptions – and, indeed, as with all Terence's ventures – there was an intimate attention to detail and an appeal to all the senses, and Terence involved himself with the design of every element in the restaurant including the construction of a mezzanine over 50 per cent of the space.

With no natural light in the restaurant, the environment could have been oppressive, especially during the day. However, an artificial glass skylight was created running the entire length of the space. Controlled by computer, the lighting behind the glass would be varied to simulate daylight and night-time, with appropriate seasonal changes. There were mirrors along the side walls and angled from the ceiling, and this made the 450-seat restaurant appear even larger. Terence and Keith worked with a host of craftspeople and artists to create the right ambience. Benchmark produced much of the furniture, including zinc-topped tables, mosaics were created by Emma Biggs and Tessa Hunkin for the crustacea altar, Philippe Starck created the toilet-cubicle handles, Jasper Conran produced the staff uniforms, and Terence designed conical ice buckets that have a direct antecedent in his fifties conical flowerpots. As with the Gastrodrome restaurants, diners would be able to see into the kitchen, and there was again an offer of different eating styles: the casual and quick antipasta bar devised by Tom Conran, the restaurant itself, and a *salon privé*.

The skill in the design was in the moulding of the individual elements of the various contributors into a cohesive whole – making the contrasts work. Although Terence's former pupil Min Hogg had once criticized Terence for paring down design 'until really there is nothing left', his design for Quaglino's was flamboyant and far removed from the minimalism much favoured by other stylish restaurants. The supporting pillars, for example, were decorated in powerfully coloured shapes by eight different artists.

With a thousand people to be fed daily by the fifty-seven chefs, the control of systems had to be perfect, and much time and money was invested in computerization. As with the other restaurants, the principle was good-quality ingredients cooked simply – spiced lamb, poussin, ribs of beef, calf's liver, lobster salad, dressed crab and *fruits de mer*.

When Quaglino's opened on St Valentine's Day 1993 under manager Eric Garnier and chef Martin Webb, it was to huge press coverage and high expectations. The verdict from all perspectives was almost universally positive. The architectural magazine *Blueprint* voted it restaurant of the year for its design, and Egon Ronay in the *Guardian* wrote:

Beyond creative brilliance in design, consummate managerial skill and high-quality food for mass pockets, Quaglino's . . . has obliterated all excuses for

The newly opened Quaglino's – Terence and Joel Kissin, 1993

poor food, bad service and high prices. My prediction is that we shall look back on Quaglino's as an epoch-making restaurant.

It was also packed from the moment it opened. To get a table at Quaglino's customers would have to book weeks in advance. In its first year Quaglino's turnover was £9 million.

There was some sneering, however – mostly in the *Sunday Times*. Rhoda Koenig bemoaned the emphasis on design:

Quaglino's is the model of the post-post modern restaurant in which cuisine takes a back seat to design – not to mention marketing.

While Christa D'Souza, with undisguised snobbery, was appalled at the clientele:

It has been impossible to hide the Essex element at Quaglino's because the restaurant is so large. Far from being buried, the leopard-print brigade can't help but play a prominent part in the show.

Both jibes missed the point. Accessibility was the idea behind Quaglino's. Terence had set out to create a restaurant where everyone would feel comfortable. He believed everyone should be able to experience the quality of the food and the ambience. What he was trying to re-create in London was the lack of social pretension that he had seen in all the big brasseries in France. As Terence said, 'It's meant to be a spot that welcomes not only a businessman but his chauffeur.' This wasn't mere press-speak, but at the heart of his long-held adherence to making good taste popular. Nor would Terence ever put design above food – in fact he would rank design below food and service in the important attributes of a restaurant. However, the key to Terence's success was that he made the three elements work so cohesively together that each complemented and enhanced the others. Each of his restaurants has this cohesion and a clear position in the market-place.

Although the restaurant operation is now big and requires structures and delegation of authority, it also benefits from Terence's active involvement. Whereas the systems within Storehouse always seemed to be beset with problems, the computerized restaurant systems work efficiently. The difference seems to be that he has an intimate appreciation of the workings of a kitchen, whereas at Storehouse and Habitat he would delegate the systems side completely because he wasn't much interested in the logistics of distribution. From a financial perspective the systems are such that rapid and accurate data are provided on a weekly basis. It means that costs and margins are always being reviewed and any problems are picked up immediately. Terence's involvement also extends to eating regularly in his restaurants – *le patron mange ici* – and making suggestions about the dishes each restaurant should serve or how they should be presented. Keith Hobbs can remember Terence sending a memo to the chef at The Neal Street Restaurant telling him to make the chips longer. He believes the key to Terence's success is the control of quality:

> Terence is so fussy about the quality of food and the style. The chefs feel involved because normally they're shareholders, and the service is good because the organization is very personal and the staff see him all the time. We have a very low turnover of people.

After his personal low in 1990, when he had lost control of Storehouse, Butlers Wharf was in receivership and he had been written off by almost everyone, Terence has clawed his way back to a new high – and one that was all the more pleasurable through his intimacy with work colleagues who shared his vision. In many ways it was 1964 all over again.

In October 1992 Terence opened a second Conran Shop – on the Parisian Left Bank, on the corner of the rue du Bac and rue Babylone. The French style that had so influenced Terence was being offered back to the French in a new guise. Under the direction of Michel Cultru, who is chief executive of the Conran Shops, the new store has all the style and quality of its English counterpart. In the same month, Terence became involved again with his former protégé, Rodney Fitch. Fitch & Co. had been hugely successful during the 1980s, but an expensive and ill-fated office move in the depths of recession had undermined the company. Although Terence was still joint president of RSCG, he invested £1 million to keep Fitch afloat. The potential conflict of interests between RSCG and Fitch caused a furore, however, and Terence was debarred from taking an active part in the management of Fitch.

The Conran Shop, Paris – exterior, 1992

A final irony was the sale of Habitat to the Swedish home-furnishings company IKEA, which had discussed the possibility of acquisition when Terence was chairman of Storehouse. After the years of deConranization, the new managing director of Habitat, Vittorio Radice, determined to take Habitat back to its roots – to Terence's original vision:

> Habitat today could be the best home furnishing chain in the world if the original concept hadn't been murdered. When Terence Conran first opened stores they were in beautiful buildings – a restored church in Tunbridge Wells, a 1920s cinema in London's Kings Road, a grand hotel in Bristol, an old Spitfire factory in Manchester – all these were wonderful, individual, special to their towns. Then they started opening in huge sheds in edge of town sites, next door to B & Q, MFI, Do-It-All. They even opened seven Habitat stores in BHS. All this diluted the image, took it down market. I think that was a tremendous mistake.[1]

1. Lucia van der Post, 'Aiming to shake the shabby out of Habitat', in *Financial Times*, 17 October 1992.

CHAPTER TWELVE

BIG AND SMALL

Terence has proved in the last few years that he still has the ability to read a market and deliver what it wants. His failure, if it can be termed as such, was his inability to turn BHS round. In retrospect the merger between BHS and Habitat Mothercare was not ill-conceived, but it was badly managed. Terence – like many of his eighties contemporaries – got too big too quickly.

Terence's successes, both in restaurants and in retailing, have resulted from the clarity of his vision, his absolute commitment and complete attention to detail. The vision itself was not contrived, and nor was it driven by the pursuit of monetary gain: rather, it was born out of his fundamental beliefs and his desire to give people something better than they already had. His critics would argue that 'better' was very much a personal definition, but to the people who bought their furniture at Habitat, Terence did seem to offer a new and more relevant way of living. When the company was relatively small, there were enough disciples to ensure Terence's ethos was also the company's; the problem with the later scramble for growth lay not so much in a compromise of his vision – he still believed in providing good quality – but in his inability to persuade those he worked with of the validity of what he was trying to do. With Storehouse there was no sense of one company being driven forward by the ideas of one person: rather, there was a series of fiefdoms with an array of counter-vailing ideas.

Looking back, Terence can now see that he was over-ambitious and overextended:

In some ways I regret what happened to Habitat and in some ways I regret my ambition. On the other hand I say it had to be done. I didn't do it terribly well, I didn't do it to my satisfaction, but at least I did it. And now I'm back really enjoying what I do. The pleasure now is that I have no shareholders or city analysts to worry about. I still want the businesses to be influential and profitable, but I'm doing it for my own enjoyment.

Spurred on by the optimism of the mid-eighties, which suggested the economy and the stock market could only go one way, he fell into the trap of believing big is best. Priscilla remembers having a conversation with him in Milan, about the BHS merger:

> I said to him, 'Why on earth are you taking on this giant company, which doesn't seem to have anything to do with us?' And he said, 'Because I've discovered I'm rather good at it.' I said, 'But don't you think you're better at making sure the handle on a teapot is perfect?' He told me I was a very small merchant.

Terence has always been susceptible to the idea of being bigger. He thinks there is something unsettling about standing still: there is a restlessness that can be satiated only by new challenges. His mother instilled in him the need for achievement, and he has never stopped trying to prove himself, to overcome the sense of his own limitations. In some areas, such as the look of a product or the design of a restaurant, he has acquired enormous self-belief and purpose, but in others the seeming confidence that he exhibits to the outside world is a cover for his underlying self-doubt. He needs to demonstrate to people that he is strong and in control. Partly he does this by challenging conventions – by doing things that others believe are wrong or doomed to failure. Partly he communicates it by assertiveness and bullying. Those who know him well, however, recognize this side of his character for what it is – a smokescreen.

Although Terence finds it difficult to show emotion, he is nevertheless an emotional person, and occasionally the emotions burst forth in a display of either temper or warmth. In recent years two events in particular have hit him hard.

The first was the death, in November 1992, in a freak shooting accident of his friend and long-time collaborator Oliver Gregory.

Although Oliver had become somewhat removed from Terence's business world, they remained close friends and regularly played chess together. Terence may be unsentimental about the past, but Oliver was his main link with the early days of Habitat: together they had created the Habitat style. Preoccupied as Terence was in the early 1990s with his restaurant business, there was, as in all untimely deaths, a sense of guilt about things left unsaid. Oliver's death also brought home to him a sense of his own mortality – something that made him feel uncomfortable. As Sean Sutcliffe says, 'Mortality is a subject Terence is scared of, but it's not something he wants to discuss.'

The second trauma was the break-up of his marriage to Caroline. He had suffered deeply when Caroline had been very ill with cancer in the mid-eighties, and had become very frightened at the prospect of losing her. Until then he had always tended to take her for granted. Terence let Caroline lead a life of her own and believed that her freedom was important. However, Sean thinks that, while she appreciated the freedom, what she really needed was to be valued and supported.

With his focus on his own work, Terence had never really given her that. After her illness, Caroline started training to be a counsellor. Terence, who believed that people should be able to control their own lives without the help of others, pooh-poohed it – he saw it in the context of rich people doing goody-goody things. However, the training brought home to Caroline the lack of emotion in their marriage and she decided that she wanted to develop her life independently of Terence. Sean says, 'Caroline can be quite prickly, but she's very soft and caring. She gave her life to supporting Terence, and he took her for granted. Terence was incredibly self-reproachful when she left. He said, "If only I could have shown my emotions more." '

Terence, as many have attested, is both enormously rewarding to be with and also potentially damaging. Often his long-time work colleagues, such as Francis Bruguière, Pauline Dora, Geoff Davy and Maurice Libby, recognized the negative side of his character, but there was nevertheless a thrill about being in Terence's circle. Francis Bruguière says, 'I've met some interesting people in my life, but I would put Terence at the top. He's extremely interesting to know and to work with. He is unique and imaginative.' Pauline Dora adds, 'He's the greatest marketer and merchant I've ever met.'

At home Terence could be very jolly, but also very cruel – he felt a need to take his frustrations and irritations out on someone, and the person who was most often in the firing-line was Caroline. Often she would not react to Terence's taunting, but when he pushed her too far she would walk out of the room – Sophie can remember a lot of slamming doors when she was growing up. It was almost as if bottling up his positive emotions made Terence show more of his negative ones. After Caroline left, Terence was vulnerable and did talk about his emotions. However, this seems to have been a transitory need – as Sean says, 'He's put the stopper back in now.'

While his relationship with Caroline was suffering, his interaction with his children was improving. He had found it difficult to relate to them when they were children, but as adults there was common ground. The four eldest have all been involved in his businesses: Sebastian at the Conran Design Group, Jasper in designing clothes and fabrics for the restaurants, Tom helping with the Bibendum Oyster Bar and the antipasta bar at Quaglino's and Sophie in buying for The Conran Shop. Terence enjoyed working with his family – it gave him the sense of togetherness that he found difficult to achieve at home – and Sophie in particular relished the experience of working in the family business. Sebastian, however, found it hard, as he put it, being 'son of God'. The employing of family might smack of nepotism – certainly it would be true that the Conran name would open the door in the first place – but the working relationship was businesslike. Jasper says, 'When you work with him, he talks to you about the idea and the concept. He gets you excited, and then you're handed over to the money people, who tell you you've got to do the job for nothing.'

The shared interest of Shirley and Terence in their children's careers also managed to bring about a reconciliation between the two of them. The break-up of their marriage had created much bitterness, but with Shirley's success as a writer she became more confident and willing to forget their past differences – even though she had created a black picture of a Terence-like, obsessive designer in her first major novel, *Lace*. Terence even says that he gave Shirley the idea for the much talked about goldfish episode in that book:

I'd been to this extraordinary wild, midsummer party in Finland. A group of young men went into the lake and came out with nets filled with sticklebacks. Then they introduced these little fish into the, er, private parts of some vodka-soaked ladies. I told Shirley all about this scene . . . [1]

Occasionally, both Shirley and Terence will make negative references to each other in press interviews, but as Terence has mellowed in the post-Storehouse days, the comments seem to have become less pointed. They seem to enjoy each other's company, and take pride in the achievements of their children. Shirley says:

Terence wasn't a very interested father when the children were growing up, but now he appreciates his children. He's very interested, very helpful and very involved, in a way that most men couldn't be. I remember one birthday party of mine when Terence owned The Neal Street Restaurant. It was the four of us [Shirley, Terence, Sebastian and Jasper] around the table, and ideas just went zooming round. It was very buzzy and very exciting.

When Shirley launched her 1992 book *Crimson* – which, in a reference to her own past, has as one of its themes the importance of women controlling their own finances – she chose Quaglino's for the party. Although Terence stole some of Shirley's limelight by being seen with a new twenty-three-year-old girlfriend called Sunita Russell, the location was a symbol of buried differences.

Terence had always been highly attracted to women, and

1. Hunter Davies, 'Wanted: something else to design', in the *Independent*, 16 March 1993.

they found his mixture of strength and fragility alluring. Fiona MacCarthy remembers a dinner party where Terence announced that the only two things really worth living for were food and sex. Terence enjoyed the excitement of affairs and, like so much else in his life, his relationships often involved women who were connected to his work. Priscilla thinks the affairs were a form of abuse, but Terence is someone who always needs new challenges – whether they be business or women – and simply seems to have always had a casual and very non-British attitude towards sex. Roger Seelig remembers going to an exhibition at The Boiler-house and meeting a very attractive girl wearing a silk pyjama suit. He took her out to dinner and to bed. When Roger next met Terence he told him about the encounter. Terence simply said, 'We always did have some of the same tastes.' Of course, whatever the motivation for the relationships, the negative side to them was the difficulty they created in his marriage to Caroline, and as the years went by this became more like a companionable relationship.

Outside his marriage, Terence has been a very loyal person, and one of his great qualities has been to inspire dedication and loyalty in others. At Habitat's thirtieth birthday party, held in the newly revamped Kings Road shop in May 1994, Terence was the guest of honour. The affection felt for him by employees and colleagues from the previous three decades was palpable. He revelled in the renewed success of Habitat, and they in the memory of the excitement of working in a shop that changed people's lives. Terence has repaid the loyalty of those he believes in by supporting people in new ventures, giving advice, and providing opportunities. At the V & A, Elizabeth Esteve-Coll took over as director from Roy Strong in 1988, and started a process of radical change. She received an almost universally bad press, but Terence endorsed what she was doing and gave her support. Similarly, when Roger Seelig was arrested in the wake of the Guinness scandal over illegal share support, his bail was set at £250,000. The first two names he put forward to stand bail were Terence and Paul Hamlyn, but Roger made it clear to his solicitor that others should be asked instead if there was any hesitation from either of them. Both readily agreed.

Terence knew that Roger's negotiating style was aggressive, but he believed absolutely in his integrity. When they had been putting together their deals in the eighties Terence had seen how Roger always cleared his decisions with his managers at Morgan Grenfell.

When occasionally people were disloyal to Terence, he was personally hurt – he always felt honesty should be reciprocated. What he seemed to fail to appreciate was that others were sometimes jealous of his success, whereas jealousy doesn't seem to have been part of his make-up. In a sense this has been a blind spot – Terence seems to have assumed that the people around him either had or should have had the same set of values as himself. Jasper says that his father 'doesn't believe people have intrinsically bad taste. It's beyond his ken to understand why people should want something in a shade of blancmange pink or want shag-pile carpets.' However, this blind spot has also been a strength, in that he was never deterred from doing things because of someone saying that people were happy with what they were being offered: he believed that he could change people's lives by providing something different; he ignored all the class precepts of the British and tried to reach as large a market as he could. The writer and restaurant critic Loyd Grossman once said of Terence:

Conran is very interesting because he's combined the fields of design, retailing and manufacturing, and in the design world he is a sort of Rambo figure. One always thinks of the popular conception of a designer as some poncy Italian, sitting around in a silk suit, designing coffee tables that cost £25,000. What Conran has done is he has said, 'Look, good design is not the province of the very rich, or the very well born. I'm going to make good design available to everyone, and I'm going to make good design an essential part of retailing and good manufacturing practice.' So what he's done is to take design out of this ludicrous, pretentious, airy-fairy, ivory tower that it lived in and made it an acceptable part of everyday life. He's given design a good name.[2]

2. *The South Bank Show*, London Weekend Television, October 1987.

This egalitarianism is also part of the reason why Terence's contribution to design is so well valued abroad – especially in France. There, by 'the Law of Exotic Validation', as Stephen Bayley puts it, Habitat is regarded as a French enterprise. For someone who had fallen in love with France as a twenty-one-year-old and had long been influenced by its food and lifestyle, this is a fitting reward – as indeed is Terence's having been made a Commandeur des Arts et des Lettres by the French Minister of Culture, Jack Lang, in 1992 – an award that delighted him.

Many people have described Terence as a Renaissance man – probably in the sense that, like one of his heroes, Leonardo da Vinci, he has interests that range far and wide. But unlike Leonardo, who was never very good at finishing things, Terence learned from his mother the importance of perseverance and of completing what he had started. However, there is also another sense in which Terence is 'Renaissance'. The dignity of man that Giotto affirmed is also a concern of Terence's. Without trying to be portentous, Terence's achievements are humanistic. He has in all his enterprises put customers at the centre and offered them something enhancing. When he rails against architects or politicians, it is invariably their cynicism he derides. Truth is what he values most – in people, buildings and products – and the criterion against which, for him, reproduction furniture, post-modernist architecture and microwaved pre-prepared food fail.

Although he may have mellowed, Terence has lost none of his passion on those subjects dearest to his heart. When, in 1994, he appeared on BBC TV's *Question Time*, he forcefully rebutted the description by the then transport minister, John MacGregor, of the Arts as 'worthy causes'. Similarly, the occasion of The Design Museum's fifth birthday party, which in a reprise of Terence's fiftieth birthday party featured the ever-young George Melly and spectacular fireworks, was seized as an opportunity to berate industry and government. He pointed out that the museum had received more support from foreign companies, such as Tokyo Design Network, Fiat and Sony, than from UK business, excepting his own charitable foundation. Similarly he criticized the politicians:

Design when it is intelligently used is, as I am sure everybody here would agree, an essential component of the quality of life . . . It is also an essential component of industrial competitiveness. Alongside innovation (and the two are closely linked), it can do more to add value to industrially manufactured products than anything else. Why government cannot recognize this simple economic fact is beyond me, and how the President of the Board of Trade can issue a diatribe on competitiveness without once using the word 'design' is scarcely believable.

Terence's career seems ever upward. By 1994 his businesses were turning over £50 million (five times the 1990 turnover) and employing some 800 people. In addition to a 20,000-square-foot Conran Shop that opened in the Shinjuku district of Tokyo in 1994, another Conran shop is planned for Marylebone High Street to serve customers in North London. A restaurant with over 700 seats, called Mezzo, opens on the site of the old Marquee Club in London's Soho in September 1995. Hotels in Vienna and Dublin are on the drawing board at Terence's design consultancy, CD Partnership, along with plans to convert the 50,000-square-foot Bluebird Garage on the King's Road (opposite the site of where The Orrery once was) into a food store, florists, kitchen shop and café: a West London Gastrodrome. He has also designed a new apartment for himself and his companion, Victoria Davis, at the top of his office building in Shad Thames. And he continues to publish books on the home, the most recent of which is *The Essential House Book* (1994). The energy with which he pursues these varied projects is reminiscent of the early days of Habitat: he may not be the complete workaholic he was then, but there is the same enthusiasm – and a tightly knit team working together towards a common goal.

Terence's overall influence on the way we live our lives should not be underestimated. There may still be plenty of aficionados of the Laura Ashley style, but Habitat and its catalogues, Terence's books and, in a more limited sense, The Conran Shop have changed the way at least some people decorate their homes. The cultural historian Christopher Frayling says, 'Terence has had more impact on design than The Design

Council and the government put together.' This has been achieved not through the originality of any specific design, but by the way products have been put together and merchandised. Terence provided people with choice where before there had been none.

In restaurants, the landscape of eating-out has been transformed. After the war the British restaurant was an uninspiring place. In his 1948 biography, the restaurateur Marcel Boulestin wrote of English waiters:

Some . . . such as the old provincial waiters are not educable. I saw two superb examples. One of them, who served an abominably corked Lafite, confided the secret to me: 'What can you expect, sir, when the cellarman keeps the bottles lying down so that the wine touches the corks?' Another time I saw to my great surprise an Yquem 1921 on the wine list, and I told the waiter to serve it properly cold. 'Oh, you need not be afraid here, sir,' he said proudly. 'Our white wines are always in a refrigerator.'[3]

In the fifties some better restaurants emerged, in terms of both food and décor – not least of them being the Chanterelle that Terence designed for Walter Baxter. However, it is only in the last twenty years, with Terence at the forefront, that London has started to produce real world-class restaurants and that the British have become more sophisticated as restaurant consumers. As with Habitat, Terence has helped to educate and develop a market from a small base, and has introduced his customers to other cultures – through everything from the ubiquitous Japanese paper lampshades to the Magistretti chair to rare grilled tuna with salsa. As Loyd Grossman says, 'Terence has convinced people that restaurants are a legitimate form of entertainment – in fact Terence has made spending money a legitimate cultural event.'

Terence has also been a key influence in changing the face of retailing, both in the creation of Habitat and in the design of other retail chains. He more than anyone transformed the idea of

3. Stephen Bayley, *Taste* (Faber and Faber, 1991), p. 188.

shopping, to its being seen as an enjoyable occasion rather than a necessary one, and helped make retailers the power they are today. Terence believes this is his greatest business achievement:

> I am proud that after 30 years Habitat is still around and doing well. But what I feel proudest of is altering people's opinions of what retailers can achieve. As a result, the public has become aware of how design can improve the quality of life.[4]

The combination of all these activities – retailer, restaurateur, designer, and writer – demonstrates the breadth of his achievement. The depth has been in helping to transform society and its values. Some might argue that the new values are not universally positive, but for those people who enjoy Quaglino's or still relax on a Habitat sofa or cook with a chicken brick, Terence has shared his ideal of the good life in a very real way.

4. Alastair Horn, 'Designs on a simple life', in *The Business Magazine*, April 1994.

Overleaf: Terence's Shad Thames apartment

PHOTO CREDITS

INDEX